BETWEEN EAST AND WEST

Rochester Studies in Central Europe

(ISSN 1528–4808)

Senior Editor: Ewa Hauser, Director,
Skalny Center for Polish and Central European Studies,
University of Rochester

Post-Communist Transition: The Thorny Road
Grzegorz W. Kolodko

Globalization and Catching-up in Transition Economies
Grzegorz W. Kolodko

Polish Formalist School
Andrzej Karcz

Music in the Culture of Polish Galicia, 1772–1914
Jolanta T. Pekacz

Ideology, Politics and Diplomacy in East Central Europe
M. B. B. Biskupski (Ed.)

Between East and West: Polish and Russian Nineteenth-Century Travel to the Orient
Izabela Kalinowska

BETWEEN EAST AND WEST:
POLISH AND RUSSIAN NINETEENTH-CENTURY TRAVEL TO THE ORIENT

Izabela Kalinowska

UNIVERSITY OF ROCHESTER PRESS

First published 2004

University of Rochester Press
668 Mt. Hope Avenue, Rochester, NY 14620, USA
www.urpress.com
and of Boydell & Brewer Limited
PO Box 9, Woodbridge, Suffolk IP12 3DF, UK
www.boydellandbrewer.com

ISBN: 1-58046-172-7

ı oo4 ı92713 ⟨

Library of Congress Cataloging-in-Publication Data

Kalinowska, Izabela, 1964-
    Between East and West : Polish and Russian nineteenth-century
travel to the Orient / Izabela Kalinowska.
        p.cm. — (Rochester studies in Central Europe, ISSN 1528-4808)
Includes bibliographical references and index.
    ISBN 1-58046-172-7 (hardcover : alk. paper)
    1. Polish literature—19th century—Asian influences. 2. Russian litera-
ture—19th century—Asian influences. 3. Mickiewicz, Adam, 1798-1855.
Sonety krymskie. 4. Pushkin, Aleksandr Sergeevich, 1799-1837—
Criticism and interpretation. 5. Orient—In literature. 6. Orientalism in
literature. 7. Poles—Travel—Orient—History—19th century. 8.
Russians—Travel—Orient—History—19th century. 9. Orient—
Description and travel. 10. Orientalism. I. Title. II. Series.

PG7020.A8K35 2004
891.709'325--dc22

                                                                2004017410

A catalogue record for this title is available from the British Library.

Book Design: Christine Menendez
This publication is printed on acid-free paper.
Printed in the United States of America.

*I dedicate this book to my children, Marysia and Krzyś,
the best companions for any journey*

Contents

Illustrations

Acknowledgments

The following institutions provided generous grants that funded research on this project while I was a graduate student: the American Council of Learned Societies, the East European Program and the Kennan Institute of the Woodrow Wilson Center, the Kościuszko Foundation, the Sendzimir Foundation, and the Social Science Research Council.

Timothy Madigan, editor at the University of Rochester Press, and Ewa Hauser, series director, generously agreed to consider the manuscript for publication and provided much-needed advice and encouragement throughout the publication process.

Congenial library personnel at numerous places offered me valuable guidance and assistance. I would like to single out Ryszard Matura of the Bibliothèque Polonaise in Paris as well as the staffs at the libraries of Polish Academy of Arts and Sciences in Cracow and the Pushkinskii Dom in St. Petersburg.

I owe a debt of gratitude to my teachers at Yale: Vladimir Alexandrov, Katerina Clark, Monika Greenleaf, Robert L. Jackson, Ryszard Nycz, Aleksander Schenker, Edward Stankiewicz, and Tomas Venclova.

Numerous colleagues and friends provided advice and various kinds of help: Nike Agman, Elena Boundina, Nikos Chrissidis, Halina Filipowicz, Emilia Hramov, Charles Musser, Elżbieta Ostrowska, Anna Reczyńska, Jackie Reich, Agata Adamiecka, Christina Bethin, and Agnieszka Skrodzka-Bates. A special thanks to Lee Blackwood for editorial assistance during the last stage of the manuscript's preparation.

INTRODUCTION

The rapid development of cultural studies in the 1970s spurred the growth of a large and now well-known literature devoted to analyzing the West's interaction with the vast regions of the world that fell under Western Europe's control in the nineteenth century. The most familiar concept associated with this school of analysis is "Orientalism." This term gained wide currency thanks to the writings of Edward Said. He defined the concept as "a discourse by which European culture was able to manage—and even produce—the Orient politically, sociologically, militarily, ideologically, scientifically, and imaginatively during the post-Enlightenment period" (*Orientalism* 3). Central to this definition is the assumption, substantiated by Said with an impressive array of evidence, that Europe's colonial incursions in the "East" were facilitated by all nature of texts, including those ostensibly uninvolved in imperial politics. Said pioneered the study of the web of mutual dependencies between literary activity and political power. In the process, he charted the path for the most serious reconsideration up to that point of the relationship between culture and imperialism.

Contemporary postcolonial theory's genealogy extends directly back to Said's original work. This school of analysis applies a dichotomy that divides the world neatly into the West—which in the nineteenth century invariably denoted Europe—and the East. This omnipresent methodological framework has engendered one notable, but heretofore largely ignored gap. Colonial and postcolonial theorists' bipolar worldview has precluded any examination of the vast territories of the European "inbetween," the region known traditionally as Eastern Europe. As the examples of the Habsburg, Hohenzollern, Ottoman, and Romanov empires demonstrate, in Europe's eastern half imperial expansion and the ensuing subjugation and exploitation of ethnic and national groups unfolded in a

manner thoroughly comparable to the more familiar extra-
European developments. Furthermore, although the colonial dominance of England, France, Belgium, and Portugal waned by the
1950s, until 1991 the Soviet Union remained in place as arguably
the greatest empire in modern times.

Why has postcolonial theory failed to tackle such an obvious
subject as Russian and then Soviet imperialism? Primarily because
academic Marxism has played a determinative role in formulating
and propagating the postcolonial agenda. Much like interwar
Europe's communist and leftist intellectuals, who turned a blind eye
to the Stalinist horrors, post-colonial theory has failed to turn its
critical eye to the Soviet Union. The self-proclaimed proletarian
state's Marxist roots meant that it was, by definition, a stringent
antagonist of western imperialism and thus could or even should not
be lumped into the same category as Great Britain and the others.[1]
Curiously, the veil of postcolonial silence over the other Europe has
extended to the analysis of pre- and post-Soviet Russia's imperial
policies as well.

In *Culture and Imperialism,* Said acknowledges that his discussion omits the Austro-Hungarian and Russian empires, inter alia.
"What I am saying about the British, French, and American imperial experience," he asserts, "is that it has a unique coherence and a
special cultural centrality" (xxii). This circumscribed contention
would leave an inhabitant of Latvia, Kazakhstan, or—even more
so—Chechnya, to name but a few, feeling at the least nonplussed, if
not denigrated. Victims of Russian then Soviet and then renewed
Russian aggression after 1991 could easily brandmark the same
kind of "coherence" and "cultural centrality" within the Russian-
Soviet-Russian imperial enterprise.[2] To be sure, colonial discourse
analysis does provide the starting point for any investigation of the
mutual implication of political power and culture in cross-cultural
encounters together with the attendant dimension of identity formation. However, the theory's self-imposed limitations need to be
exposed and the concomitant shortcomings elucidated to generate
new insights.

This study scrutinizes Polish and Russian texts of travel to lands
that the Slavic writers considered to be part of the Orient and that
today are known as Crimea, the Caucasus, and the Middle East.
Larry Wolf authoritatively establishes that by the end of the eighteenth century the Eastern Europeans found themselves transformed

into Europe's others as Western European civilization discovered an inferior "complement, within the same continent, in shadowed lands of backwardness, even barbarism" (4). Paradoxically, in the nineteenth century scholarly and literary Orientalism enjoyed great popularity in Eastern Europe in part because the Eastern Europeans desired to participate as equals in the intellectual life of Europe. For some Polish and Russian writers, travel to the East provided a way to assert their own westernness and hence Europeanness. Historically, both Slavic nations always existed in close proximity to the Muslim world. Similar to Spain and Sicily earlier in the millennium, each of them experienced extensive exposure to a fusion of western and eastern cultural traditions.

Andrzej Walicki, the most prolific English-language scholar of Polish nationalism, highlights a crucial feature of early-modern Polishness: the gentry's deep-seated suspicion of everything western. The *szlachta* was "much more tolerant of oriental influences that reached them through the Muslim peoples—Turks and Tatars— against whom the Sarmatian Commonwealth waged constant wars under the banner of defense of Christianity," preventing, for example, the Ottoman conquest of Vienna in 1683. Walicki explains further that "this peculiar 'easternization' of Poland was a result of the transformation of the medieval, ethnically homogeneous Polish monarchy into a part of a multiethnic, multireligious, federal republic of the gentry, known as the Polish-Lithuanian Commonwealth" (*Philosophy and Romantic Nationalism* 9).

Whereas Polish statehood was always inextricably linked with Catholicism, it was Byzantine Orthodoxy that consecrated Russian statehood. From its inception, Muscovy therefore had a much more integral link to the East than did the premodern Polish state. Evoking parallels to Sarmatianism's *antemurale christianitatis* doctrine, Muscovy defined itself in opposition to the Mongols, who in the thirteenth century had overrun and viciously sacked its predecessor, Kievan Rus, the first East-Slavic state. Russia's proximity to the non-Christian East came to find expression in the belief that Russia embodied a unique—and superior—synthesis of western and eastern civilizations. The fundamental dividing line between Catholicism and Orthodoxy meant that in the early-modern period Poland and Russia were firmly embedded in two distinctly different cultural spheres. And yet overarching, culturally meaningful parallels in their relative positions vis-à-vis the East can be traced back to the period predating the modern period, the chronological arena for this current study.

Despite their long-standing and indigenous tradition of interaction with the East, by the nineteenth century Western European models of cultural interaction with—and hence construction of—the predominantly Muslim, Romantic Orient exerted a strong influence on Polish and Russian cultures. The investigation of the degree and the character of this dependence on Western European orientalist discourse provides one of this study's main lines of analysis.

Although the two Slavic nations shared this intersection of western and native cultural traditions that shaped their nineteenth-century encounters with the East, the growing political empowerment of Russia and the disenfranchisement of Poland differentiates the Polish and Russian perspectives. Despite its fateful inability to modernize on par with Western Europe, imperial Russia acted as a recognized Great Power whose political power was on the rise. Meanwhile, the Poles found themselves relegated to the class of imperialism's victims, acquiring, in the opinion of Karl Marx, the status of "a revolutionary nation" because of the threat a resurrected Polish state posed to the imperial status quo in Eastern Europe (Walicki, *Philosophy and Romantic Nationalism* 361). Precisely this striking and fascinating power disparity between the two Slavic nations inspired this study's juxtaposition of Polish and Russian texts. The fact that the Russians were colonizers and the Poles were the colonized creates fruitful terrain for exploration, one that has gone largely understudied up to now.

In 1795, the Polish state disappeared from the map of Europe for 123 years. Russia was the driving force behind the three Polish partitions, and it was Russia that, between 1815 and 1915, retained control over the core Polish lands as well as what was by far the largest of the three partitions. The two anti-Russian uprisings launched by the Poles, the 1830 November Uprising and the 1863 January Uprising, resulted in the progressive intensification of Russian control. By the end of the nineteenth century, the universal political and cultural restrictions characteristic of tsarist rule everywhere were augmented by increasingly harsh measures designed to root Polishness out of Polish society. These included the elimination of all vestiges of Polish state administration, wide-ranging confiscation of Polish estates, attempts to impede the development of a modern national consciousness among the Polish peasantry, and extensive Russification of the educational system. In 1830, the authorities closed the University of Wilno, an institution whose immense significance for Polish cultural life emanated well beyond the Russian partition. One year later, the same fate befell the University of Warsaw. In 1869, a Russian university in the former Polish capital became the only institution of higher education in the Russian-ruled Polish lands. In retaliation for the January Uprising, Russification of the Polish school system began. By 1868, all school instruction in the partition was conducted in Russian, while the authorities also prohibited all Polish-language cultural events, with the exception of Catholic masses.

One must situate Marta Piwińska's description of the protagonist of Polish Romantic literature in this context. "Prison and banishment [made up] the Polish 'journey to the East,'" she notes. It was a journey "into a greater alienation, into a denial of one's self as a Schillerian creator of progress and freedom, to a cell, to loneliness, to denigration, to hatred. Here—surrounded by gendarmes, sentenced to death or banishment, faced with his nation's bondage—the hero always recognizes himself in the ultimate alterity of imprisonment. This means that he comes to an awareness of himself in his cursed 'Polish' destiny" (91). Piwińska's formulation is justified and characteristic of the predominant opinions about Polish nineteenth-century culture. But it does not account for Polish writers' continuing participation in European intellectual developments and fashions of the day, including Orientalism. Statelessness did render Poland incapable of interacting with the East as extensively as Russia did. The partitions largely severed Poland's diplomatic and trade contacts with the East. Once the Russian authorities shut down the University of Wilno, institutionalized oriental studies in the territories of the former Commonwealth ceased.

Nonetheless, Polish literature of the period abounds in broadly defined voyages of exploration. Moreover, despite the varying degrees of restrictions placed on the writers' freedom, the Polish *voyage orientale* did manifest certain similarities to its Western European counterparts. A salient question arises here: did Polish writers merely replicate the patterns of western discourse, or did their own experiences with imperial subjugation lead them to find their own alternative ways of describing and relating to the oriental Other? Formulated differently, does a text of a cross-cultural encounter originating in the consciousness of a colonized European

invariably have to expound the same constructions of the oriental
Other as the texts produced by European colonizers?

Roman Koropeckyj's analysis of Mickiewicz's "Crimean
Sonnets" adds an important dimension to this discussion.
Koropeckyj attributes to the most prominent Polish Romantic Adam
Mickiewicz the capacity "to replicate in the 'Crimean Sonnets' the
imperial discourse about Russia's relationship with its Muslim
world that created an implicit bond between the young Polish poet
and his Russian readers" (671). This study's interpretation of the
"Crimean Sonnets" contests Koropeckyj's interpretation. But his
provocative reading does foster the realization that a group whose
identity rests on its own oppression may at the same time be engaged
in a discursive ensnarement of somebody else. The ordering of the
chapters in this study does reflect an impulse to grant agency to the
colonized—it begins by discussing the work of Mickiewicz and
other Polish writers. Simultaneously, however, the analyses of Polish
orientalist literature presented here afford the opportunity to put
these texts' anti-imperialist characteristics to the test.

The Polish historian Andrzej Chwalba argues that Polish historiography has tended to ignore the Polish collaboration with the
partitioning powers in the nineteenth century. "The researchers'
attention has concentrated, among other things," he says, "on Polish
greatness, true or invented, on heroic and romantic deeds and the
subsequent repression of the partitioning administrations, on
national and class struggles, on the examples of Polish and Russian
revolutionary solidarity. Historians were to provide us with consol-
ing pictures of national glory, improve the atmosphere, and help us
deal with complexes, to pour into the weary minds and hearts hope
. . . . In effect, we were satisfied with stereotypes that were heartwarming for the spirit, the stereotypes we believed in and the ones
we made others believe." Following Chwalba's cues for a new kind
of historiography, postimperial rereadings of Polish literature and
culture should transcend heartwarming stereotypes and drive home
the fact that heterogeneity characterized nineteenth-century Poles'
encoding of otherness in literary texts. Such rereadings should challenge and qualify the dominant discourse of oppression and solidi-
fy the realization that a whole range of political attitudes developed
among the Poles.

The extent of Russia's involvement with the East during the period studied here mirrored the tsarist state's firm ensconcement as an

imperial Great Power in Eastern Europe. Peter the Great and then Catherine the Great implemented a concerted program of imperial expansion in the eighteenth century. In the nineteenth century, Russia came to wield substantial military and political influence in the Caucasus and in Central Asia, where it competed successfully, first with Persia and then the Ottomans, and subsequently with France and, most significantly, Great Britain. As Katya Hokanson points out, nineteenth-century Russian culture produced "the literary equivalent of colonization, with all peoples appropriated for Russian literary representation subject to the Russian poet-tsar, for the poet was placed squarely in a position of power vis-à-vis the poetical people and places. The new imperial subjects were coming under the wide-ranging imagination and representation of the Russian poet" (340). Russian literature flowered in the same period that Russian imperial expansion was coming into its own. This dynamic appears to make Russian culture a ripe subject for colonial discourse analysis in the Saidian tradition.

A relatively recent study of Russian imperialist discourse, Ewa Thompson's *Imperial Knowledge: Russian Literature and Colonialism*, makes ample use of postcolonial theory. Unfortunately, the book stumbles in its analysis because its author ignores the pitfalls created by a wholesale adaptation of ready-made theoretical models. The avoidance of the epistemological deficiencies that become apparent in *Imperial Knowledge* lies at the heart of this study. A look at some of these shortcomings sheds light on important features of this study's approach to the material it examines.

Since postcolonial theory offers a politically engaged, radical reexamination of culture, it harbors the risk of confining literary texts to the level of political slogans. Such constricting militancy afflicts *Imperial Knowledge*. What is the source of this attitude in this particular instance? Thompson's study does adopt the legitimate perspective of a dispossessed Polish post-colonial-slash-post-Soviet subject for the analysis of Russian (imperial) culture. But the author's reliance on popular prejudice in place of a balanced analysis of the authors and the texts she discusses constitutes a major flaw. The forceful imposition of communism by Poland's eastern neighbor solidified the Poles' preexisting negative stereotype of Russia and the Russians. Popular opinion in Poland considered the Russians to be crude, barbaric people, capable of little more than mindless violence. This negative attitude extended to the Russian language, the enforced second language of the entire Soviet Bloc. Everyone in Poland studied it, but few learned it. This set of negative attitudes—including gratuitous comments on the Russians' linguistic inferiority—inflects Thompson's study of Russian literature. In the context of scholarly literary studies, such emotional anti-Russian prejudices denude the author's argument of credibility.

Thompson, for example, misses the irony of Pushkin's "Journey to Arzrum," an oversight made even more apparent by her failure to refer to Monika Greenleaf's nuanced interpretation of this text. Likewise, she claims that Pushkin's "Bronze Horseman" "promotes hero worship in the Carlylean sense"(78-79). Yet a reader can only arrive at such a conclusion by confining the interpretation to the poem's "Introduction," while any consideration of the entire text must render "the hero worship" thesis untenable. Thompson's claim that Russia's greatest poet was nothing more than "the crudest jingoist" is equally unjustified (67). But it is not quite as odd as the compensatory epithet of "nouveau-riche" she attaches to Pushkin (76). These and other flaws overshadow some of the important observations Thompson makes concerning the continued lack of interest in any type of postcolonial reevaluations of Russia itself (33-35) and the reasons why the major postcolonial theorists have ignored Russia and the Soviet Union (34-39, 46). While attempting to expose the workings of Russian literary imperialism, Thompson activates the same mechanism of negative stereotyping whose eradication she advocates.

The neat, oversimplified division between the imperial Russians and their subaltern victims, between "them" and "us," makes it impossible to account for a whole range of transitory phenomena. The Polish writer Jan Potocki played an active role in the Polish Enlightenment reform project that futilely sought to thwart Russia's policy of destroying the Commonwealth. He also happened to be among the first travelers who began mapping the Caucasus for Russian imperial conquest (Beauvois). Potocki's further plans complicate matters even more. Hoping to benefit from his ties to Prince Jerzy Adam Czartoryski, the Pole who served as Tsar Alexander I's foreign minister from 1801 to 1810, Potocki went so far as to hope to assume a ministerial position that would have allowed him to take charge of Russia's policies towards the southeast (Kukulski 13). We will never know whether Russia's expansionist policies would have taken a different turn under his guidance.

According to Thompson, "there is no denying the welcoming attitude with which the Russians have treated defections from German, Polish, Ukrainian, Lithuanian, Latvian, or Estonian nationhoods into their own. Not only were those defectors accepted as Russians, but they were accepted with gratitude" (21). Yet who, one has to ask, were the accepting Russians? The famed Polish Orientalist-turned-Russian writer Julian Sękowski was equally distrusted and disliked by his Polish and Russian contemporaries. Another Pole who became a Russian writer, Tadeusz Bułharyn vel Fadei Bulgarin, denounced his Russian friends who participated in the reformist Decembrist conspiracy that came to a head in 1825 (Gomolicki 25). On the other hand, the literary circles of St. Petersburg and Moscow warmly received Adam Mickiewicz, an enemy of the Russian state whom the authorities expelled from Wilno into Russia proper. Some of the Polish bard's Russian friends, including the eminent poet and critic Petr Viazemskii, cherished his friendship long after Mickiewicz established himself in Paris as a vehement, uncompromising critic of imperial Russia.

These examples all illustrate that alongside an analysis of the dominant discourse of Russian imperialism one has to allow room for the analysis of literary and cultural phenomena that do not fit the dominant pattern. Despite their own experience of imperial subjugation at the hands of Russians, some Poles promoted Russian imperialism's goals both in Poland and, most notably, in the East. On the other hand, some Russian writers used their orientalist texts to oppose or question Russian autocracy. To revisit Said, "the difficulty with theories of essentialism and exclusiveness, or with barriers and sides, is that they give rise to polarizations that absolve and forgive ignorance and demagogy more than they enable knowledge" (*Culture and Imperialism* 31).

American Slavists have led the way in exposing the mechanism of Russian orientalist discourse and in demonstrating the phenomenon's complexity. In her study of nineteenth-century Russian authors, Susan Layton identifies a whole range of attitudes towards Russian imperial expansion in the southeast. "Total complicity in imperialism," she writes, "was the mode of ephemeral orientalia, especially prominent in the 1830s. At the polar opposite, *Hadji Murat* denounced the subjugation of the Muslim tribes as vile aggression." Layton places Pushkin, Bestuzhev Marlinskii and Lermontov, writers who were in the Caucasus as exiles, in the "middle ground."

They "endorsed [Russian] imperialism in certain ways, while taking issue with it in others" (9). The perpetuation of autocracy in tsarist Russia created a *sui generis* situation. Even the native elites, including those active in literature, faced serious limitations to their personal freedom. Consequently, the literary figure of the captive in Russian orientalist literature does more than simply project a Westerner's emotional anxieties. It is important to recognize that in the Russian Romantic tradition "the treatment of society and the hero's estrangement from it is nothing new ... it follows the Byronic example" (Hokanson 346). But, as Harsha Ram argues, "the Russian artist, while seldom denouncing the empire explicitly, provided an alienated prism through which to contemplate the 'prison of all nations' in which both the Russian and the highlander were—however differently—trapped" ("Prisoners of the Caucasus" 14).

This study transports the investigation of Russian Orientalism into new territory. It follows Russian writers out of the Crimea and the Caucasus to the Holy Land and, in the case of Pushkin's later Caucasian poetry, back to Russia. Signs of disaffection with western orientalist discourse's influence surface in Russian accounts of travel to areas outside the boundaries of the empire, including the Holy Land. Pushkin's later Caucasian poetry, written around the time of his journey to Arzrum in 1829, bears traces of a similar distancing from the western textual Orient. At the same time, the new format of a cross-cultural encounter provided by the pilgrimage account makes the voicing of alternative, anti-imperial sentiments less likely. The pilgrimage ushers in an intensified negative valorization of any differences whatsoever, including religious, ethnic, and national ones. Pushkin's turn away from the Orient and towards Russia in his Caucasian cycle does not produce the same result, although the poet does demonstrate a greater readiness to assert the correctness of Russia's imperial claims in other texts written around the same time.

In sum, Polish and Russian writers' participation in the discourse of Orientalism may but does not necessarily have to reproduce the structures of dominance embedded in western Orientalism. Thus, their literature may or may not legitimize colonialism. The Slavic writers examined in this study used the orientalist framework in a dichotomous way: either to subvert the empire or to advance imperialist thinking. Furthermore, an author's conscious distancing from western patterns of oriental travel does not usually indicate a subversive intent vis-à-vis the empire. More so than Polish Holy

Land pilgrimages of the time, Russian pilgrimages revived a pre-Enlightenment mode of relating to the world that emphasized the travelers' cultural exclusiveness. This attitude diminished the possibility of entering into a dialogue with the surrounding otherness. The residue of Enlightenment thinking that provided the impulse either to write about the Other or to acknowledge the Other in oneself could therefore create a platform for antiimperialist resistance in the literatures of Polish and Russian Romanticism. But articulating such sentiments from within a tradition that rejected Enlightenment universalism proved to be much more difficult.

This dualism lies behind the study's questioning of one of the basic tenets of postcolonial theory: the mutual implication of knowledge and power that purportedly sprang from Enlightenment philosophy. According to the introduction to an anthology of post-colonial theory,

> Orientalism's enormous appetite for forms of knowledge—scientific, historical, geographical, linguistic, literary, artistic, anthropological—derives in part from its location within the period of the Enlightenment. The Enlightenment's universalizing will to knowledge (for better or worse) feeds Orientalism's will to power. The latter then stands as an example of the production of knowledge as (certainly on balance, if not categorically) negative stereotyping, Othering, dominatory." (Chrisman, Williams 8)

This analysis of nineteenth-century Polish and Russian texts casts doubt on postcolonial theorists' wholesale rejection of the ideological heritage of the Enlightenment. Tsvetan Todorov stakes out a position that better corresponds to the picture that emerges from the readings offered here. He maintains that two forces work to deflect the Enlightenment spirit. One is ethnocentrism, defined as a situation in which "the subject identifies her own values, naïvely or disingenuously, with values in general; she projects the characteristics proper to her own group onto an instrument designed for universality" (*On Human Diversity* 389). The other is scientism, the evocation of a scientific ideology to justify social and political practices (393). While criticizing the perverted version of Enlightenment, Todorov strongly opposes the assertion that "colonial imperialism is intrinsically connected with the universalist ideology." Instead, he points out that "colonialist politics is prepared to use any means at hand, it makes undiscriminating use of all the ideologies that come its way, universalism as well as relativism, Christianity as well as anticlericalism, nationalism as well as racism" (388).

The analytic concepts of postcolonial criticism do contain indispensable reference points for an analysis of Eastern European travel to the East. That being said, neither the early work of Edward Said nor later postcolonial studies offer a fully satisfactory blueprint for the interpretation of Eastern European Orientalism. To be effective, such an analysis must transcend the simple division of the textual East into the European "writing of empire" and the contestatory, non-European "writing in opposition to empire" (Boehmer 5). Eastern European travel accounts function on several levels as works of interpretation and translation. As such, they provide a fascinating repository of the authors' attempts to locate their own cultures in the intermediary space between the East and the West.

Closer scrutiny of oriental travel texts produced by Poles and Russians demonstrates that not only do they differ from their western models in significant ways, but that they also have features that distinguish the Russian texts from the Polish ones. The specificity of the Polish and Russian texts is grounded in the two societies' own longstanding traditions of direct contacts with the Muslim world, as well as in the particulars of their sociocultural development. Thus, even though the Slavs applied intellectual categories borrowed from the West, they looked at the East through the lenses of their own cultures.

The records of individual oriental voyages found in works of literary Orientalism document a quest for cultural self-definition. This is the case with Adam Mickiewicz's "Crimean Sonnets," Aleksandr Pushkin's Caucasian poetry, and with other nineteenth-century accounts that, despite their original popularity, subsequently suffered marginalization. Accounts of pilgrimages to the Holy Land represent an especially interesting case. Even though such pilgrimages involved the crossing of many national and cultural borders, they often entailed a journey to an area with which the traveler claimed to posses intimate spiritual familiarity by virtue of his identification with the Christian tradition and his internalization of biblical geography. Both the literary texts that might not be readily identified as travel accounts as well as the lesser-known pilgrimage accounts contain valuable clues about the writers' understanding of themselves and their cultures.

The first chapter, "Travel, Orientalism and Dialogue in Adam Mickiewicz's *Sonnets*," looks at Mickiewcz in Crimea. The highly intertextual character of Mickiewicz's *Sonnets*—including the "Crimean Sonnets"—makes the sequence very much a product of European literary Orientalism. And yet this cultural context allowed Mickiewicz to produce a text that is not subsumed by the discourse of colonialism, but that, instead, opens the possibility of a multilayered dialogue with another culture. Chapter two, "Polish Nineteenth-Century Travel to the Orient: Scholarship, Poetry, Politics," discusses the types of cultural burdens and dependencies identifiable in the accounts of Polish travelers to the Middle East. Drawing on the examples of several Polish writers, but especially Juliusz Słowacki and Władysław Wężyk, it examines how the textual and cultural traditions of western Orientalism, on the one hand, and Polish nationalism, on the other, influenced Polish literary travelers. "Empire in the Background: Russian Oriental Travel From Crimea to the Holy Land," the third chapter, draws primarily on the writings of Andrei Murav'ev and Petr Viazemskii. It concentrates on how these writers used their pilgrimage accounts first to appropriate, and then to distance themselves from western Orientalism. Chapter four, "Aleksandr Pushkin's Caucasian Cycle: From the Orient Back to Russia," presents a close reading of a cycle of poems written by Pushkin around the time of his second trip to the Caucasus in 1829. Pushkin introduced Russia to western-style literary Orientalism in the early 1820's. But in the text of the Caucasian cycle Pushkin carefully distances himself from the many western influences that figured so prominently both in his earlier southern poems and in Mickiewicz's sonnet sequence.

Polish and Russian writers' textual encounters with the East speak to the ways they thought about their own cultures. The texts analyzed here are more than documents of individual quests and discoveries. They are fundamental sources for reflections on the cultural history of an epoch. An examination of Polish and Russian literary accounts of travel to the Orient heightens our understanding of these two nineteenth-century Slavic cultures and the tension inherent to their coexistence.

The legacy of national consciousness that extends back to the nineteenth century remains an important element of Eastern Europe's intellectual and social tapestry. One need only think of the debates surrounding Poland's accession to the European Union in May 2004 as well as the ongoing arguments about Russia's "true" identity, be it within or at the doorstep of Europe. Just like the literary figures featured in this study, contemporary Poland and Russia are in the process of defining themselves in ways that are at once similar and dissimilar and no less riddled with contradictions than were the Polish and Russian encounters with the "East" of nearly two hundred years ago.

NOTES

1. Anticolonialist statements were a continuous and obligatory element of Soviet rhetoric throughout Soviet history. As late as 1985, the editors of an anthology of Russian and western oriental poetry introduced the volume with the mandatory dose of Leninist holy water: "In 1918, upon meeting with S. F. Ol'denburg, the most remarkable representative of classic Russian orientalism, V. I. Lenin said: 'This is your task. Go to the masses, to the workers and tell them about the history of India, about all the ages of long sufferings of those multi-million masses, unfortunate, enslaved and oppressed by the English, and you will see how this will resonate with our proletarian masses" (*Vostochnye motivy* 3). For most of Soviet history, the anticolonialist rhetoric provided a smoke screen for the Soviets' own expansionist and colonialist endeavors.

2. The only point where Eastern Europe is implicitly present in Said's work is his analysis of Conrad's *Heart of Darkness*: "Never the wholly incorporated and fully acculturated Englishman," Said notes about the native Pole, "Conrad therefore preserved an ironic distance in each of his works" (*Culture and Imperialism* 25).

CHAPTER 1

Travel, Orientalism, and East-West Dialogue in Adam Mickiewicz's Sonnets

Wytężylo się me oko
Tak daleko! Tak szeroko!
Że więcej świata zasięga,
Niż jest w kole widnokręga.

I strain my eyes and my sight reaches
so far and so wide that it embraces
more than the frame of the horizon.

A. Mickiewicz, "Farys"

The involuntary traveler is not always an enthusiastic tourist. Political exiles who focus on the causes of their displacement and on the losses they have suffered often show little interest in their new surroundings. This type of nostalgic dejection did not stifle the creativity of Adam Mickiewicz, Poland's most celebrated exile. Nor did it determine the mood of the poetry written during his first experience with exile. While spending time in the south of the Russian Empire, Mickiewicz, like Farys, the hero of one of the poems he authored during this Russian phase, looked far and wide. He used his creative genius to reach beyond the horizons of Polish literature. The two poetic cycles Mickiewicz published in unison in 1826 under the common title *The Sonnets* provide a fascinating record of this journey, which was at once physical and intellectual.[1]

The Sonnets are a unique travelogue. Mickiewicz's stay in Odessa, particularly the sightseeing trips he took from there into Crimea, enhanced his interest in Orientalism and inspired a multifaceted dialogue with what his contemporaries would have termed oriental cultural traditions. The poet's biography, *The Sonnets'* critical reception, and the history of the sonnet as a genre form the background for an analysis of the volume's inner dynamic, and, ultimately, its intriguing fusion of eastern and western literary traditions.

The Sonnets engage both the long tradition of European sonnet writing as well as all the major intellectual currents that shaped modern Europe. But Mickiewicz is far from Eurocentrism. The rich tapestry of subtextual influences in this poetic sequence extends well beyond this continent. The superficial and, for the most part, mediated oriental borrowings in vocabulary and imagery are not the only things that point in this direction. More significant are the common narrative-structural characteristics that link *The Sonnets* with the *qasidah* of classical Arabic literature. A longer poem, the latter can be described as "a series of pictures conveying different aspects of Arabian life, loosely bound together in a conventional order" (Gibb 18). In a qasidah, the description of a journey and the development of the poem's proper subject follow the opening lines commemorating the beloved. Mickiewicz's conscious adoption of the qasidah template means that the concept of an "oriental travelogue" assumes a new significance when applied to his sonnet sequence. In no way do *The Sonnets* affirm Europe's dominance and its superiority over the cultures of the East. To the contrary, they survey and illustrate the benefits of a creative engagement born from literary travel to the Orient.

The Road to Crimea

In 1824, tsarist officials became aware that Mickiewicz and some of his fellow students belonged to what was deemed a subversive organization. Known as the Philomaths (Filomaci), it was designed to promote scholarship and self-reliance among students at the University of Wilno, a hotbed of Polish nationalist activity. After being jailed, Mickiewicz and his friends were expelled from Lithuania and ordered to settle in one of the non-Polish provinces of the Russian Empire. That fall, Mickiewicz arrived in St. Petersburg. Aleksandr Shishkov, the conservative writer and the tsar's minister of national enlightenment, may have let the exiles express preferences about where they wanted to work (Gomolicki 11). Mickiewicz received a teaching post at a Gymnasium in Odessa. He reached this port city in February 1825, but the job there never materialized. Mickiewicz was not keen on working as an educator anyway, and he busily went about cultivating friendly relations with Odessa's multi-ethnic high society.

One of Odessa's central social figures was Karolina Sobańska, née Rzewuska. The daughter of a Polish aristocratic family, Sobańska was already surrounded by the atmosphere of scandal that was to accompany her throughout her life. Separated from her first husband, Sobańska ran the household of General Ivan Witt when Mickiewicz met her (Slisz 49-51). Witt soon played a central role in the unmasking of the Decembrist conspiracy in the southern part of Russia. In Karolina Sobańska's miscellany, separated by just a couple of pages from Aleksandr Pushkin's "What in my name . . ." Mickiewicz, in a hand equally as fine as the Russian poet's, recorded:

> Niedbam co się na ziemi, co w niebiosach dzieje,
> w tobie widziałbym tylko moją przyszłą dolę
> w tobie złożyłbym duszy i rozum i wolę,
> Pamiątki nawet serca głęboko zagrzebię.
> Abym nigdy nic nieczuł oddzielnie od ciebie.[2]

> I care not what happens on earth, or in the heavens,
> I wish to see my future existence in you,
> I want to cede to you my soul's reason and will,
> I would even deeply bury my heart's memories
> Not to feel anything apart from you.

Reflecting back on his time spent in Odessa, Mickiewicz writes in a letter to Margaret Fuller: "I was beginning to form an attachment to this lady, but I was too sentimental and I wanted to be the only one. She would only have me as one of many. I held a grudge against her for a long time. Finally, I understood that she was right and that her actions were correct. I now remember her fondly" (*Dzieła*, XVI, 115). When he penned this fatalistic amorous confession many years after his stay in Odessa, Mickiewicz provided a testament to the fact that his earlier feelings towards Sobańska had extended well beyond the conventions of a salon conversation.

Around the end of August 1825, Mickiewicz set off on one of his trips to Crimea. According to Władysław Mickiewicz, the poet's son and one of his first biographers, Sobańska suggested the trip to the picturesque peninsula (W. Mickiewicz 31). The participants in the Crimean excursion made for an intriguing cast of characters. Apart from Sobańska, a yet-unknown secret police informant, the party included her former husband; her brother, the would-be writer

Henryk Rzewuski; General Witt with his proven track record of service to the tsar's police; a police informant named Aleksandr Boshniak, who was later involved in the surveillance of Pushkin in Mikhailovskoe; and, finally, a certain Kałusowski, an administrator of the Sobański estate.[3] After crossing the sea to Sevastopol, the Sobańskis and Witt established themselves in Evpatoria. Rzewuski and Kałusowski occasionally accompanied Mickiewicz during his

Figure 1: "Adam Mickiewicz na Judahu skale" by Walenty Wańkowicz. A lithograph from an oil painting reproduced in S. S. Landa, ed. Adam Mitskevich, *Sonety,* p. 65. The original painting, one of Mickiewicz's most often reproduced portraits, is in the Literary Museum in Warsaw.

excursions to various places in Crimea. At other times, Mickiewicz only had the Sobański's Cossack or a Tatar guide as a companion (W. Mickiewicz 208-13).[4]

In December 1826 in Moscow, Mickiewicz published his first volume of poetry written in exile, *The Sonnets*. The modestly named edition contained two cycles of poems—a sequence of twenty-two love sonnets commonly referred to as the Odessa sonnets, and eighteen sonnets titled the "Crimean Sonnets." Mickiewicz inscribed the following quotation from Petrarch on the volume's title page: "Quand'era in parte altr'uom da quel, ch'io sono" (When I was partly a different man than I am now). Preceding the "Crimean Sonnets" was an epigraph from Goethe's *West-Oestlicher Divan*: "Wer den Dichter will verstehen, muss in Dichters Lande gehen" (If one wants to understand a poet, one must venture into the poet's land). Even though many considered Sobańska, the poet's lover and the femme fatale of Odessa society, to be the implicit dedicatee of at least some of the Odessa sonnets, the Crimean cycle is the one that bears an explicit dedication: "to the companions of the Crimean journey." The text's prose annotations, customary for orientalist poetry, included references to Hammer, Murav'ev-Apostol, Sękowski, and Pushkin.[5] In addition, the first edition featured a Persian translation of one of the sonnets authored by Mirza Djafar Topchy-Bashy.[6]

The Sonnets' publication unleashed the most heated literary debate in the history of nineteenth-century Polish literature prior to the anti-Russian uprising of November 1830. Most reviewers interpreted them as a powerful statement in an ongoing debate over Polish national literature's very concept and form. In the center of the literary maelstrom stood a question that to this day continues to ensure *The Sonnets'* undiminished status as a fascinating object of analysis: what was the nature and the extent of the poet's reliance on models and material that the critics perceived to be of foreign provenance?

Maurycy Mochnacki, one of the heralds of Romanticism in Poland, welcomed the appearance of Mickiewicz's poetic work, which he characterized as a highly significant cultural event. Mochnacki waxed grandiloquent about the *The Sonnets*, asserting that

> the combination of the boldest and most colorful eastern imagi-
> nation with the melancholy loftiness of the northern Romantics,
> the blending of the sounds of southern Arabic poetry with the

> dark, sentimental sensitivity of today's poets; finally, the molding
> of a complex totality out of the spirit of the forgotten masters of
> modern European civilization and its thoughtful idealism—all of
> this characterizes the general effect on the reader's mind pro-
> duced by the contemplation of this most uncommon work, this
> singular poetic creation. (Billip 83)

It was precisely *The Sonnets'* admixture of Orientalism and
European idealism that so impressed Mochnacki and provoked
severe criticism from other reviewers. The more conservative mem-
bers of the Warsaw literary world heaped anger and ridicule on *The
Sonnets*. In Kajetan Koźmian's assessment, for example, Mickiewicz
had ventured much too far into unfamiliar territory. *The Sonnets'*
imagery and language contained purportedly alien elements that
posed a threat to Polish national culture (Billip 334-42).

Why the Sonnet?

Franciszek Salezy Dmochowski, another influential figure in Polish
literature, focused his ire on Mickiewicz's choice of the sonnet. He
dismissed the sonnet as a literary form that failed to facilitate the
free and accurate expression of emotions, and he wondered whether
the poet's inspiration could survive the constricting limits imposed
by the sonnet's rigid form. Even in Italian poetry, Dmochowski
argued, the sonnet rarely succeeded in capturing the voice of the
heart. Instead, it merely expressed flirtation and wit. Since, in his
estimation, the sonnet's form overshadowed its subject, success
could be achieved only by those sonnets that were "light, smoothly
written, witty, and harmonious in their choice of words, rhymes, and
the composition of the stanzas" (Billip 72). According to
Dmochowski, Mickiewicz's sonnets suffered from deficiencies in
most of these areas. Nor was this to be seen as surprising, given
Mickiewicz's supposed attempt to straightjacket "a subject that is so
rich, so new and fresh . . . in the narrow, uncomfortable frames of
the sonnet" (73).

   After Dmochowski's pronouncements, commenting on *The
Sonnets'* perceived limitations developed into a tradition shared by
both their critics and their admirers. Writing about Mickiewicz's
work at the beginning of the twentieth century, Julian Klaczko
laments the poet's choice of "that fourteen-line frame, where every-

thing seems to be calculated to limit the free strivings of the heart, to reduce poetry to the level of an intellectual game" (Zgorzelski 117). Czesław Zgorzelski, the author of one of the most sensible analyses of *The Sonnets,* quotes Klaczko and reaffirms his view of the limiting character of the sonnet's narrow structural strictures. Zgorzelski's analysis concludes with an understated yet all-encompassing criticism of the sonnet. Mickiewicz succeeds, he notes, in breathing life into the "stone-like, mathematically determined contours of the sonnet" (118).

What were the broader cultural implications of the Polish poet's decision to use this particular literary form? Franciszek Malewski, the poet's close friend and fellow exile, provided one explanation. According to Malewski, Mickiewicz first intended to write a narrative poem (poema) set in Crimea. Mickiewicz's concern that his work would share too many similarities with Byron's *Childe Harold* purportedly led him to abandon this original concept. And yet, in reality, the decision to go with a sonnet sequence in lieu of a narrative poem was not at all surprising for a poet of Mickiewicz's generation. Romanticism resurrected the sonnet. When August Schlegel held his Berlin Lectures from 1801-04, his authoritative remarks had a formative impact on the emerging Romantic movement. Schlegel went so far as to praise the sonnet as the highest of all lyric forms (Schlegel 241-50). The sonnet appealed to Romantic sensibility as a literary form that, despite its appearance of rigidity, encompassed either parallel or opposed vantage points. The sonnet's binary structure made it well suited to the narration of a nineteenth-century travelogue. Furthermore, as a literary form with presumably oriental origins, the sonnet provided the perfect medium for describing a journey to the Orient itself.

The author traditionally uses the sonnet's two quatrains to introduce and then develop a theme. This prescription often renders the sonnet's octave descriptive in character. The tercets contain either a meditation on the main theme, or an antithetical statement. As a result, the sestet—in contrast to the descriptive octave—may be reflexive. Wacław Kubacki places the "Crimean Sonnets" squarely within the tradition of Romantic ideology. He elucidates some of the reasons underlying the sonnet's appeal to the Romantics, whose aesthetic sensibility was marked by a quest for a literary synthesis. Not only does the sonnet stand at the crossroads of epic, lyric poetry, and drama (it can include elements of dialogue), it also traditionally encompasses descriptive and lyrical elements, and, most crucially, a dual structure defined by the division into octaves and sestets that formally expresses the sonnet's thematic dynamic (Kubacki 156). The combination of these traits invites exactly the kind of synthesis that lay at the heart of Romanticism's raison d'être.

At the core of the Romantics' worldview was their fervent belief in the multifarious character of being, symbolically manifested in reflections, shadows, and echoes. The sonnet offers the possibility of thematizing its structure's duality, and it allows the poet to explore a plethora of parallels and antitheses. Mickiewicz's "Crimean Sonnets" furnish a rich ground for the analysis of parallel motifs and structures. Throughout the cycle, the sestets enter into an array of relationships with the octaves. For example, sonnet VI, "Morning and Dusk" ("Ranek i wieczór"), contrasts the day's changing times—morning in the octave and evening in the sestet—with the prevailing sadness of the lover whose own mood does not change with the coming of the evening. Sonnet II, "Calm at Sea" ("Cisza morska"), constructs a metaphor of the Traveler's mind by contrasting the apparent calm of the sea's surface in the octave with the activity of hidden underwater sea life revealed in the sestet. Memories of the past are less likely to disturb the Traveler at times of emotional upheaval than at moments of peace. In sonnet V, "View of the Mountains from the Kozlov Steppes" ("Widok gór ze stepów Kozłowa"), the octave and the sestet belong to two different speakers, each of whom assesses reality from a different perspective.

Similar interrelationships exist between consecutive sonnets, such as the humorous pair of sonnets XVIII and XIX of the Odessa sequence. The former, "The Visit" ("Do D.D. Wizyta"), features an impassioned subject upset with a stream of visitors who persist in engaging in small talk when he would rather be enjoying a moment of intimacy with the hostess. The latter, "To the Visitors" ("Do wizytujących"), then presents a distant, omniscient voice offering practical advice to the visitor: when one comes across two people who may be seated precariously close to one another, or whose clothing is somewhat disheveled, it is advisable to say good-bye and to depart. Mickiewicz ingeniously shifts from the subjective perspective in XVIII to the omniscient vista in XIX.

On other occasions, he gives adjacent sonnets of both sequences titles that indicate either reflected or inverted images. Some titles evince a tendency to incorporate into the picture another, or, at times, the other perspective. For example, sonnet VI, "Bakczysaraj," precedes "Bakczysaraj by Night" ("Bakczysaraj w nocy"); sonnet XI, "Aluszta by Day" ("Ałuszta w dzień"), comes before "Ałuszta by Night" ("Ałuszta w nocy"). Sonnets VIII and IX, "Potocka's Grave" ("Grób Potockiej") and "Tombs of the Harem" ("Mogiły haremu"), form an additional "thematic" pair. The same is true for sonnet XIII, "Czatyrdah" and sonnet XIV, "Pilgrim" ("Pielgrzym"). The dialogical interplay within individual sonnets and between the sequence's consecutive poems goes hand in hand with the dual structure defined by the collection's division into two distinct parts, the Odessa sonnets and the "Crimean Sonnets." These innercyclic relationships encourage the reader to seek out larger units of meaning as they emerge within each sequence as well as to identify and reflect on the elements that may link these heuristic units.

Mickiewicz does signal a sequence by grouping sonnets of the second cycle under a unifying title. Yet numerous original readers of *The Sonnets* failed to correlate the inner dynamic of the "Crimean Sonnets" to the organization of a travelogue. Since the form's inception, sonnet writers have often grouped their poems into sequences. Michael Spiller points out that sonnets in a sequence may be "arranged to unfold a story to the extent that the people and objects in it are presented as they would be in a novel, with descriptions of place and time and character." He also characterizes the "narrative [as] an uncommon kind of linkage, since its demands tend to obliterate the internal wholeness of single sonnets" (*The Sonnet Sequence* 140). The "Crimean Sonnets" display the characteristics of all the different "ways of aggregating" discussed by Spiller: they are lyric, philosophical, and topographical. But it is the narrative of travel that provides the overarching and most important nexus. Mickiewicz's journey has a clearly marked departure, passage and point of arrival. At the same time, the sequence's sonnets retain their wholeness as discrete pieces of a larger work. In fact, each sonnet's dual structure allows the poet to capture the twofold character of a nineteenth-century travelogue.

The "Crimean Sonnets" as a Travelogue

In eighteenth-century Western Europe, the popularity of foreign travel and travelogues grew dramatically to unheard-of proportions. The Grand Tour's perceived educational value spurred this development.

As the public expressed growing interest in such accounts, travelers who embarked on "educational" trips began to publish factual, "objective" accounts of their experiences while underway in foreign lands. In this mode, driven by a thirst for knowledge, the traveler viewed himself as a researcher dedicated to verifying existing information and to acquiring new knowledge. Observation and instruction had to supplant any self-referential, autobiographical urges harbored by the traveler (Batten 1-46).

In Laurence Sterne's 1768 *Sentimental Journey*, travel functions as a mere pretext for an examination of the self in relation to others. Sterne's criticism of the established norms of the Grand Tour literature marked a turning point in the history of travel writing as a genre. Chateaubriand's travel narratives then shifted the writer's attention even more decisively away from descriptions of the external world and towards intimations of the traveler's own inner states. Most nineteenth-century accounts do infuse elements of an enlightened journey into the portrayal of a sentimental journey. Their authors often supplement descriptions of the visited places with intimations of "internal landscapes." The result is a record of the traveler's emotions as they unfold against the backdrop of the traversed lands. The travel writer had a dual purpose. One was to satisfy those readers who were interested in the tour-guide component of travel descriptions. The other was to portray the journey as a catalyst for a wide range of emotions invariably discussed in a manner that incorporates some obligatory historiosophical musings. Seweryna Wysłouch argues that the object of perception *per se* does not come into focus in the "Crimean Sonnets." The sequence can hardly serve as a guide to Crimea (Wysłouch 50, 51). Yet, the journey's physical motions and the subject's immediate impressions of the sites lead his mind to produce a binary composition.

The sonnet's structure corresponds perfectly to a Romantic travel account's two-faceted character. The first four sonnets of the Crimean sequence establish the pattern. The octave records the sensory impressions of the journey. The sestet transmits the thoughts and emotions stimulated by these impressions. The sestets, with their emphasis on the poet's state of mind, mirror the descriptive octaves' topographical narrative. The poet's feelings are either in conflict or in harmony with the surrounding world. The pattern established in the first four of the "Crimean Sonnets" breaks down in the fifth, when a more intricate octave-sestet relationship comes to the fore.

For example, the fifth sonnet's sestet complicates the duality by introducing the voice of the Tatar Mirza. However, in the last sonnet, "Ajudah" (XVIII), Mickiewicz reverts to the pattern established at the sequence's outset; he records visual impressions in the octave and reflects upon them in the sestet. This restoration of the octave-sestet dynamic serves to underscore the "Crimean Sonnets'" travelogue-like character. In keeping with the genre's tenets, the landscapes of the Traveler's soul conform to his impressions of the foreign lands.

Ostensibly, travel in the "Crimean Sonnets" denotes movement in space. In "Bajdary" (X), the Traveler offers the following topographical description:

> Lasy, doliny, głazy, w kolei, w natłoku
> U nóg mych płyną, giną jak fale potoku.[7]
>
> Woods, valleys, cliffs, in swarming chain,
> Beneath me flow, vanish like ripples in a stream.

But any journey inevitably becomes associated with a chronological progression. In both the Odessa cycle and the "Crimean Sonnets," Mickiewicz takes advantage of the sonnet's dual structure in a manner that enables him to communicate a tension between the present and the past. The present usually lures the Traveler, enticing him to enjoy life and to submit to the flow of events. On the other hand, the Traveler's past experiences, his memories of the people and places he has left behind, are no less compelling. In the Odessa sonnets, sonnet XII, "Do . . ." ("To . . ."), features a telling contrast between octave and sestet. In the octave, the subject flirts with the current object of his desire, who lights an "unholy fire" of carnal desire in his heart. Meanwhile, the sestet establishes that his place is in reality "among the cemeteries and coffins of the past." The dangled promise of instant gratification does not overpower the longing for the past, a longing that transcends pleasure.

A tension between the Traveler's experience of the present moment and his memories of the past marks the first of the "Crimean Sonnets," which initiates the reader into the poet's conceptualization of the journey as movement in space. The first phrase in the sonnet—"I sailed onto . . ."—denotes that the Traveler is already on his way. All of the ensuing verbs are conjugated in the present tense. This grammatical choice gives the octave the character of a reportage-like narration. Mickiewicz uses the sonnet's first part to foreground the immediate, all-engulfing immensity of the "dry ocean" of the steppe. The perspective's perfect horizontality further delineates the illusion of a vast space concocted by the sonnet. This view of the landscape is first violated when the persona looks upwards. Having failed to discern a road ahead of him in the seemingly endless space, the Traveler resorts to looking up at the stars for guidance.

The beginning of the sestet arrests the Traveler's movement in space, as he exclaims: "Stójmy!"(Let's stop!). At the same time, Mickiewicz's poetry guides the reader through a progression from the visual immensity in the octave to the audible detail in the sestet:

> . . . słyszę ciągnące żurawie,
> Słyszę, kędy się motyl kołysa na trawie.
> Kędy wąż śliską piersią dotyka się zioła.

> I hear the cranes flying,
> I hear where the butterfly hovers on a blade of grass.
> Where the snake's slick breast touches the grass.

While the poem's last two lines buttress the impression of the steppe's silent vastness, the subject's thoughts move far beyond his immediate surroundings:

> W takiej ciszy!—tak ucho natężam ciekawie,
> Że słyszałbym głos z Litwy—Jedźmy, nikt nie woła.

> In such silence! So curiously, I strain my ear
> That I would hear a voice from Lithuania—let's go, no one is calling.

Just as he does in other sonnets of both sequences, Mickiewicz builds "The Akerman Steppes" ("Stepy Akermanu") on a series of oppositions between the octave and the sestet. Movement in space and the recording of visual impressions dominate the octave, while the sestet transposes movement into stillness. Aural effects begin to dominate, as audible details focus the reader's attention on the steppe's great silence. This atmosphere stimulates reflection as the poem's focus shifts to the temporal dimension of travel. The anticipated "voice from Lithuania" signals the homesickness gripping the Traveler's heart. But the exile cannot hear the voice, which is incapable of overcoming the tremendous physical distance separating him from his yearned-for Lithuania, a distance vastly greater than the space bounded by the steppe's endless horizon. In addition, the use of the verb's conditional form "słyszałbym" ("I would hear," "I would like to hear") signals doubt as to whether anybody in the remote homeland is indeed summoning. It is the plot of memory that preoccupies the poet. The painful awareness of his own absence and the fear of being forgotten are amplified because his thoughts dwell on Lithuania.

Mickiewicz reverses a situation described by Chateaubriand. In one of the most oft-cited passages of *Travels in Greece, Palestine, Egypt and Barbary*, the Frenchman calls the name of Leonidas where Sparta once stood:

> A mixture of admiration and grief checked the current of my thoughts, and fixed me to the spot: profound silence reigned around me. Determined, at least, to make echo speak in a spot where the human voice is no longer heard, I shouted with all my might—"Leonidas! Leonidas!" No ruin repeated this great name, and Sparta herself seemed to have forgotten her hero. (138)

Leonidas is dead, and although modern Greece may well have forgotten him, Chateaubriand claims for himself the right to remember by calling out the ancient hero's name. "The Akerman Steppes" reverses this dynamic between the one who is remembering and the one being remembered. Unlike Leonidas, who belongs to the distant past, Mickiewicz's subject is present, alive and ready to hear the call. But nobody summons him. Has Lithuania forgotten her native son? Departure, like thoughts of death, often provokes the one who is departing to think of what if anything will remain of him in the memory of others. The semblance between departure and death works both ways: while others either experience or fail to experience the loss of the one departing, the Traveler is challenged by his loss of everything familiar.

Ignacy Hołowiński authored one of the most popular Polish nineteenth-century pilgrimage accounts after he journeyed to the Holy Land from his native Ukraine in 1839. Hołowiński informs his readers that

> just as I had crossed into the endless Cherson steppes, this desert landscape offered a true reflection of my situation. Alone, without

> friends and acquaintances, without substantial funds, I had
> crossed into some wild lands full of danger. I felt like an orphan,
> and this was a solemn moment in my life. The clear night gazed
> silently with its sparkling stars. In front of me and behind me the
> empty steppe. The quick movement of the carriage, the monoto-
> nous drone of a bell and of the driver placed me in a heretofore-
> unknown emotional state. With my eyes fixed on the sky, and
> constantly shedding a tear of prayer, I spoke with God, whose
> mercy and help I asked for myself, a poor pilgrim. (1)

Both the landscape Hołowiński describes in this passage as well as
the emotions he intimates show a clear resemblance to Mickiewicz's
"Akerman Steppes." The similarity between the two texts attests to
the universal qualities of experiencing departure. Both Mickiewicz
and Hołowiński tap into the reservoir of the most intimate losses to
give expression to their feelings as travelers who have ventured far
from home.

Once the departure has taken place, every traveler grapples with
overcoming the resulting grief. Often, this challenge proves to be as
painful as mourning. Freud's essay "On Mourning and
Melancholia" contains the first and most succinct description of this
process. In this event, the usual reaction to the "loss of a loved person, or to the loss of some abstraction that has taken the place of
one such as fatherland, liberty, an ideal, and so on" changes into a
pathological fixation on the loss (Freud 125).

Mickiewicz's persona successfully resists Freudian melancholia.
The last words of the "Akerman Steppes"—"jedźmy, nikt nie woła"
(let's go, no one is calling)—suggest that the Traveler has mastered
the temptation to dwell on the feelings of loss. However, further
developments in the sequence demonstrate that his reconciliation
with the loss of everything that he associates with his homeland is
not complete. Grief will resurface in subsequent, systematically
recurring sonnets of recollection and mourning. Sonnets I, II, VIII,
and XIV belong to this group. Both the Traveler's progress and the
cycle's inner dynamic motivate their positioning within the cycle.
The first and second sonnets describe an early stage of the journey,
when memories of departure are still fresh. In the following sonnets,
thoughts of home overpower the Traveler when his journey's pace
slackens and the world around him falls into silence.[8] The tension
between the past and the present moment underlies not only individual sonnets. It runs through the entire cycle of the "Crimean
Sonnets," and it is just as perceptible in the Odessa sonnets. Two

instincts compete for the Traveler's attention. One demands unfailing loyalty to the past. The other urges him to enjoy the present moment. The form of the sonnet and the sonnet sequence enable the poet to articulate the ensuing dialogue.

Dialogue and Sublimity

Paul Oppenheimer identifies an integral link between the sonnet's birth and the development of the modern mind. "The idea of turning inward, implicit in the form of the sonnet," he notes, "contained a dangerous question" that worked to undermine the medieval system of beliefs (*The Birth* 4). The alterity incorporated into the sonnet's form and meaning enables the poet to question and subvert established truths. The sestet's division into two parts mirrors the structure of the octave. But there is an obvious difference. The six lines of the sestet contrast with the octave's eight-line arrangement. The sonnet's ninth line brings a twist: "a sudden turn of thought, an abrupt transformation of theme" (Oppenheimer, "The Origin" 293). Hence, the sonnet encompasses both similarities and contrasts. Its space contains room for differences of opinion. The poem's very form questions the possibility of a single and final meaning.

The octave-sestet relationship is inherently dialogical; it engenders an intratextual dialogue leading to the discovery of meaning. Like the Bakhtinian self, the sonnet "is never whole, since it can only exist dialogically" (Clark and Holquist 65). In his poetic travelogue, Mickiewicz uses the formal, preprogrammed and readily apparent difference between the octave and the sestet to symbolize the dialogue produced by the Traveler's encounters with a new, culturally distinct environment. The cycle's fifth sonnet, "View of the Mountains from the Kozlov Steppes," exemplifies this dynamic. In it, the Traveler asks questions about the awesome spectacle of Crimean nature. His Tatar guide, Mirza, provides the answers and becomes an indispensable source of information. The Easterner enables the Traveler to comprehend the surrounding foreign environment. Precisely because the Other is present, an enlightening dialogue proves to be possible. This relationship entails the absolute necessity of a dialogical engagement with the Other, and it applies even to the experience of sublimity, which in the traditional Western European context is invariably predicated on a solitary quest.

Figure 2: "Tatar Messengers in Crimea" by Raffet. Reproduced in Anatole de Demidoff, *Voyage dans la Russie méridionale et la Crimée par la Hongrie, la Valachie et la Moldavie exécuté en 1837*. Paris, 1840. Between pages 478-479.

The fifth sonnet contains the cycle's culminating moment, the point where the Traveler's metamorphosis into the Pilgrim signals that the journey has assumed a new dimension. Just like Byron's Childe Harold, Mickiewicz's Pilgrim is not underway to a specific sanctuary. But the journey's transformation into a pilgrimage does emphasize its spiritual dimension. Pilgrimage signifies an inward quest, not merely a journey in space. A pilgrim's progress towards a holy place is concurrent with a search for sublimation.

The Romantics transposed the Absolute onto the world outside of churches. Their holy places were not confined to repositories of holy relics and sites of miracles. A distinguishing feature of the Romantic mind was its quest for the divine in nature.[9] In *The Beauties of Christianity* Chateaubriand pronounces that

> There is a God: the plants of the valley and the cedars of the
> mountain proclaim him; the insect hums his praise; the elephant
> salutes him with the rising day; the bird warbles his praise
> among the foliage; the lightning announces his power, and the

ocean declares his immensity. Man alone has said, "There is no God." Has he then never in adversity raised his eyes towards heaven; has he in prosperity never cast them on the earth? Is Nature so far from him that he has not been able to contemplate her works, or, does he consider them as the mere result of chance? But how could chance have compelled crude and stubborn materials to arrange themselves in such exquisite order? (95)

In the two sonnets preceding "View of the Mountains," a violent sea storm confronts the Traveler. This direct experience of nature's supreme, inscrutable power brings with it an inward liberation from the bounds of established society. After he has severed his links to the "old world," the Traveler in "View of the Mountains" finds himself at the foot of a mountain. The scale of the natural wonder towering over him exceeds his comprehension. The octave consists of a series of questions:

> Tam? Czy Allah postawił scianą morze lodu?
> Czy aniołom tron odlał z zamrożonej chmury?
> Czy Diwy z ćwierci lądu dźwignęli te mury,
> Aby gwiazd karawanę nie puszczać ze wschodu?

> There? Did Allah raise a wall from a sea of ice?
> Or for his angels cast a throne of frozen cloud?
> Or did the Divs lift these ramparts from half a hemisphere,
> So as not to let the caravan of stars pass from the East?

The awesome spectacle of nature thrusts the Traveler's psyche into a state in which "either mind or object is suddenly in excess— and they both are, since their relation has become radically indeterminate" (Weiskel 4). Faced with this overwhelming sensation, the Pilgrim can do only one thing: ask questions. His inability to grasp fully the object and to find words adequate to describe it symbolizes the mind's relation to a transcendent order. The same process of transforming the sight of a natural phenomenon into a symbol of the Absolute organizes sonnet XIII, "Czatyrdah." "The sublime," Thomas Weiskel notes, "is a stunning metaphor" (4). The wonders of Crimean nature evoke a series of metaphors from the mouths of both of Mickiewicz's travelers, the Eastern European Traveler/Pilgrim and the Eastern Mirza.

The octave in "View of the Mountains" allows Mickiewicz to maintain the descriptive character of the sonnet's first two stanzas.

In the sonnet's second part, Mirza answers the Traveler's questions. He tells his companion that he has been there; that he is familiar with the astounding phenomenon. Mirza knows and furthermore understands the mystery behind the mountainous landscape's sudden and imposing appearance.

> Tam? Byłem! Zima siedzi, tam dzioby potoków
> I gardła rzek widziałem pijące z jej gniazda.
> Tchnąłem, z ust mych śnieg leciał, pomykałem kroków.
>
> Gdzie orły dróg nie wiedzą, kończy się chmur jazda,
> Minąłem grom drzemiący w kolebce z obłoków,
> Aż tam gdzie nad mój turban była tylko gwiazda.
> To Czatyrdah!

> There? I've been there! Where winter lives; the beaks of streams
> and the rivers' necks drinking from her nest I saw there. I
> exhaled, snowflakes fell from my lips, I rushed
> along paths not known to eagles, where the clouds' journey ends,
> I passed by thunder, sleeping in a cradle of clouds, until only the
> star was above me.
> That is Czatyrdah!

The Tatar has been to the highlands, a place where no terrestrial sovereign can control him, a place of beginnings and ends. Mirza can therefore interpret for the Pilgrim the mystery behind the natural wonder. Mickiewicz features Mirza's sage words in the sestet, the part of the sonnet essential to the poem's meaning. By positioning the Tatar here and not elsewhere, the poet highlights the oriental subject's superiority vis-à-vis the western Traveler.

Mickiewicz's choice in this instance contradicts the scheme first described by Edward Said in *Orientalism*. The Saidian paradigm of orientalist discourse posits the Westerner a priori as the creator, as the one "whose life-giving power represents, animates, and constitutes the otherwise silent and dangerous space beyond familiar boundaries" (*Orientalism* 57). Yet, in "View of the Mountains," Mirza has the final word as he exclaims, "That's Czatyrdah!" The poem's last phrase spills over the sonnet's purportedly constricting boundaries to form the last stanza's fourth line. To the Pilgrim's ears, the mountain's name rings like a revelation: the mountain and the sublime have become one. The sonnet's rigid structure cannot restrain the Traveler's emotions. The sonnet's last regular stanza segues into the Pilgrim's emphatic: "Aa!!" This ingenious finale, a feature that enraged some of the Warsaw literary critics, both inter-rogates and revitalizes the sonnet's established form.[10] The dialogue between the Pilgrim and Mirza structures the sonnet, while the prominent formal innovations highlight the dynamic of their rela-tionship. Mickiewicz proffers his own paradigm, one that is hetero-geneous from the point of view of the traditional orientalist and postcolonial theoretical canon. The Polish poet's astonishing artistry reinvigorates the old literary form and signals its new potential.

"View of the Mountains" portrays Czatyrdah as a nurturing source for the streams and rivers that drink from the peak's wintry nest. For the poet, the physical approach to what becomes the sub-lime in nature constitutes a pilgrimage to the source of creation. Mickiewicz's Pilgrim comes into the foreign land with an open mind. No past experiences burden him, and he appreciates Mirza's value as an interlocutor and interpreter.

"Any investigation of alterity," Tzvetan Todorov informs us, "is necessarily semiotic, and, reciprocally, semiotics cannot be conceived outside the relation to the other" (*The Conquest of America* 157). Only the mediation of the Tatar, who is both independent and dif-ferent from Mickiewicz's Pilgrim, enables the latter to interpret the sign inscribed in Crimean nature. Moreover, Mirza's presence vali-dates this experience. At stake, then, is more than just the interpre-tation of signs. To cite Bakhtin again, one could envision Mickiewicz subscribing to the notion that "as the world needs my alterity to give it meaning, I need the authority of others to define, or author, myself. The other is in the deepest sense my friend, because it is only from the other that I can get my self" (Clark and Holquist 65). The Pilgrim/poet reaches his ultimate destination by having traveled a route that sets him apart from other Romantic travelers. He eschews solipsism and comes to discover the sublime through dialogue with the Other.

After "View of the Mountains from the Kozlov Steppes," *The Sonnet's* persona continues on a largely dialogical journey through the mountainous peninsula. The next three sonnets present Crimea from the Pilgrim's perspective. But Mirza's voice returns in "Graves of the Harem" (IX). "Czatyrdah" (XIII), "The Road Along the Precipice of Czufut-Kale" ("Droga nad przepaścią w Czufut-Kale") (XV), and sonnet XVI, "Mount Kikineis" ("Góra Kikineis"), like-wise belong to the Tatar.

"The Grave of the Countess Potocka" (VIII) has the Pilgrim pause over the alleged grave of Maria Potocka. In his notes, Mickiewicz points out a local legend that gained a new lease on life thanks to Pushkin's "Fountain of Bakhchisaray" ("Bakhchisaraiskii fontan"). According to the legend, Potocka was a prisoner of the harem. The Pilgrim relates his situation to the predicament of the captive Polish woman. She died confined to the harem, pining for her native land, and he, too, will meet his end in loneliness. In the next sonnet, "Graves of the Harem" (IX), the Pilgrim's reflections on Potocka's fate find a parallel in Mirza's own meditation on the graves of the harem's other inhabitants. The cover provided by the women's graves is like the veil that protects a Muslim woman's face from a stranger's gaze. The hand of an "infidel" left a trace on this veil in the form of names carved on the graves. Both an infidel's gaze and the grave inscriptions are equally insulting, according to Mirza. Significantly, he does not find offense in the Pilgrim's gaze: "I have allowed him [to cast a glance]—forgive me great Prophet!" The earlier positioning of the Pilgrim and Mirza vis-à-vis each other in "View of the Mountains" has already established a bond connecting the Tatar and the Pole. The pairing of the two sonnets, "Grave of the Countess Potocka" and "Graves of the Harem," in which the Pilgrim and Mirza respectively pause over the graves, suggests a similarity of sensibilities between the two travel companions. On a certain level, they perceive the world in similar ways, and their shared perceptions allow them to forge a bond of mutual understanding. Mirza interprets the tears in the Pilgrim's eyes as a sign of empathy. The Tatar notes that the Pilgrim was "the only one among foreigners who gazed with tears in his eyes." The insights into the Pilgrim's exile-induced loneliness communicated by the previous sonnet, "The Grave of the Countess Potocka," do raise the possibility that Mirza's assumption could be wrong. The Pilgrim's tears may flow from the memories of his own past. Nonetheless, the tear that originates in the Pilgrim's contemplation of the loss of his homeland does fall, in a gesture of empathy, on Crimean graves.

At the same time, Mickiewicz juxtaposes the two poems so as to signal the differences between the two travelers, and it is evident that these differences stem from their diverse cultural heritages. The two sonnets' titles—"The Grave of the Countess Potocka" and "Graves of the Harem"—set Mirza and the Pilgrim apart. The sonnet pair's language and imagery further reinforce and substantiate this differentiation. The two men are equal, but also different. The Pilgrim occasionally attempts to cross the cultural divide by, for example, adopting an oriental manner of speech. This is true especially of "View of the Mountains from the Kozlov Steppes." But the pairing of "The Grave of the Countess Potocka" and "Graves of the Harem" sets the tone and firmly inscribes the East-West division.

Towards the end of the cycle, the Pilgrim begins to speak more and more with his own voice. Mickiewicz tones down his oriental stylization, thereby indicating that his European subject has overcome the initial temptation to identify himself with the eastern Other. In the ensuing sonnets, the poet brings the differences in Mirza's and the Pilgrim's understanding of the world into stark relief. And yet in no way does the two companions' awareness of alterity imply enmity. Quite the opposite—in a sign of far-reaching understanding between the two cultures, alterity denotes mutual empathy. The divide between the Pilgrim and Mirza is not a precipice but rather the foundation for their dialogue. Because they communicate in a way that produces knowledge, their exchange takes on epistemological proportions.

In "Czatyrdah," Mirza affirms the splendor and greatness of the natural phenomenon that so enthrall the Pilgrim in "View of the Mountains from the Kozlov Steppes." In contrast to the Pilgrim, the Tatar speaks about Czatyrdah with a calm that stems from his knowledge of an established cosmic order and from his unwavering belief in the existence of such an order.

Mickiewicz does not stop after "View of the Mountains" has established the Tatar nobleman's prominent role as an indispensable guide and interpreter of signs. The sonnets "The Road Along the Precipice" (XV) and "Mount Kikineis" (XVI) deliver the same message. In the former poem, Mirza addresses the Traveler with a series of imperatives: "Say a prayer, drop the bridle, turn your face to the side"; "Do not look there"; "Do not point your finger there"; "And do not let your thoughts move in that direction." In "Mount Kikineis," Mirza interprets the world for the Pilgrim in a way that evinces obvious similarities to "View of the Mountains." The Tatar once again demonstrates his interpretive superiority. He proffers seemingly paradoxical explanations for natural phenomena and again transforms the surroundings into a metaphor,

> Spójrzyj w przepaść—niebiosa leżące na dole,
> To jest morze—wśród fali zda się że ptak-góra,

Piorunem zastrzelony, swe masztowe pióra
Roztoczył kręgiem szerszym niż tęczy półkole,

I wyspą śniegu nakrył błękitne wód pole.
Ta wyspa żeglująca w otchłani—to chmura!
Z jej piersi na pół świata spada noc ponura
Czy widzisz płomienistą wstążkę na jej czole?

To jest piorun! (. . .)

Look into the chasm—the skies lie below,
That's the sea—among the waves it seems that the mountain-bird,
Struck with thunder, its mast-like feathers
Spread in a circle larger than a rainbow's hemisphere,
And covered the blue expanses of water with an isle of snow.
That isle sailing in the abyss—a cloud!
From it the sullen night descends upon half the world;
Can you see the glowing ribbon on its forehead?
That is lightning!

This sonnet invites an analogy to Kaja Silverman's analysis of the metaphor. In *The Subject of Semiotics*, she scrutinizes a fragment from Proust's *Remembrance of Things Past*, noting that

> Elsir's paintings are organized around visual metaphors and metonymies which blur the boundaries between sea and land without reducing them to a single term. The sea makes the viewer think of the land, and the land of the sea. In these metaphors and metonymies the primary and secondary processes reach an ideal accommodation. Metaphor and metonymy can thus be seen as signifying formations which facilitate a movement back and forth—a "transversality"—not only between the two elements which they conjoin, but between the primary and secondary processes, the unconscious and the preconscious. (110)

Similarly, in "Mount Kikineis," the metaphor once more presents a way of looking at the world. In the words of August Schlegel, "all things are related to all things; all things therefore signify all things; each part of the universe mirrors the whole" (Wellek 41).

Although the Pilgrim generally recognizes Mirza's superior position as a guide, a certain degree of tension nonetheless does inject itself into their relationship. "The Road Along the Precipice" has Mirza telling the Pilgrim to turn away; not to point in the direction of the precipice; not to let his thoughts wander. In the following sonnet fragment, Mirza characterizes all of these actions as dangerous:

I myśli tam nie puszczaj, bo myśl jak kotwica
Z łodzi drobnej ciśniona w niezmierność głębiny,
Piorunem spadnie, morza do dna nie przewierci,
I łódź z sobą przechyli w otchłanie chaosu.

And let not your thoughts stray there, for thoughts let loose are
like an anchor thrown out from a small boat into an immeasur-
able depth,
They will go down with the speed of lightning, but will not reach
the sea's bottom,
Instead they will overturn the boat and drag it down into the
abyss of chaos.

The Pilgrim, however, does not heed Mirza's advice. He does look, and he catches a glimpse of something he is unable to name. This behavior is consistent with the identity assumed by the Pilgrim. A nineteenth-century European intellectual who has lost the certainty granted to people by religion, he is striving to find his own answers to the recurring eschatological questions that preoccupy him. The Pilgrim rejects the confines of "the magnifying glass and the eye" just as Mickiewicz himself did in his 1822 ballad "Romanticism" ("Romantyczność"), the seminal manifesto of pre-1830 Polish Romanticism. Whatever the Pilgrim sees defies rational explanation. His glance into the precipice violates both the laws of Mirza's religion as well as the dictates of reason. One interpreter describes this situation in the following terms:

> A precipice, in the sense of a mountainous chasm, embodies the physical situation and becomes, at the same time, an epistemo-logical metaphor. ...two people poised above the precipice at Czufut-Kale, these are two individuals who confront the unknown, and each of them will choose a different path, will adopt a different posture. For Mirza, it is a secret of Nature, and he does not seek its clarification, for the Creator himself has made it so. The pilgrim, remembering the master's [Mirza's], instructions, seeks to deepen his understanding. (Zawadzka 123)

In a repetition of the formative template established in "View of the Mountains," Mirza's calm in the later sonnet, "Mount Kikineis," contrasts prominently with the Pilgrim's querulous restlessness. The character whom Mickiewicz presents as an oriental paragon benefits from an ability to accept the cosmic order of things, a trait that the western Pilgrim clearly lacks. Mirza's interaction with the surrounding world communicates security and certainty, precisely those feelings that the Pilgrim needs. But he must pointedly grapple with his western ballast when trying to inculcate these feelings within himself.

Imperial Entanglements

The representation of other peoples, especially in East-West relations, has become one of the central questions for much of contemporary critical discourse. For the most part, contemporary Polish scholarship has not taken up this politically charged issue. And yet, any nuanced understanding of the "Crimean Sonnets" must devote attention to the representation of otherness. The key to understanding the entire volume lies in Mirza's status within the world of Mickiewicz's poetic cycle and the discursive choices made by the Polish bard. Does Mickiewicz replicate the patterns of Western European Orientalism? More specifically, is the Pilgrim's companion in the Crimean journey a stereotypical orientalist creation? The following section discusses a whole range of existing and possible interpretations in order to arrive at a satisfactory answer to these questions.

The Polish scholar Janina Kamionka devotes considerable attention to the subject of Romantic travel. She concludes her remarks on the "Crimean Sonnets" by contending that in Crimea the Pilgrim sees almost exclusively landscapes, even though he closely observes the signs of human existence and action throughout history. According to Kamionka, Mickiewicz's account does not contain the things that usually provided the impetus for sojourns to the South and the East. She notes that

> Living people are missing, as are their customs, their appearance, their temperament, their costumes, their activities, etc. The eastern markets, the popular legends, the people in general—all are missing: there is only the sober comrade of the journey.... Only the narrator, the speaking subject, is a fully developed figure. He is the only one who is richly portrayed, constantly present, and who possesses depth. (154)

One would look in vain in the "Crimean Sonnets" for a trove of ethnographic information on the Crimea, which Mickiewicz himself characterizes as "the Orient in miniature." On the surface, living people and their settlements form only a small part of the Crimean landscape in Mickiewicz's cycle. In "Bakhchisaray by Night," we see them dispersing after a religious service. The plural dative pronoun "nam" (to us) used by Mirza in "Czatyrdah" implies the presence of a Tatar community. Roman Koropeckyj points out that Mirza himself is "never objectively described by the narrator of the cycle, never even glossed in the notes" (666). Indeed, it is the incorporation of Mirza's voice into the "Crimean Sonnets" that hints at the most significant aspect of a Crimean presence within the sequence. Without the objectivizing burden of ethnography, Tatar otherness enters the stage in the person of the Traveler's guide.[11] The Traveler/Pilgrim speaks more often than Mirza does. Nonetheless, five of the sonnets feature as their lyrical subject the Tatar, who is thus guaranteed a prominent position in the cycle.

Kamionka suggests that Mirza lacks sufficiently eastern traits; that he functions "merely" as a travel companion. Mirza, in fact, does not fit the stereotype of the so-called "free Arab." This Romantic construct portrayed the inhabitants of the Orient as independent and brave, proud, passionate and spontaneous. This mythical Arab often behaved like a misanthrope, a trait indicative of his nineteenth-century European origins. This literary myth's scholarly antecedents extended back to the Enlightenment. In his 1784 *Ideen für Philosophie der Geschichte der Menschheit,* Johann Gottfried Herder compared the Arabs' kingdoms with a southern Tatary and thus made the two types of oriental polities interchangeable. For the leading German Enlightenment thinker, the Arabs reveled in their freedom and derived great pride from their heritage, their nobility, their families and their god. Herder uses an analysis of old Arabian poetry to buttress the claim that the Arabs'

> propensity to adventure, love, and glory; and even their love of solitude, thirst of vengeance and wandering life, were all incentives to poetry, and their muse distinguished herself by splendid imagery, pride and grandeur of sentiment . . . (593)

Leon Borowski, one of Mickiewicz's teachers at the University of Wilno, devoted a section of his *Remarks on Poetry and Rhetoric* to oriental poetry. In it, he repeats almost verbatim some of Herder's pronouncements about the Arabs and expounds on them by emphasizing the perceived poetic character of the Orientals' thoughts and deeds. Mickiewicz had to be aware of both Herder's and Borowski's ideas about the Arabic Orient. Had the poet taken his cue from the scholarly and literary fashion of the day, his familiarity with literary Orientalism could have easily transformed Mirza into a conventional embodiment of easternness and overt otherness redolent with well-worn stereotypical traits.

But Mickiewicz's literary account of the Orient went further than the reigning convention. The Pilgrim's view of Mirza betrays only trace amounts of the free Arab's colorful and radically different character that so inflamed the western imagination. The absence in Mirza of many of the characteristics often imposed on contemporary inhabitants of the East by western travelers explains Kamionka's contention that Mirza is not "different" enough to assume the role of the oriental Other. This contention, however, fails to notice one crucial thing. The absence of distinguishing traits that would make Mirza stand out in his easternness preempts any attempt to typecast the Tatar as a superficial element of oriental stylization. Rather, Mirza occupies the position of a speaking subject who participates actively in a dialogue.

Mirza combines wisdom with calm acceptance of the laws of nature. Viewed through the prism of the determinative literary antecedents of Mickiewicz's time, Mirza is closer to the eighteenth-century image of a noble savage than to a typical nineteenth-century Oriental. But as Halden White argues, European writers developed the concept of the noble savage not to dignify the native, but rather to demote the idea of nobility. The creation of the noble savage was, accordingly, entirely motivated by domestic needs and interests (183-96). Evaluated as a way of representing otherness, the status of an eighteen-century noble savage does not differ much from that of the free Arab of the following era.

A Saidian analysis would see both as symptomatic of the egoistic and ethnocentric character of all European ventures into the Orient. Viewed from this perspective, Mirza could be interpreted as representing yet another attempt to indulge in a selfish appropriation of another culture that has been conveniently stylized to fit the purpose. And Mickiewicz would have to be seen as one of many European writers whose need to assert the superiority of Europeanness inevitably led them to exercise discursive control over non-Europeans. The Saidian paradigm presents imperial conquest as one of the logical consequences of this type of discursive pursuit.

The very definition of otherness compels the affirmation and imposition of prevailing norms as a way of countering the Other. Failure to do so would infect hegemonic western discourse with a fatal contradiction.

Some traditional and recent interpretations of the "Crimean Sonnets" situate Mickiewicz squarely within the hegemonic European literary tradition. Juliusz Kleiner, one of the foremost Mickiewicz scholars, relies unambiguously on the determinative notion of Eurocentric thinking. Kleiner's interpretation of the sequence eschews any critical questioning of the interpretive tradition that alleges appropriation of the Orient for the express purpose of enabling western self-expression. Kleiner satisfies himself with the claim that eighteenth-century writers used Orientalism to camouflage their critiques of various aspects of domestic politics. Likewise, for the Romantics, Orientalism purportedly provided a mask that allowed them to liberate themselves from the bounds that Europe seemingly imposed on the writers' imaginations and passions. Kleiner's Mickieiwcz subscribes to this tradition: his Mirza serves as a convenient disguise for the author of the "Crimean Sonnets." Kleiner draws on "Czatyrdah" to illustrate his argument, asserting that Mickiewicz's oriental stylization breaks down in the lyrical voice's final address to the mountain. The reference to Bóg (God) rather than Allah reveals that the actual speaker in this sonnet, the one who expresses his religious feelings, is not Mirza, but the author himself (535-37).

Wacław Kubacki's excellent analysis of the same sonnet weakens the validity of Kleiner's example by demonstrating how Mickiewicz combined elements of Muslim and Hebrew Orientalism (89). Contrary to Kleiner, Roman Koropeckyj is fully cognizant of the dangers of a discursive involvement with Orientalism. But he reaches a conclusion about Mirza that is nonetheless in sync with Kleiner's. For Koropeckyj, Mirza is "something of an occidental ventriloquist's oriental dummy, wearing a turban and mouthing a stylized, syncretic language" (666). This relationship between *The Sonnets'* subject and Mirza constitutes, according to Koropeckyj, yet one more indicator of the degree to which Mickiewicz depends on the colonizing orientalist discourse. Like Kleiner, Koropeckyj runs roughshod over the nuances apparent in the Traveler/Pilgrim-Mirza relationship. As demonstrated above, this relationship's dialogical character situates Mirza firmly outside the overdetermined orientalist paradigms.

Many Polish scholars subscribe to a politically opposite interpretation of the affinities between Mirza and the Pilgrim. These
readings define the Pole and the Tatar as embodiments of their
respective homelands. Mickiewicz draws the readers' attention to
the parallels between Crimea and Poland, both of which are victims
of Russian imperialism. This patriotic interpretive line contends
that the "Crimean Sonnets" transmit an antiimperialist message,
one diametrically opposed to the Saidian interpretation.[12]

For example, the presence of ruins in Mickiewicz's Crimean
landscapes does not denote, as such an interpretation of the trope
would have it, that the poet sees the Orient as speechless and impo-
tent. Since Russian imperialism victimized both Crimea and Poland,
those who detect in Mickiewicz's work the intent to affirm stateless
nationalism's viability construe the ruins as a symbol of Crimea's
past glory and, by association, as a symbol of Poland's lost statehood. The "Crimean Sonnets'" contemplation of history's vanitas
may also contain an element of hope; the ruins hold forth the promise that the empire that has so wantonly engulfed the Pilgrim's and
Mirza's unfortunate homelands must also fall. Jerzy Świdziński
detects political overtones that determine meaning in the sonnet
cycle. He asserts that Mickiewicz had one sole purpose when he
penned it: to express political dissent. Oriental stylization thus provided a mechanism for pulling the wool over the tsarist censor's
eyes. Swidziński records that

> several pictures of the steppe, the sea, the mountains, the moun-
> tain valleys, the southern sky, of the ruins and two human settle-
> ments absorbed by the landscape sufficed to hide political allu-
> sions, to create a tragic vision of the land of exile, and, finally, to
> dissipate the myth of the Arcadian land of bounty and beauty.
> (79)

This particular interpretation defines the "Crimean Sonnets" as an
early variation on a theme later developed so famously by
Mickiewicz in "Digression" ("Ustęp") of *Forefather's Eve, Part III*,
the work that established him as a harsh, uncompromising critic of
imperial Russia's ruthlessness.

Several factors make it plausible to consider the poet a conscious
propagator of anticolonial discourse: the context of his stay in
Russia; the circumstances of his journey to Crimea; the reality of his
political exile; and the company of people who were on the side of

his oppressors. When Mickiewicz dedicated the "Crimean Sonnets" to the companions of his Crimean journey, those individuals' unsavory secrets were hardly a secret to him. He knew that Boshniak was a spy. He also suspected what role Witt and his informants—including Karolina Sobańska—had played in the unmasking of the Decembrist conspiracy, the participants in which were notably more sympathetic to the Polish cause than was the tsarist autocracy (Gomolicki 93). Seen in this light, Mickiewicz may very well have conceived the "Crimean Sonnets'" dedication "to the companions of the Crimean journey" as a device for placating the censor. Perhaps what he saw as the successful use of such a device encouraged the poet to hone it further in his 1828 narrative poem *Konrad Wallenrod*, a benchmark work of nineteenth-century Polish Romantic nationalism. *Wallenrod's* preface goes so far as to praise Tsar Nicholas I for his tolerance and to ennoble the repressive autocrat as "the father of many nations" who "grants them the possession of material as well as spiritual goods" (*Dzieła* 2, 318).[13]

Świdziński's reading defines the "Crimean Sonnets" as, first and foremost, the cry of an exile consumed by thoughts of his tragic situation and engaged in an active attempt to rebel against a system of oppression. The Tatar companion's presence merely provides further evidence of the oppression he is chafing against. But just as Roman Koropeckyj's labeling of Mickiewicz as an imperialist fails to interpret the Crimean sequence satisfactorily, neither does reducing the "Crimean Sonnets'" message to a call for political dissent offer a fully tenable interpretive framework. Świdziński's circumscribed take on the work in the 1970s most likely grew out of an intentional choice to oversimplify Mickiewicz so as to engender a reading that communicated a subversive message directed against the realities of communist Poland. By this point, the post-1956 loosening of the intellectual straightjacket in the People's Republic had progressed to the point that all manner of artistic and scholarly texts contained between-the-lines messages of defiance against the political status quo.

Świdziński, however, retrofits the Pilgrim with the distinguishing traits of Konrad from *Forefathers' Eve, Part III*. These two figures belong to disparate stages of Mickiewicz's life and literary career, and the poet conceived and articulated them in different ways. Overall, optimism—not tragedy—characterizes the experiences of Mickiewicz's Traveler/Pilgrim in the "Crimean Sonnets." By the time his journey concludes, he has overcome the feelings of loss, and the discovery of the positive sublime has cast everything in a new light. "Ajudah" (XVIII), the last sonnet, depicts the Pilgrim as someone entirely free of bitterness. In the words of Tadeusz Boy-Żeleński—one of interwar Poland's preeminent literary figures—the November uprising of 1830 hit Mickiewicz "like a rock on the head" (15). In the wake of this failed bid for independence against overwhelming odds, Polish literature could no longer accommodate the type of discovery and the type of poetry displayed in Mickiewicz's Crimean work.

In addition, while he was in Odessa and Moscow, Mickiewicz's feelings towards Russia and the Russians were more ambivalent than Świdziński suggests. The Polish poet did identify Russia's government with imperialist oppression, but sympathy and respect for many of the people whom he encountered during his Russian exile counterbalanced—to a degree—his negative assessment of tsarist Russia's international role. Boy-Żeleński rightly notes that, even though Mickiewicz was a political exile while in Russia, the experience imbued him with a sense of liberation. The country's rich cultural life impressed Mickiewicz and helped him mature as a poet (14). Moreover, a limited and limiting interpretation of the "Crimean Sonnets" which confines them to a covert political statement effaces Mickiewicz's genuine interest in the Orient and in Orientalism and misses the broader philosophical issues broached by the work.

The two contradictory interpretations of Mirza as the oriental Other bring Polish culture's peculiarities into stark relief. Mickiewicz's encounter with Crimea reflected an intellectual crisis that was Western European in origin and that led the poet to participate in the discourse of Orientalism. At the same time, Polish colonial dispossession colors the "Crimean Sonnets." More important, this paradox demonstrates that narrow ideological readings of the cycle are unsatisfactory. For Mickiewicz, the Crimean journey facilitated liberation into a universally human, not a specifically Polish condition.

Postcolonial criticism has both developed and partly placed itself in opposition to the views articulated by Said in *Orientalism*. Some postcolonial theorists have advocated that subjugated (subaltern) cultures should occupy a subject position. Others have pointed to the multifaceted character of the non-Westerners' relationship with western cultural influences. Such postcolonial developments

encourage a movement away from categorical statements and legitimize a search for a middle ground. Without denying that academic
as well as literary Orientalism played a role in mapping the Orient
for conquest, it may be useful to point out that late-eighteenth-cen-
tury and nineteenth-century interest in the Orient was multifaceted.
Alongside a selfish appropriation of elements of eastern culture
either for the purpose of reevaluating the West through the creation
of superficial oriental Others, or for the purpose of imperial conquest, the process of gathering information about eastern cultures
initiated in the eighteenth century and continued into the nineteenth
century formed one of the elements that led to the birth of modern
humanism. Humanism itself has been denounced for its attempts
to impose essentializing patterns of development on non-western
contexts. And yet it is an ideology that has to be credited with
acknowledging the equal status of all cultures.[14] It was primarily this
humanist aspect of Western European Orientalism that appealed to
Mickiewicz. In the relationship between the Pilgrim and Mirza the
Polish poet produced a humanist blueprint for relating to representatives of other cultures. His text promotes respect for difference
without transforming that difference into a fetish.

Mirza is not a noble savage. He does not just function as an alle-
gorical embodiment of the virtues that are to expose the corrupt,
civilized world's vices. Neither does Mickiewicz's Traveler/Pilgrim
project his personal anxieties on to the Tatar. Mirza becomes an
ontological Other in the positive sense of the word. The mediation
of an Easterner renders the space beyond the borders of that which
is familiar accessible to the Westerner. As this analysis has emphasized throughout, Mirza plays a role much closer to that played by
the Bakhtinian Other. Dialogue with the Other leads to the affirmation of one's own existence. This affirmation comes after the realization that

> I cannot perceive myself in my external aspect, feel that it encom-
> passes me and gives me expression . . . . In this sense, one can
> speak of the absolute aesthetic need of man for the other, for the
> other's activity of seeing, holding, putting together and unifying,
> which alone can bring into being the externally finished person-
> ality. (qtd. in Todorov, *Bakhtin* 95)

Mickiewicz's Orientalism is more than a superficial masquerade.
The pattern of relations to the Other that emerges from the

"Crimean Sonnets" allows for communication between individuals of different cultural backgrounds. Dialogism becomes a celebration of alterity (Clark and Holquist 65). The sonnet does not constrict the Muslim inhabitants of Crimea. It provides the necessary structure for introducing into the cycle a voice that represents them. Debating the degree of Mirza's authenticity makes no sense—the Polish poet's authorship is unquestionable and therefore the Tatar cannot be authentic. Far more important is the great prominence his voice assumes within the cycle: Mirza operates as an authoritative interlocutor who offers answers to the Traveler's questions. The location of the Tatar's voice in the sestet provides yet another example of a perfectly harmonious interplay of form and meaning in Mickiewicz's Crimean cycle.[15]

Mickiewicz and Eastern Literary Traditions

Any consideration of the cultural ramifications and consequences of Mickiewicz's choice of the sonnet must take into account this literary form's genealogy. In his analysis of the "Crimean Sonnets," Wacław Kubacki points out that the Romantics were aware of the sonnet's oriental origin (157). He refers to several nineteenth-century sources that consider the affinities between the *ghazal* and the sonnet (95-97). Like the sonnet, the ghazal has a regular metric and rhyming pattern. Both the ghazal and the sonnet contain elements of description and introspection. Kubacki also mentions a lecture delivered by an Italian scholar, A. Cappeli, at the University of Wilno in 1817. Capelli discussed eastern influences in Petrarch (97). Mickiewicz's notes to the "Crimean Sonnets" cite Josef von Hammer's *Geschichte der schoenen Redekuenste Persiens*. Von Hammer asserted elsewhere that the Italians borrowed from the Arabs the form of the *ottava rima* and partially that of the sonnet, as well as the latter's name (Hammer-Purgstall 21). Nineteenth-century scholarship's and literature's preoccupation with Orientalism meant that the sonnet's genealogy could only have heightened the Polish poet's curiosity about this literary form. The prevalence of orientalist interests among the faculty and many of the alumni of Mickiewicz's Wilno alma mater has been well documented (A. Zajączkowski, *Orient jako źródło inspiracji*). Mickiewicz doubtlessly associated the sonnet with its supposed oriental origin.

The dialogue between Mickiewicz's Pilgrim and the Muslim Mirza in the "Crimean Sonnets" forms a reenactment of a cultural exchange that took place long before this literary encounter was devised. The sonnet sequence presents a perfect medium for the writing of an oriental travelogue. At the same time, Mickiewicz's choice of the sonnet for the cycle takes us back to this literary form's inception. Unlike nineteenth-century sources, recent studies of the development of the sonnet often ignore the possibility of an Arab influence. Paul Oppenheimer focuses on the influence of classical Greek and Roman literatures, while Michael Spiller emphasizes the influence of Provençal poetry in the development of the sonnet (Oppenheimer, *The Birth* 22-25; Spiller, *The Development* 15-27). For the purpose of an analysis of the "Crimean Sonnets," Mickiewicz's own belief in the sonnet's oriental origin is what matters. Yet, given the cultural milieu that surrounded the sonnet's first appearance, the hypotheses of two centuries ago may indeed deserve some credit.

The first European sonnets were written at the court of Emperor Frederic II of Sicily in the first part of the thirteenth century. Twenty-five of the thirty-five original sonnets known from the period are attributed to the Emperor's notary, Giacomo da Lentino, who is usually credited with the invention of this poetic form (Wilkins 463). Should the sonnet's structure indeed be Giacomo's ingenious literary invention, the cultural context in which this discovery appeared is certainly a factor to consider. Frederic II was Sicily's third Christian ruler after its recapture from the Arabs, who had ruled the island from around 902. According to W. M. Watt, Sicily prospered under Arab rule, and Islamic culture took firm root there (5). The Norman knight Roger recaptured Sicily. Watt explains that

> In the reconquest of Sicily material motives seem to have been stronger than religious ones, and in many respects it remained a part of the Islamic world. The externals of the life of some of the later rulers seemed to contemporaries more Muslim than Christian. In particular Roger's son Roger II (1130-54) and the latter's grandson Frederick II of Hohenstaufen (1215-50) have been called "the two baptized sultans of Sicily." (5)

In "The Invention of the Sonnet," Wilkins asserts the sonnet's Sicilian origins. He also speculates that the sonnet's sestet might have derived from the Arab *zagal* (107-108). Oppenheimer points out that Wilkins abandoned this idea in a subsequent publication ("The Origin" 289). Oppenheimer himself recognizes that the atmosphere of the court of Frederic II, "the most brilliant, intellectual, and literary emperor of the age," provided the necessary environment for the development of the sonnet. "The nature of the new lyric, the sonnet," continues Oppenheimer, "with its capacity for self-confrontation, corresponds perfectly to the questioning, 'modern' spirit of Frederick's own life and career, in which accepted forms and modes of thought, including those of the Church itself, were subjected to constant challenge" (300). Like others, though, Oppenheimer stops short of considering a direct Arab influence on the birth of the sonnet. A systematic investigation of the history of this verse form, and even more so of the merits of the different hypotheses that explain the sonnet's origin, exceeds the scope of this study. In a bibliographical essay, Michael Spiller observes that towards the end of the nineteenth century

> nationalism had bedeviled discussions of the sonnet with two controversies: was the sonnet in its origins French/Provençal or was it a native Italian creation?—an issue of more than academic interest during the Italian struggle for independence in the nineteenth century. (*The Sonnet Sequence* 161)

One can only hope that a similar rendition of Eurocentric particularism has not prevented western scholars from recognizing that what Oppenheimer identifies as the inception of modern poetry in the West began, in all likelihood, as a dialogue with the East.

By the time Mickiewicz wrote about Crimea, there was nothing original in transforming a journey to the East into a modern pilgrimage. Mickiewicz followed in the footsteps of some formidable predecessors. But pilgrimages have always been conceived as journeys towards a source of an essential truth, and, as such, they have tended to reaffirm that single truth. By contrast, Mickiewicz, in his journey towards the wellspring of human creativity, emphasizes the continued importance of dialogue. The dialogical relationship of Mickiewicz's Traveler/Pilgrim to Mirza, his guide, reenacts the original, seminal exchange between the East and the West that led to the inception of the sonnet. Since the sonnet's oriental origin may have led Mickiewicz to adopt the form of the sonnet sequence for his oriental travelogue, the analogy between the two sonnet sequences and the forms of Arabic literature may go even further. Indeed, considered in their entirety, the Odessa sonnets and the "Crimean Sonnets" form a narrative that closely resembles an older form of Arabic poetry from which the ghazal is said to have evolved, the *qasidah*.

The Qasidah Connection

In his lengthy analysis of the "Crimean Sonnets," Wacław Kubacki stresses that parallel structures form the backbone of the sonnets. However, he overlooks that an investigation of any such structures should also account for the fact that *The Sonnets* contained not one, but two sonnet sequences. The sequence that precedes the Crimean travelogue, the so-called Odessa sonnets, has received far less attention than has the former one, not only in Kubacki's monograph, but in the work of other scholars as well. Even fewer have looked at the volume in its entirety. Czesław Zgorzelski is one of the few to consider the possibility of viewing *The Sonnets* as a unit.[16]

Zgorzelski presents an interesting investigation of the two cycles' inner dynamic. He points out stylistic and thematic continuities: within certain groups of sonnets, certain motifs arise, continue and subside. He also points to the sonnets that both sum up the developments of a part of the cycle and foreshadow its further course. He talks about the cycles' progression, in which a certain dialectic seems to operate on at least two levels. On a metaliterary level, the first cycle evinces a clear progression of literary conventions: from sonnets that borrow from Petrarch, through sentimental poetry and the poetry of Romantic disenchantment, to irony that brings all social forms and literary conventions into question, and to the sober realism in the sonnets that come near the cycle's end. Mickiewicz clearly emphasizes the literariness of his own utterance. Zgorzelski observes that

> One can trace the hand of the master, who does not intend to conceal his activity. Quite the contrary: he is interested in providing a crafted, literary form for his utterance. In this group of sonnets one can hear a rich tradition of several centuries. They resound with echoes of Petrarch in the way they present the sorrows and joys of an ideal love. Just as in the following group one will hear the echoes of Byron. (105)

On another level, underneath the literary conventions, there is what Mickiewicz's friend Tomasz Zan referred to as the "journey of the heart" (Billip 337). The Odessa sonnets present subsequent phases of a relationship: from a pure fascination with the beloved through the relationship's ripening to disenchantment. The last three sonnets of the first cycle provide a synthesis of the different stages of an emotional journey that continues throughout *The Sonnets'* first part. "Danaids" (XXI) ends with this *summa summarum*:

> Danaidy! rzucałem w bezdeń waszej chęci
> Dary, pieśni i we łzach roztopioną duszę
> Dziś z hojnego jam skąpy, z czułego szyderca.

> Danaids! Into the abyss of your desire I have thrown
> Gifts, songs, and a soul melted in tears;
> Today no longer generous, I have become a miser, no longer tender, I am now a jester.

Zgorzelski rightly points out that this sonnet does not mark the end of the road for *The Sonnets'* persona. The journey breaks out of the boundaries of the first cycle and continues into the second, Crimean, cycle. Just like in the previous cycle's successive love episodes, the following stages of the journey through the steppe, by sea and through the mountains mark the Traveler's subsequent transformations. In Zgorzelski' s words: "We first see him with a grimace of Byronic disbelief on his face, but later, in front of the majestic beauty of nature, he changes into a pilgrim who stares at the skyrocketing greatness of Czatyrdah" (117).

The thematic and structural continuities that unite the two sonnet cycles justify viewing the entire collection as a single sequence. The Odessa sonnets and the "Crimean Sonnets" complement each other just as the sestet complements the octave. But a much sharper correspondence exists between the narrative structure of Mickiewicz's *Sonnets* and the primary form of classical Arabic literature: the qasidah. Mickiewicz was certainly familiar with this literary form. During the time of his Russian exile, the poet authored two translations from the French of Arab qasidahs, "Szanfary. A Qasidah from the Arabic" ("Szanfary. Kasyda z arabskiego") and "Almotenabby," and one original poem, "Farys. A Qasidah Composed in Honor of Emir Tadj-Ul-Fekhr" ("Farys. Kasyda na cześć Emira Tadż-Ul-Fechra ułożona"). Scholars interested in Arab influences in Mickiewicz's poetry have analyzed all three poems (Uziębło, Benda, Segel). Even though the same authors refer to the "Crimean Sonnets" as Mickiewicz's best "oriental" work, they do not at all consider the possibility that Arabic literary forms served as a subtext for the sonnet sequence.

Aleksander Chodźko, Mickiewicz's friend, and himself a student of oriental literatures, authored a narrative poem titled "Derar. An Eastern Tale in Two Qasidahs" ("Derar. Powieść wschodnia w dwóch kasydach"). Chodźko provides a definition of the qasidah in an introduction to the poem. This definition indicates that the author conceived the bipartite narrative of "Derar" in imitation of the qasidah (*Poezje* 117—118). According to Józef Bielawski, the qasidah—a "narrative poem with a goal"—is the most refined form of Old Arabic literature. There are two main parts to a qasidah: "one is more conventional, less diversified, the other one, where the poet addresses the main subject and reaches his end, is more diversified" (27). Although other authors explain that the qasidah traditionally developed a tripartite structure and consisted of an amatory prologue, a disengagement, and the main theme, they acknowledge that the poet was free to allow himself a certain degree latitude within this structure.

In the *nasib*, the qasidah's first and more conventionalized part, the poet often travels with companions and comes across the site of a former encampment. He halts his journey, and in his memory he goes back to the happy times he spent there with his beloved. In his analysis of the qasidah, Abdulla el Tayib, writing about the nasib, notes that

> The mention of the abode, or indeed anything associated with it, evokes memories of the beloved and of past hours of happiness. The poet's heart is moved by anything reminiscent of it—the name of a land, its sand dunes, its hills, the stars that indicate the way to it to the traveler . . . (46)

In keeping with this tradition, Chodźko precedes the first part of his narrative poem with the following epigraph: "In the evening I stopped by the site where she had stayed. I asked questions of this place, but it could not answer. No one lived there any more" (*Poezje* 119). Mickiewicz's sonnet VIII from the Odessa cycle, titled "To the Niemen River" ("Do Niemna"), sums up the developments of the sequence's preceding poems. Even though Mickiewicz published an earlier version of this sonnet in 1822, here, in the context of the sequence, the poem possesses all of the characteristics of the nasib.

Niemnie, domowa rzeko moja! Gdzie są wody,
Które niegdyś czerpałem w niemowlęce dłonie,
Na których potem w dzikie pływałem ustronie,
Sercu niespokojnemu szukając ochłody?

Tu Laura, patrząc z chlubą na cień swej urody,
Lubiła włos zaplatać i zakwiecać skronie,
Tu obraz jej malowny w srebrnej fali łonie
Łzami nieraz mąciłem zapaleniec młody.

Niemnie, domowa rzeko, gdzież są tamte zdroje,
A z nimi tyle szczęścia, nadziei tak wiele!
Kędy jest miłe latek dziecinnych wesele?

Gdzie milsze burzliwego wieku niepokoje?
Kędy jest Laura moja, gdzie są przyjaciele?
Wszystko przeszło, a czemuż nie przejdą łzy moje!

Niemen, river of my home! where the waters flow
That once I drew with youthful hands,
Where later I swam to the wild notch
Searching for cool respite for my unruly heart

Here Laura, looking proudly at the reflection of her beauty,
Liked to braid her hair and her forehead with flowers to adorn
Here, her picture painted on the bosom of a silver wave
I spoiled not once with my tears, a hot-headed youth.

Niemen, river of my home, where are those waters,
And with them all the happiness, so many hopes?
Where has the joy of my childhood gone?

Where would the storms of my rebellious age be more dear?
Where has my Laura gone, where are my friends?
Everything has passed, everything, but why not my tears?

Another feature of the nasib deserves mention in this analysis. The portrait of the beloved that emerges from the nasib is often equivocal:

The inamorata is often said to belong to an enemy tribe, and thus she serves the double role of a person sought after, but also proudly rejected when her demands grow excessive. (Abdulla El Tayib 44)

The tension that mounts in sonnets XII through XX of Mickiewicz's Odessa cycle leads to the realization that the beloved's demands have grown excessive. The subject proceeds to reject his lover. Independently of whether or not Karolina Sobańska was *The Sonnets'* addressee, the beloved of the Odessa sonnets appears to be a great deal closer to the inamorata of a qasidah than she is to Petrarch's Laura.

How do the "Crimean Sonnets" compare to the following parts of the qasidah? The epigraph that comes before the second part of Chodźko's qasidah reads: "Happy is the caravan that has you as the companion of her nocturnal journeys. The glow of your face illuminates the caravan's path" (*Poezje* 119). The epigraph signals that the description of a journey constitutes the main component of the qasidah's second part. Abdulla El Tayib writes: "The disengagement (*takhallus*) forms the second section of the qasidah, in which the poet makes his way out of the nasib towards the main motive of his qasidah." This is accomplished by describing a journey which the poet may have undertaken "to console himself and forget her (his) beloved in pursuing some other serious purpose, or to desert her just as she has done to him" (52). The same author provides several examples of "the disengagement." For example, Labid in his Mu'allaqah "severs the rope of amity with his inamorata of the nasib in retaliation for her turning away from him, and consoles himself by traveling on a swift-riding camel in pursuit of a more serious purpose" (54). Passing from a description of the second to the third part, El Tayib notes that

> The takhallus journey expresses the attempt at seeking relief from the intense emotion of the nasib. The "journey," pictured in terms of camel, desert and sympathetic communication with aspects and phenomena of nature, symbolizes the poet's endeavor to change from an introvert to an extrovert mood. The path of the journey leads into the main theme, with which comes the ultimate sense of relief. (56)

The "Crimean Sonnets" approximate both the "disengagement" and the "main theme" of the qasidah. Interpreted as a description of a journey—in large part on horseback—the sonnets correspond to the takhallus of classical Arab poetry. Throughout the journey, the poet gives his readers hints as to his ultimate destination. Sonnets V and XV are especially suggestive: both of them record the experience of sublimity. Approaching the sublime in nature constitutes a pilgrimage to the source of creation. The last of the "Crimean Sonnets," "Ajudah," is nothing less than Mickiewicz's "Exegi monumentum." Here the poet arrives at a reaffirmation of his identity and his creative energy. The journey to the realm of the absolute results in songs that will not perish.

The similarities between the structuring of the qasidah and the narrative dynamic of *The Sonnets* as a unit explain Mickiewicz's decision to publish both cycles, the Odessa sonnets and the "Crimean Sonnets," in one volume. A sustained heterogeneous view of culture emerges as the most significant ideological consequence of the subtextual relationship between Mickiewicz's sonnet sequence and the qasidah. The undercurrent of oriental influences in *The Sonnets* represents a nourishing, identity-forming relationship between what Mickiewicz and people around him would have referred to as the West and the East, without necessarily recognizing that the realm they inhabited was itself situated in an intermediary space.

Souvenirs and Lasting Impressions

Mickiewicz found still another way of bringing the East into his oriental cycle. He asked Mirza Djafir Topchy Bashy, whom he met through Józef Sękowski, to write an introduction to *The Sonnets* in Persian and to provide a translation of one of the poems. Aleksander Chodźko, who was not only Mickiewicz's close friend but also a student of Topchy Bashy, provided the latter with the sonnet's literal translation.[17] Mickiewicz intended to incorporate the translation into *The Sonnets*' first edition, but technical difficulties delayed its printing and it came off the press too late to be included in all of the edition's copies.[18]

Mickiewicz also attempted to study Persian. In a letter to Józef Kowalewski, the poet writes: "You ought to know that I am going to enter the oriental field. I am reading a history of oriental literature, and I have even translated six poems from Mirhonda's history from Persian, nota bene from the original" (*Listy* 283). Obviously, his linguistic endeavors could not rival those of Sękowski and this is why he needed Topchy Bashy's assistance in the translation intended for *The Sonnets*. Since most of Mickiewicz's readers were not able to read Persian, for the majority of them the text could only function as a visual attraction. It played the role of a souvenir that the traveler brought from a far away journey and put on display for visitors in his house. In addition, the text of Topchy Bashy's introduction served as a sort of a cultural imprimatur. Although he was not a Crimean Tatar, Mirza Djafar Topchy Bashy boasted a sophisticated knowledge of the culture into which Mickiewicz ventured during his journey. He could therefore evaluate the Polish poet's account from that culture's perspective and legitimize Mickiewicz's voice.

It is likewise significant that Mickiewicz selected "View of the Mountains from the Kozlov Steppes" for translation into Persian. The sonnet constitutes a dialogue between representatives of two different cultures. With the translation, Mickiewicz found yet another way to reach out to the Orient. It is another part of a dialogue that began when the poet decided to go to Crimea and familiarize himself not only with the sounds and sights of the peninsula, but also with its culture.

The East-West cultural dialogue structures every aspect of Mickiewicz's poetic travelogue. Far from being limited to the introduction of oriental imagery and language, through their form the "Crimean Sonnets" approximate oriental genres. Finally, the interaction between the Traveler/Pilgrim and Mirza presents not only the most tangible, but also the most important facet of the dialogue.

The Sonnets and Polish National Culture

Both the Commonwealth and the partitioned Polish lands were geographically and culturally close to the Orient, and they provided fertile ground for the renewed cultural and scholarly interest in things oriental that characterized Europe's intellectual atmosphere in the late 1700s and 1800s. The great ethnic diversity in the eastern Polish borderlands must have facilitated such interests. But this proximity to the Orient went hand in hand with a long history of political and military conflicts with Tatar and Ottoman neighbors that intensified especially in the seventeenth century and that spawned a tradition of anti-Muslim prejudice. In his notes to the *Collectanea*, an anthology of Turkish sources for the study of Polish history, Józef Sękowski speaks out against such prejudice. Sękowski argues against historiographic mythmaking and for using Ottoman sources to arrive at a more balanced view of Poland's history. "Our century is too enlight-

ened to take offense at what people of a different faith say. Prudent
tolerance is required of both sides. For the sake of truth and knowledge, let us make a noble sacrifice of our self-adulation," argued the
author (1, IX). In the introduction to his work's second volume,
Sękowski observes that,

> Imbued with the prejudices of our civilization, which we consid-
> er to be the only one, we have come to view the Turks as a nation
> bereft of education while, after all, there can exist two complete-
> ly different, dissimilar, but equally good civilizations . . . . On
> what grounds could we require that all people accept our system
> of beliefs, that they accept as beautiful that which we find beau-
> tiful . . . that they look at the world from the same perspective as
> we do, a perspective additionally colored by a charming prism of
> our self-delusions which we as a habit take to stand for reality.
> (2, VIII–XII)

When he wrote *The Sonnets*, Mickiewicz clearly shared
Sękowski's attitude towards the cultures of the East, even though the
ideological trajectories that the two men of letters later followed
were not always consistent with their earlier beliefs. In *The Sonnets*,
the realization that mutual openness and dialogue between the cultures of the West and the East may be beneficial to both sides follows from the belief that there may be two different but equally
good civilizations. Frustrated with the critics' response to *The
Sonnets*, Mickiewicz further articulates his views concerning relations between different cultures in his polemic "On Warsaw Critics
and Reviewers" ("O krytykach i recenzentach warszawskich").
Countering the opinions of those who criticized his openness
towards foreign influences and who feared that this attitude would
bring the downfall of national culture, Mickiewicz maintains that

> . . . predictions concerning the imminent collapse of literature
> and taste in Poland appear to be baseless—at least no such threat
> emanates from Romanticism. The history of world literature
> demonstrates that the collapse of taste and a dearth of talent
> have everywhere resulted from one cause: from limiting [the cul-
> ture] to a certain number of truths, thoughts, and opinions
> whose exhaustion leads to [the culture's] starvation and death
> because of a lack of nourishment. This [process] brought about
> the collapse of Byzantine literature, the greatest heir to the mon-
> uments of Greek [culture]. While isolating itself from the Franks
> and the Arabs, Byzantine literature refused to accept new forms

as the centuries passed. A similar exhaustion affected French literature in the last century. During the times of the Jesuits here in Poland, precisely the people most versed in the rules of rhetoric—professors of rhetoric and clergy—disseminated bad taste. General ignorance resulted not from the introduction of foreign scholarly principles, but rather from the strict adherence to the old methods. When Konarski sought to prove the necessity of the French language, the Jesuits' students and supporters expressed their outrage at this innovation—just as the students and supporters of the Warsaw school inveigh against English and German literature. (5, 316)

Of course, it was not just the influence of English and German ideological trends on contemporary Polish literature that the "Warsaw school" critics feared. The critical response to *The Sonnets* demonstrated that any perceived contamination with eastern influences— no matter whether they were coming to Poland directly from the East or were mediated by the West—was certain to cause the conservatives to sound the alarm.

Mickiewicz responded to his critics with the unequivocal assertion that any culture's well-being depended on its openness to foreign influences. Such a dialogical view of intercultural communication implies a nonadversarial relationship between national cultures: "He often spoke of the approaching times/ when nations, having forgotten animosities/ will unite in a great family," wrote Pushkin, remembering Mickiewicz's Russian exile in his 1834 poem, "He Lived Among Us." "On Warsaw Critics and Reviewers" elicited an early manifestation of Mickiewicz's belief in the brotherhood of nations that later formed an important part of his ideological credo. But the prophetic internationalism of Mickiewicz's 1832 *Books of the Polish Nation and the Polish Pilgrimage* (*Księgi narodu i pielgrzymstwa polskiego*) may, to a contemporary reader, seem pretentious and exclusive because of the work's strongly nationalist tone. In contrast, the concept of national culture that emerges from *The Sonnets* and the polemical formulations of "Warsaw Critics" retains its appeal. Nearly two hundred years after their writing, these texts still point to a way of reconciling globalizing tendencies in culture with efforts to preserve native distinctions.

Safeguarding a national culture against all foreign influences and, on the other hand, narrowly interpreting all orientalist discourse as imperialist master discourse both obliterate the possibility of a nonviolent discursive relationship. At the sonnet's origin lies an identity-forming cultural exchange, not aggression projected on to the Other. Mickiewicz reaffirms this exchange in his sonnet sequence. To discover one's own creative energy one must undertake a journey into the land of the (other) poet. The displacement that came with exile allowed Mickiewicz to recognize and respect the difference of the Other and to embrace the otherness within himself. Within a postcolonial theoretical perspective, *The Sonnets* occupy a space that "opens up the possibility of a cultural hybridity that entertains difference without an assumed or imposed hierarchy" (Bhabha 4).

NOTES

1. Parts of this chapter have been previously published in *The Polish Review* and in *Slavic and East European Journal.*
2. Karolina Sobańska's miscellany is part of the collection of the Pushkin House in St. Petersburg. Item number 244, page 60.
3. S. S. Landa hypothesizes that Mickiewicz's presence in Witt's retinue must have been connected with the general's ongoing investigation of the brewing political conspiracy that culminated with the Decembrist uprising. By keeping a close eye on Mickiewicz, Witt may have hoped to discover the Polish poet's ties to Russian revolutionaries (Landa 240).
4. The excursion described in Władysław Mickiewicz's monograph was, most likely, one of several trips Mickiewicz made to the Crimea in the course of his stay in Odessa (Rymkiewicz 255).
5. By appending notes to the "Crimean Sonnets" Mickiewicz followed a convention established by other Romantic poets, including Pushkin. Susan Layton and Monika Greenelaf comment on the character and function of notes appended to Russian orientalist poetry. Layton concludes that, at the time, "no dichotomous style of thought prevailed, declaring *either* literature *or* science, *either* imagination *or* verifiable data. To the contrary, writers and readers in the 1820s entertained notions of poetry's potential as artful fact rather than frivolous artifact" (34). Greenleaf points out that both Byron and Pushkin used notes as "opportunities for stylistic disengagement" (118). Mickiewicz's notes are free of an ironic interplay with the text of the sequence proper. Rather, they validate *The Sonnets* as an oriental travel narrative.
6. Topchy-Bashy was a Persian who grew up in Tiflis. He taught oriental languages at the University of Petersburg along with Osip Senkovskii.
7. All of the quotations from *The Sonnets* come from a facsimile of the original 1826 Moscow edition (Zgorzelski). The original spelling varies on occasion from correct forms of contemporary Polish. All the translations into English are my own, unless otherwise indicated.
8. Edward Stankiewicz has analyzed the tension between visual and auditory impressions in the sonnets. He asserts that "the progressive journey in space is

thus at each point stalled by a retrospective journey in time, and under the surface of the outer, exotic world flows an undercurrent of the poet's innermost longings and aspirations." He then notes that "while the eye looks ahead into the darkness, seeking the guiding stars, the ear listens to voices of the past, to that which is intimate and dear, but remains silent, because it is prompted only by memory, by an act of the mind" (496-98).

9. In the most extensive up-to-date analysis of Mickiewicz's Crimean cycle, Wacław Kubacki identifies the sublime as one of the main elements of the "Crimean Sonnets'" poetics. He points out that Mickiewicz read Pseudo-Longinus' treaty "On the Sublime" in the course of his studies in Wilno. He names *The Sonnets'* stylistic elements that correspond to pseudo-longinian prescriptions (questions, series of verbs without conjunctions, particular use of tenses, etc.). He also discusses the concept of sublimity in Friedrich Schlegel, and a number of other figures of the same period, and he emphasizes that Romantic sublimity was discussed and understood in conjunction with Orientalism. He also remarks that the experience of sublimity constitutes the subject matter of "View of the Mountains" and "Czatyrdah" (Kubacki 44-72, 318).

10. Dmochowski, for example, notes that "in the ensuing part of the sonnet the Sultan's ceremonial dress and, in Mirza's response, the necks of the rivers, the beaks of the streams drinking from the nest, the clouds' journey and, finally, the 'A!!' ending the sonnet—all this—instead of grandeur—creates a strange and ridiculous impression" (Billip 76).

11. It may be useful to contrast the lack of ethnographic detail and description in the "Crimean Sonnets" with the abundance of this type of material in Anatoly Demidoff's 1837 Crimean travelogue. Unlike Mickiewicz, Demidoff, an enthusiastic advocate of Russia's territorial expansion, provided a wealth of ethnographic information about Crimea's native inhabitants, including the Tatars. The following comment, which concludes one of the account's ethnographic sections, reveals the exploitative nature of such intelligence gathering: "he [the Tatar] is naturally lazy, and he delights in his own laziness; but, nevertheless, he is capable of enduring the hardest and most painful toils" (344).

12. Megan Dixon presents an interesting interpretation of the "Crimean Sonnets" and "Digression" from *Forefathers' Eve Part III* that develops along similar lines. Mickiewicz's "construction of sympathy" expressed in the relationship between the Pilgrim and the native, concludes Dixon, "becomes a strategy to rewrite the Empire's view of itself, and to create a powerful picture which will resonate in the minds of the ostensible conquerors" (692).

13. Mickiewicz included the text of the preface in a Russian edition of *Wallenrod*. The poem's later editions did not include this text.

14. In *Orientalism*, Said identifies "sympathy" as one of the currents within eighteenth-century thought which formed the foundation of modern Orientalism. However, Said claims that this sympathy was merely a substitute for earlier Christian supernaturalism that served as a prerequisite to the accumulation of people and territories in which modern Orientalism has been implicated (123). As noted above, Megan Dixon comments on this aspect of Said's theory and its applicability to Mickiewicz's poetry.

15. I have analyzed the relationship between the Traveler/Pilgrim and Mirza of the "Crimean Sonnets" in "The Dialogue Between East and West in the *Crimean Sonnets.*"

16. As Rolf Fieguth points out, the thesis of the two-sonnet cycle's compositional unity has been suggested by several scholars, including Furmanik, Borowy, and Weintraub (91). Zgorzelski's investigation of *The Sonnets'* intercyclic linkages presents the most interesting study of the cycle's compositional unity.

17. Introducing an oriental sample into a nonoriental text was not Mickiewicz's ingenious invention. Here again he probably followed the example of Sękowski, the man whose work may have kindled his oriental interests in the first place. In 1824, the famous Polish Orientalist published a study titled *Supplement a l'histoire generale des Huns, des Turks et des Mongols*. An introduction in Persian, written by the author himself, preceded the French text of the study. The edition also included some of Sękowski's translations of poetry into various oriental languages.

18. In a letter to A. E. Odyniec, Mickiewicz writes: "Have the copies of a Persian translation of the sonnet sent from Petersburg arrived? I will send you a Polish translation of Djafar's interesting introduction at a later point. This translation was to be included in the edition, but it came out too late because of the lithographers and my agents, and now it is no longer needed" (Danilewicz 309).

CHAPTER 2

Polish Nineteenth-Century Travel to the Orient: Scholarship, Poetry, Politics

Talking about travels someone once noticed: I do not really care what you saw, but I am interested in how you saw it.

Maurycy Man, *Journey to the East*

In his biography of Jan Potocki, Aleksander Brueckner describes Potocki as Poland's first tourist and first travel writer. Brueckner goes on to identify a paradox, noting that, "as far as I know, there is no other nation as well traveled as the Poles that would produce such scarce travel accounts" (12). In fact, some Polish travelers made the trip to the East well before Count Potocki embarked on his voyages. For example, Mikołaj Krzysztof Radziwiłł "Sierotka" traveled to Jerusalem in 1582 and produced an account of his journey that deserves a place among the early-modern classics of the oriental travel genre. Unfortunately, the original Polish version of Radziwiłł's account was not published until 1925. Polish nineteenth-century travelers knew it only from abbreviated and retranslated versions. Likewise, contrary to Brueckner's contention, many other Polish travelers who went to the Orient in the years following Potocki's enlightened voyages actually did leave written descriptions of their journeys. But even those accounts that were published and enjoyed certain popularity among contemporary readers ceased to function as familiar reference points because they subsequently dropped out of the canon of Polish nineteenth-century literature. Moreover, Polish scholars have downplayed the oriental context of this period's literature. In a preliminary study of the Orient as a source of literary inspiration in Poland published several decades ago, Ananiasz

Zajączkowski appealed to scholars of Polish literature to produce a serious study of nineteenth-century literary Orientalism (*Orient jako źródło inspiracji* 12). Until now, few of them have responded to his call.[1]

Nineteenth-century Polish encounters with the East provide an excellent, if understudied, measure of the fate that befell the Poles after the partitions of the late eighteenth century and then in the wake of the failed anti-Russian uprising of November 1830. Polish oriental voyages from this period also provide insight into the Poles' attempts to narrate their own identity while grappling with the distinctive lynchpin of their national existence from 1795 onwards: stateless nationhood. Commentators have often overlooked the uniqueness of Polish oriental experiences despite the fact that Polish Orientalists' careers and, even more so, Polish writers' depictions of their own travel experiences in the Orient offer revealing windows into Polish culture's inbetweenness. The paradoxes of Polish Orientalism help illuminate the crucial period in Polish cultural history when, after the calamity of the Commonwealth's destruction, Polish scholars, intellectuals, politicians and writers began to articulate and refine a basic concept of modern Polishness.

One of the basic texts for the study of Russian Orientalism, Krachkovskii's *Sketches on the History of Russian Arab Studies* (*Ocherki istorii ruskoi Arabistiki*), includes an entire section devoted to oriental studies at the University of Wilno. Julian Sękowski was just one of the university's many Polish graduates who entered Russian imperial service as an oriental specialist. His work and service as the head of the Oriental Institute in St. Petersburg earned him international fame as an Orientalist as well as the reputation of a traitor to the national cause among his compatriots. Two influential professors in Wilno, Godfryd Grodek and Joachim Lelewel, worked on oriental subjects, and contact with these mentors encouraged talented students to direct their scholarly endeavors to the East (Reychman, "Zainteresowania" 74). Many a youthful, enthusiastic Wilno Orientalist's subsequent career gave concrete meaning to one of the key ideas of the emerging ideology of a nation in bondage— to the concept of *wallenrodyzm*.

Mickiewicz's narrative poem *Konrad Wallenrod* tells the story of a Lithuanian captive-turned-Teutonic knight. He advances to the position of the Order's grand master, all the while developing a plan to bring about the knights' downfall so he can save his own country.

Mickiewicz's contemporaries read the work as a sraightforward call to political and military action designed to evict the Russians from the large chunk of the Polish lands they controlled. But *Wallenrod* also expounded on the dilemmas of a colonized subject living out his life as one of the colonizers.[2] As Maria Janion notes, as early as their school days, the Wilno Philomaths debated whether or not to accept regular employment in the service of the Russian Imperial government (84). Entering into the service of the Russian Empire was the norm for Polish oriental specialists. They did so despite their abiding condemnation of Poland's subjugation to Russia. The following two examples illustrate the contradictions inherent to this situation.

One of the many colorful figures in the group of Polish oriental scholars, Ignacy Pietraszewski, resolved to become a serious student of the Orient partly in reaction to the publication of Julian Sękowski's *Collectanea*. Sękowski was, in his view, a renegade, someone who was "once . . . a Pole then a Russian writer." This characteristic, together with the negative image of Poland that Sękowski's anthology purportedly painted, offended Pietraszewski (Ogrodziński ix). In response, Pietraszewski set out to master Turkish so he could accurately translate Ottoman sources on Poland. Ironically, not only did Pietraszewski follow Sękowski to St. Petersburg, where he was allowed to study oriental languages, though only after he appealed directly to the tsar himself. In addition, after he graduated from the Institute of Oriental Languages in 1831, Pietraszewski also entered the Russian foreign service, a step glaringly at odds with his denouncement of Sękowski's allegedly traitorous activities. Pietraszewski went so far as to state that, to his "heart's delight," the tsarist bureaucracy posted him to Turkey as a dragoman at the Russian mission in Istanbul (Pietraszewski 7). Some eight years earlier, none other than Sękowski, Pietraszewski's ideological bête noire, occupied the exact same position, which—in an interesting twist on the Poles' intermediary position beween East and West—entailed acting as a linguistic and cultural interpeter/intermediary between Russian officials and the Turks.

Aleksander Chodźko's professional travels provide another good illustration of Polish Orientalism's intricacies and complexities. The investigation of the subversive unofficial student organizations at the University of Wilno also caught Mickiewicz's good friend Chodźko in its net. Mickiewicz's association with the Philomath group earned him exile from Lithuania and set him on the path to

Crimea. Likewise, Chodźko, after a short imprisonment, left Wilno in 1824 for St. Petersburg, where he became a student of oriental languages. After graduation, Chodźko followed the same path as most of the Institute's alumni. He entered the tsar's diplomatic service, working as a dragoman at the Russian mission in Constantinople. Later, Persia became the site of his most important contribution to Russia's imperialist program in the East (Płoszewski 381).

After years of actively promoting Russia's interests in the Orient, Chodźko settled in France, where he made a career out of interpreting the Orient for the West. His work from this period displays a

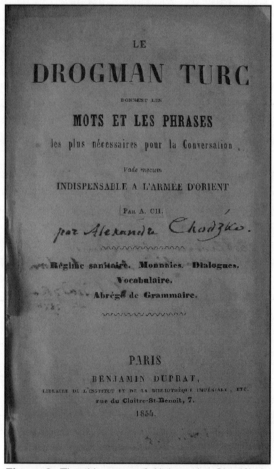

Figure 3: The title page of Aleksander Chodźko's
Le Drogman Turc (Paris, 1854).

devotion to scholarly accuracy and respect for the distinct cultural status of the objects of his analysis. But Chodźko also had a more mundane preoccupation. He assiduously appealed to the tastes of his work's immediate consumers. In his *Specimens of the Popular Poetry of Persia* (London 1842), Chodźko makes sure to include an oriental imprimatur similar to the one he helped obtain for Mickiewicz's *Sonnets*. In the introduction to his own *Specimens*, Chodźko writes that

> the best authority the compiler could find on the subject, Mahmud Khan Dumbulli, after having read thoroughly the narrative, appended to the last page his seal, with the following remark [the original text is given and followed by the translation]: "All is right, but the orthography of some Turkish words should be corrected." The learned observer means that the text of Kurroglou's own improvisations was not orthographied according to the system of the Constantinopolitan Turks. Some specimens of this text shall be given at the end of this volume, with all its original imperfections. (*Specimens* 14)

In an effort to underscore his own authority, Chodźko sets out to convince his readers of the text's authentic character and of its cultural relevance. At other moments, however, he does not hesitate to edit the Persian material to make it suit his western readers' taste. In an introduction to a selection of Persian songs, Chodźko informs that

> All the following songs, with few exceptions, came to me from the inmates of the harem of the late Feteh Aly Shah. I was favoured with them, at different epochs, by Chalanch Khan, the director of the Shah's orchestra, by Molla Kerim, his first singer, . . . names of high repute in the annals of the beau monde of Teheran. From that source, as from a central point, these songs, with their indispensable accompaniment—the dance—disseminate themselves all over the country . . . Many parts of these songs are so contrary to European manners that I was obligated to paraphrase, rather than translate them. We cannot, however, blame the Shah for taking pleasure in such productions. He was too much of a Persian to do otherwise. A Persian seeks in love only the gratification of sensuality; and his song, which expresses that love, and his dance, which is an illustration of his song, having but one tendency—the exciting of sensual desires—are sometimes obscene and revolting . . . . Persons able to consult the text of these songs will certainly admire the voluptuous elegance

> of the style in which they are written. In this respect, the erotic
> poetry of modern Persia perhaps has no equal in the literature of
> any other country. (*Specimens* 417-18)

Around the time of the first attempts to establish a faculty of oriental languages at the University of Wilno, a notice went out to the
public requesting financial support for the project. Its authors
emphasized that Poles, thanks to the sounds and other properties of
their native tongue, were better equipped to study oriental languages
than were western Orientalists (Reychman, "Zainteresowania" 77).
Chodźko fit into the category of specialists envisioned by this notice.
Though not an Oriental, he could present himself as someone who
had benefited from better access to and greater affinity with his oriental sources. At the same time, he boasted an understanding of the
western cultural context.

Chodźko's role as an intermediary between West and East
assumed an overtly political character when he entered the service of
the French foreign ministry in 1852. His tenure there coincided with
the Crimean War. While serving the French, he compiled a French-
Turkish pocket dictionary, *Le Drogman Turc*. This work bore an
unequivocal subtitle: *Vade mecum Indispensable a l'armee D'orient*.
When Mickiewicz struck out for Constantinople on his second oriental journey—the one from which he was fated never to return—
he studied Turkish from this *Vade mecum* (Zajączkowski 90). The
announcement of *Le Drogman* presents Chodźko once again as a
man well equipped to assume the task of democratizing French-
speakers' access to the Turkish language. Under the existing circumstances, the author asserts, *The Turkish Drogman* is destined to
become very popular:

> Every officer should carry it in his pocket; every soldier should
> have one in his bag. This is not a scholarly book. Our soldiers are
> not going to have the time to study the humanities in
> Constantinople.[3]

Indeed, apart from everyday phrases written in a simplified form of
the language and general information on such useful questions as
"how to rent a horse," the little book contains advice geared
towards a specific audience. For example, the section titled "The
Sanitary Regimen to be Followed in the Orient" notes that "after
work, battle, or a tiring march, one should make sure to remove

one's sweaty garments" (1). Chodźko's next assignment placed him in the service of the Shah of Persia. For several years, the Polish scholar oversaw young Persians studying in France.

Were political loyalties never permanently fixed in the oriental field? Polish Orientalists' professional careers revealed Poland to be an area of great cultural fluidity, a peculiar "contact zone," "where disparate cultures meet, clash, and grapple with each other" (Pratt 4). To start with, various and frequently contradictory impulses animated the development of Polish scholarly Orientalism. Alongside an interest in biblical studies, the growing interest in folklore and exoticism played a major role. The Western Europeans began to foster such interests already in the eighteenth century. A perceived cultural proximity to the Orient and the tradition of amateur orientalist studies nurtured by some of the magnate families—the cases of Jan Potocki and Wacław Rzewuski best illustrate this phenomenon—also inspired Poles who were willing to make a professional commitment to Orientalism.

A growing awareness of the East's strategic importance in the international arena weighed even heavier than the native Polish oriental tradition. Dismembered by the three partitions, Poland could not participate in the Great Powers' colonial contest. Yet, on occasion, the road to the state's resurrection appeared to run through the Orient. In an article written at the beginning of the 1830s, "What Do Events in the East Mean for Us?" ("Co nam wróżą wypadki na Wschodzie"), Mickiewicz expresses hope that the military conflict between Muhammad Ali, the viceroy of Egypt, and the Turkish sultan, supported on this occasion by Russia, will spread and give the Poles a chance to fight for their independence (*Dzieła* VI, 237).[4] Prince Adam Czartoryski, one of partitioned Poland's most influential politicians, and the leader of his own independence movement based at the Hotel Lambert in Paris, also appreciated the strategic importance of the East. Czartoryski's emissaries used Turkey as a base to launch military missions in aid of Caucasian mountaineers fighting against Russian rule (Reychman, *Podróżnicy* 219). In 1841, Czartoryski dispatched Michał Czajkowski to Turkey to gather information and represent Polish political interests to the Porte.[5]

At the same time, a confluence of intellectual and political aspirations led Polish orientalist scholars to serve the Romanov Empire's political interests, even though they perceived themselves to be victims of Russian imperialism on a par with the subjugated peoples of Crimea and the Caucasus. The alternative—and best-case scenario—was to work on the side of the oppressor's imperialist rivals, say, for France and thus against Russia. This option appeared to provide a way out of the "wallenrodian" conundrum.

Jan Reychman points out that the orientalist milieus in Wilno and St. Petersburg exerted a strong influence on Polish Romantic literature's formal and thematic contours. This influence also encompassed the work of Mickiewicz. "The connection between scholarly Orientalism and literary Orientalism is quite clear," Reychman contends ("Związki" 90). Like the scholarly counterpart that often informed many of its assumptions, Polish orientalist literature—in particular the literature of oriental travel—delivers ample proof that in the "contact zone" of Poland power relations extended beyond the simple patterns of domination and subordination present in East-West relations. For the Poles, literary travel to the orient constituted an exercise in negotiating their own cultural identity. Polish travelers and writers went to the Orient in part to assert their own westernness. To survey the Orient in the same manner as the Western Europeans meant to emphasize Poland's allegiance to Europe. Polish writers were therefore prone to replicate the models of cultural encounters present in Western European texts. Yet they did not participate in the West's colonizing enterprise. Rather, on the level of discourse, they faced the risk of becoming voluntary victims of colonization. In western European literature—especially in travel literature devoted to the Orient—"the view of the world as directed from the colonial metropolis was consolidated and confirmed" (Boehmer 14). But when Polish writers replicated a similar attitude while addressing Polish nineteenth-century readers, different connotations resulted. Instead of providing a measure of Poland's Europeanness, Polish travel literature about the Orient often bears signs of a discursive powerlessness and submissiveness in relation to its Western counterpart. Awareness of the Polish experience's specificity increased steadily following the defeat of the November 1830 insurrection. Polish writers had to articulate this momentous and traumatic national experience's unique character and simultaneously stress Polish participation in a culture perceived to be universally European.

As a consequence, post-1830 Polish literature of travel to the Orient appears to be no less riddled with contradictions than the professional engagements of Polish orientalist scholars throughout the century. Two sets of travel texts produced by authors of widely different stature elucidate the discursive tensions inherent to Polish culture's inbetweeness. Both travelers took voyages at roughly the same time, and both were writers. However, whereas Juliusz Słowacki saw himself as a worthy candidate for the title of Poland's first poet, Władysław Wężyk wrote sparsely and his literary output is relatively little known.

Juliusz Słowacki's Oriental Journey: from Irony to Melancholy

Słowacki set off on his journey to the East on August 24, 1836. He left from Naples and traveled to Greece, Egypt, Palestine, and Syria. He intended to compile an account of the journey in some form, but he did not produce anything even approximating a consistent oriental travelogue. The narrative poem in eight cantos, titled "A Journey to the Holy Land from Naples" ("Podróż do Ziemi świętej z Neapolu"), covers only the Greek part of the itinerary. Nor was it ever published in its entirety during the poet's lifetime. Further insights into the character of Słowacki's peregrination come primarily from a handful of poems he wrote during and soon after the journey, including the so-called letters in verse; from the letters to his mother and other correspondents written in the course of his voyage; and from two narrative poems that belong to the same period of his literary biography, "Anhelli" and "Father of the Plague Stricken" (Ojciec zadżumionych). The challenges implicit in writing from within the framework of Orientalism but from outside the western imperial power structure left their mark on Słowacki's poetry. Herein lies the explanation for two things: the poet's failure to find a form suitable for a finished travel narrative and the artistic choices made in the texts dealing directly with the journey and in other texts written around the same time.[6]

In a letter sent to an acquaintance, Zofia Balińska, on September 17, 1836, Słowacki first mentions his planned journey to the Orient, noting that

> In a couple of days I will bid farewell to the Teofils and I leave for the East: I am going to be in Greece, Egypt, and in Jerusalem .... Some sort of anxiety and longing for something undefined

compel me to move from place to place, and I perceive everything that surrounds me as if in a daze, immobile and in silence.
This has not always been the case. (XIV, 107)[7]

The opening stanzas of "A Journey to the Holy Land from
Naples" reveal a mixture of the same feelings of anxiety and uncer-
tainty along with a good dose of Romantic irony:

1

Muzo, mdlejąca z romantycznych cierpień,
Przybądź i pomóż! Wzywam ciebie krótko,
Sentymentalną bo kończy się sierpień,
Bo z końcem sierpnia i koniem i łódką
Puszczam się w drogę przez Pulia, Otrando,
Korfu . . . gdzie jadę, powie drugie Canto.

2

Tymczasem pierwsze opowiedzieć musi,
Skąd sie wybrałem, po co, i dlaczego?
Chrystusa diabeł kusił i mnie kusi.
Na wieży świata postawił smutnego
Życia nicości? i pokazał wszędzie
Pustynię mowiąc: "Tam ci lepiej będzie." (IV, 7)

1

Oh Muse, languishing due to romantic anguish
Appear and help me! I summon you briefly,
Sentimental one; August is almost over,
At the end of August, on horseback and by boat
I am setting off on a journey through Pulia, Otrando,
Corfu . . . where exactly I am off to, the second Canto will say.

2

In the meantime, the first one must tell you
Where I am coming from, why and for what reason?
The Devil tempted Christ and he is tempting me.
He put me on top of the world's tower, saddened
By life's nothingness, and showed me the surrounding
wilderness saying: "You will be happier there."

During the years following his departure from Poland, Juliusz
Słowacki had good cause to feel both unhappy and disoriented. He
left Warsaw when the November Uprising was still in full swing,
although the signs of its imminent collapse were already apparent
(Dernałowicz, *Słowacki* 30). In the post-November period, the

poet's support for the anti-Russian revolt left him with no other option than life in exile. Yet in the first canto of "The Journey," Słowacki creates a subject free of any characteristics that would mark him as a Polish political exile. The poet clearly plays with the idea of assuming the guise of a universally European Romantic malcontent who fashions himself according to the Byronic mold. His persona joins the long line of European travelers embarking on an oriental adventure. Nonetheless interpreters of Słowacki's oriental poetry tend to downplay his journey's universally orientalist dimension.

Jan Reychman formulates the following conclusion to his otherwise insightful essay on Słowacki's journey:

> The journey to the East was really not an Oriental journey. It became a great creative episode for the poet. But neither the goal he originally set for himself, nor the totality of his impressions, nor the way in which it was reflected in Słowacki's later poetry, suffices to define his journey as a manifestation of Romantic Orientalism. ("Podróż Słowackiego" 11)

And yet the same author repeatedly points out Słowacki's dependence on the text of Lamartine's oriental account. Ryszard Przybylski embraces Reychman's view of Słowacki's Orientalism. Słowacki's was not an oriental journey, he argues, because the poet was first and foremost an exile and a pilgrim (Przybylski 13). At the same time, the same author often compares Słowacki to Chateaubriand, the master of the genre of oriental travel, and someone who also spoke of himself as an exile and a pilgrim. A more recent volume of articles, *Juliusz Słowacki: A European Poet*, contains two essays that focus on Słowacki's oriental poetry. Both authors fail, however, to consider the most obvious measure of the poet's Europeanness: his involvement with the discourse of Western European Orientalism (Królikiewicz, Poklewska).

The text of Słowacki's "Journey" proves beyond any doubt that the conventions of oriental travel were very much on his mind around the time of his voyage. Moreover, just like Mickiewicz earlier in the "Crimean Sonnets," he, too, knew how to use the overdetermined, textual character of the Orient to his own creative advantage. "The Journey" functions primarily as a self-reflexive narrative; Słowacki writes about travel writing. His metaliterary commentary exposes the dangers of a textual abuse of conventions. At the outset, canto I sets the antiillusionist tone that becomes the venue for transcending the oriental travel genre. The author recommends some hotels that would be suitable for a reader intent on retracing his footsteps. He then reflects:

13
Dosyć już! Dosyć! Wyznaję ze wstydem,
Że pohamować nie umiejąc weny,
Z wieszcza zostanę prozaicznym gidem
Ja, com zamierzał wypłakiwać treny
Nad Caracciolim i kląć Ferdynanda;
Dziś piszę, jaka, gdzie stoi loccanda.

14
Bo też kto dzisiaj jest na stałym lądzie,
A jutro myśli wędrować po morzu,
A pozajutro jeździć na wielbłądzie,
Nie jedząc mięsa, ani śpiąc na łożu,
Chciałby Europę, co mu z oczu znika,
Unieść jak Jowisz przemieniony w byka. (IV, 10)

13
Enough already! Enough! I shamefully confess,
that unable to restrain my creative energy,
I will transform myself from a prophet into a common guide.
I, even though I intended to cry out laments over Caraccioli and
to curse Ferdinand,
Today I am writing about where to find what type of lodgings.

14
But it so happens that if you are on land one day,
And tomorrow traveling by sea,
And in two days you ride on camel back,
You have no meat to eat, and no bed to sleep in,
Then you would like to carry off Europa, about to disappear
from sight,
Like Jove transformed into a Taurus.

The subsequent cantos introduce variations on the different modes of self-reflexive distancing. Canto VII presents a masterful and multilayered description of the Megaspilleon monastery. Słowacki bares his literary device in this fragment of "The Journey." He takes the reader by the hand and invites an examination not only of the monastery but also of the way in which he as the author uses a variety of ingredients—including elements of familiar landscapes—to construct the site's description. Such an antiillusionist use of generic conventions, Robert Stam notes, creates "tensions which force us to reflect on the nature of the genre itself as one of the ways 'reality' is mediated through art." Stam continues,

> since the stuff of self-conscious art is the tradition itself—to be alluded to, played with, outdone or exorcised—parody has often been of crucial importance. Implicit in the idea of parody are some self-evident truths about the artistic process. The first is that the author does not imitate nature but rather other texts. (132)

As a writer coming from the gray area of a cultural inbetween, Słowacki was well positioned to produce an antiillusionist oriental narrative, one that interrogates both the Western European discourse and his own dependence on this textual tradition. Rather than satisfying himself with mere imitation, in "The Journey" Słowacki mocks European travelers and parodies the conventions of western travel narratives. Later, in the unpublished cantos of "Beniowski," the narrative poem that grew directly out of the "Journey," Słowacki speaks of oriental literary travel in the same ironic mode. When "Beniowski's" title character reaches Crimea, the narrator observes that his protagonist has just entered the realm of mosques and sonnet-shaped mountains. The desert wind blows there; witch-like Arab women use curative mud to cover a paralyzed Polish maiden held captive by a "pop," an Orthodox priest; a Turkish holy man runs around naked; and a camel, the "desert's ship," urinates unceremoniously in front of an inn (cantos VII - IX).

In both "The Journey" and "Beniowski," Słowacki parlays the self-conscious mode into irreverence not just towards his predecessors in the field of oriental travel—including his rival for the top rank among Polish poets, Mickiewicz. The self-reflexive distancing also affects the way he sees the homeland he has left behind. Canto VIII, "The Tomb of Agamemnon" ("Grób Agamemnona"), ruthlessly criticizes his countrymen who failed to secure Poland's independence. Słowacki places the blame for Poland's disintegration squarely on the Poles themselves.

16
O! Polsko! Póki ty duszę anielską
Będziesz więziła w czerepie rubasznym;
Póty kat będzie rąbał twoje cielsko

Póty nie będzie twój miecz zemsty strasznym,
Póty mieć będziesz hyjenę na sobie,
I grób—I oczy otworzone w grobie. (IV, 77)

Oh, Poland! As long as your angelic soul
Remains bounded by a degenerate shell,
An executioner will partition your flesh
And your punishing sword will not inspire fear.
You will have a hyena on your bosom,
And a tomb, and eyes that remain open in the grave.

"Agamemnon's Tomb" was the only part of "The Journey" that appeared in print in the period following Słowacki's journey to the East. Thus, the poet suppressed, for the most part, the ironic impulse that enabled him to rein in the traditions of European and Polish Orientalism. This impulse could have helped him formulate an original narrative of his oriental voyage. Instead, the published "poetic letters" and other poems from the same period often revert to oriental clichés that do not have the additional element of self-reflexive distancing that usually determined the character of his intertextual engagement with Orientalism. How do the pressures of orientalist structuring manifest themselves in these texts? What are the reasons of what ultimately has to be described as Słowacki's failure to transcend the Orient's textual character?

On October 22, 1836, Słowacki composed a poem in Alexandria that took the form of a letter to Teofil Januszewski, his maternal uncle. This work narrates the poet's first encounter with the East as it develops in a way that reflects the structure of a journey. In the first part, Słowacki remembers a space familiar both to him and the letter's addressee. Next come memories of parting with the Januszewskis and of the poet's own departure. In the poem's second part, Słowacki relates the experience of arrival initiated by the first sighting of land and reinforced by the land's steady growth as it fills the horizon. At first, he notices Muhammad Ali's palace, which, from a distance, looks like a white dove. Surrounded by a colorful crowd, the persona's perspective undergoes a change:

Tu przeszywany złotem—przetkany bławatem,
Chce być człowiek bawiącym twoje oczy kwiatem,
Nawet w ubiorach ludzi taka rozmaitość
Że cię wkrótce dusząca opanuje sytość. (I, 81)

Here embroidered with gold—woven with light blue,
the man wants to be a flower that will entertain your eyes.
Even in people's clothing—such variety,
that you will soon feel dizzy from satiety.

The sensation of touch soon augments these visual images, as a
crowd of carriers, accompanied by their donkeys, surrounds the
traveler, who is then placed on one of the animals. A succession of
images follows in the wake of the donkey's collision with a camel, the
same "ship of the desert" Słowacki later makes fun of in "Beniowski."
The subject registers seeing a complex mosaic of images: a black-clad
woman who looks like a coffin, an Egyptian peasant, a blue-garbed
fellah, an Egyptian woman carrying a vessel filled with water on her
head, people wearing European dress, beggars who resemble a flock
of storks. Słowacki intelligibly fills his poem's limited space with an
array of sensory moments whose description could easily take up
several pages of a prose account.

The sighting of the black-enshrouded, coffin-like woman—who
seems to be asking "Who am I?" foreshadows the poem's conclusion, when, after the impression-rich encounter with the colorful
gathering of people, the persona anticipates a coming encounter
with some ancient sights:

> Jutro ujrzę pomniki—trumny—katakomby—Wszystko, co
> pozostało na tym piasku z wieków
> Od Egipcjan przez Rzymian podbitych i Greków. (I, 82)

> Tomorrow I shall see monuments—coffins—catacombs—
> All that has been left on the sand from centuries passed,
> From the Egyptians through the conquered Romans and the Greeks.

The woman-coffin's centrality bespeaks Słowacki's dependence
on orientalist discourse. Embodied by the woman, the Orient asks to
be defined; it invites the traveler's interpretation. Through his overt
association of the woman with death, Słowacki's subject delineates
the interpretation's parameters. In *Orientalism*, the contemporary
Orient's alleged inability to define itself and the concomitant, repetitive western assessment of the region's perceived inadequacies operate as well-established orientalist tropes. Said establishes that

> Orientalism is premised upon exteriority, that is on the fact that
> the Orientalist, poet or scholar, makes the Orient speak,

describes the Orient, renders its mysteries plain for and to the West . . . . The exteriority of the representation is always governed by some version of the truism that if the Orient could represent itself, it would; since it cannot, the representation does the job, for the West, and . . . for the poor Orient. (21)

The Westerners' assertion about its current state of decay predetermined the Orient's perceived inability to speak with its own voice. In the Saidian analysis, such assessments had a clear ideological purpose: they provided the rationale for asserting Europe's dominance over the East. Since the Orient's glory days had long since passed, this moribund part of the world needed European tutelage (*Orientalism* 35, 57). Upon his arrival in Alexandria, the Egyptian city's silence struck Chateaubriand, one of the founding fathers of Western European Orientalism. "A fatal charm," he records, "plunged the inhabitants of modern Alexandria in profound silence." One should expect nothing else, he continues,

> from a city, of which one-third at least is forsaken; of which another third is occupied by sepulchres; while the living third, in the middle of these two extremities, is a kind of a palpitating trunk, which, lying between ruins and tombs, has not even the strength to rattle its chains. (197)

The progression from the first part of Słowacki's colorful and vibrant description of Alexandria to the focus on the coffin-evoking woman demonstrates the pressure the orientalist cliché exerted on the Polish writer's imagination. Even Słowacki's own ironic recycling of the same image in "Beniowski" does not enable him to move beyond the cliché. In the text that came after "Journey," Słowacki debases the encounter with the coffin-like woman. If in the original poem the image foreshadowed the denouement of the poet's historiosophical musings, in "Beniowski" the situation culminates in a disappointing sexual encounter:

> Czasami . . . wielkim robrontem skrzydlata,
> Bowiem kobiety wschodnie chcą być grube . . .
> Leci . . . ogromna, czarna, trumna, chata
> Jak okręt, co ma parę albo szrubę. (. . .)
> Z jedwabnym ciebie minęła szelestem,
> Oczyma . . . tylko łysnęła . . . lecz okiem
> Juz myślisz, że cię spytała: "Kto jestem?"
> Juz myślisz, że to Wenus pod obłokiem,

Że to jest ogień, który pod azbestem,
Pod niespaloną szubą i szlafrokiem
Płonie . . . i z drogi cię cnoty oddali . . .
A jeśli dotkniesz go—na popiół spali. (III, 208)

Sometimes, winged by the large robe she's wearing,
Since Eastern women want to appear fat,
There comes flying, a huge, black, coffin, hut,
Like a vessel powered by steam or by a propeller.
She has passed you with a silky whisper,
With her eyes she barely glanced but with your eye
You think already that she has asked you: "Who am I?"
You already think that it's Venus hidden behind a cloud,
That it is a fire whose flame underneath the asbestos,
Under the robe that has not caught on fire burns brightly
And it will make you stray from the path of virtue,
And it will burn you to ashes if you touch it.

The woman agrees, according to the next stanza, to a cemetery assignation. But the disgruntled traveler curses the wind that finally allows him to see what has been hidden underneath the robes. The oriental exterior's mysterious otherness excites, but closer acquaintance with it results only in disillusionment.

Disappointment with the experience of the Orient constitutes a prominent and a recurring theme in the poetry of Słowacki's oriental journey. Nor does the intellectual stimulation anticipated from an encounter with Egyptian monuments live up to the poet's expectations. In his "A Letter to Aleksander H. Composed on a Boat on the Nile" ("List do Aleksandra H. pisany na łódce nilowej"), Słowacki engages the addressee in an imaginary dialogue. He assumes that H. appreciates the East's rich cultural heritage. Słowacki himself admits that Egyptian monuments do not impress him. The works of Shakespeare, in contrast, constitute a meaningful, living monument. The Egyptian graves do not speak to him. Like the hieroglyphs, they represent empty signs bereft of decipherable meaning. Or perhaps they could—like the hieroglyphs—be deciphered, but what they contain no longer interests Słowacki. The graves of the Egyptian kings have been robbed of what was once inside of them:

Dziś gorsi i podobni do Mojżesza plagi,
Cudzoziemcy wynoszą z grobów sarkofagi.
Anglik dumny, w sterlingi zmienione na piastry,
Rzuca trupy, trumniane bierze alabastry,

I w Londynie zachwyca zgraję zadziwioną,
Wstawiwszy świecznik w próżne alabastru łono.
Rzekłbyś wtenczas, że wszystkie płaskorzeźby rusza

Chrystusową nauką ożywiona dusza.
Że pełny nauk, ciemną przyszłością straszliwych,
Grobowiec oświecony, stał się lampą żywych. (I, 94)

Today worse and yet similar to the plague of Moses
Foreigners carry out the sarcophagi from the vaults
The proud Englishman, with sterlings changed into piastrs
Throws out the corpses, and takes the alabaster
And in London he is able to impress the amazed public
By putting a candelabrum into the empty womb of the sarcopha-
gus
One could then say that the sculptures have been brought back
to life

Through the soul revived by Christ's teachings.
That filled with terrible lessons of a dark future,
The lighted tomb became a lantern for the living.

Even though Słowacki exposes and condemns the Westerners'
drive to take possession of Egyptian antiquities, this criticism does
not form the crux of the text. The ease with which Egyptian tombs
succumb to Western pillage and the tombs' and the stone coffins'
resulting emptiness symbolize the defeat of the ancient Egyptian
belief system. Słowacki juxtaposes the balm that has ultimately
failed to make the Egyptians' bodies impervious to destruction with
the balm of Christ's teaching used to anoint the souls of his follow-
ers to render them truly immortal. The image of an empty Egyptian
sarcophagus occupies the center of "The Pyramids" (Piramidy) as
well. After being dragged inside the pyramid by his Arab guides, the
poet finds himself in what he calls the hall of the King's corpse:

Sarkofag—próżny—ręką uderzyłem—dzwonił,
Jak rzecz pusta . . . (I, 85)

The sarcophagus—empty—I stroke it with my hand—it rever-
berated,
Like some thing that is void . . .

Ryszard Przybylski perceives a similarity between Słowacki's
and Chateaubriand's interpretations of the East. For both of them,

he argues, Christ's empty grave represented the spiritual victory of resurrection and provided a counterpoint to the empty graves of Egyptian kings (65-67). Przybylski, however, overlooks that this Franco-Polish convergence affirms the constricting character of nine-teenth-century orientalist discourse. As Said asserts, Western encoun-ters with the Orient became limited to "a set of references," and

> as a form of growing knowledge Orientalism resorted mainly to citations of predecessor scholars in the field for its nutriment . . . . In a fairly strict way, then, Orientalists after Sacy and Lane rewrote Sacy and Lane; after Chateaubriand, pilgrims rewrote him. (177)

A putative imperialist impulse does not explain the eagerness with which Słowacki followed this familiar pattern of structuring his experience of the Orient. Not only was he a political exile, but he wrote explicitly for a Polish reading public. Unlike Western and Eastern European Orientalists, who worked to promote the interests of imperial politics, Słowacki spoke from the perspective of a culture threatened, just like Egyptian culture, with the consequences of for-eign imperial domination. Paradoxically, perhaps his growing iden-tification with the abandoned homeland, with the suffering Poland, inhibited a more nuanced and individuated encounter with the Orient free from Western Orientalism's discursive dictates.

Ryszard Przybylski discerns in the poet approaching Egyptian shores what he deems "Antigone's complex"—an urge to find a bur-ial place for himself. Przybylski writes that

> A hundred miles away from the Egyptian shore . . . the Pole who had been adrift for a long time began to feel envious of the ashes of the dead who had a grave . . . . Every man should have a tomb, the location of which is not a trifling matter . . . . A tomb means a continuous presence among the living, in the communi-ty, in tradition. For Antigone, depositing the body of her brother in a grave constituted a religious obligation. The grave repre-sented the end of a person's earthly journey. This journey was a source of joy during life, in spite of all the suffering that was part of it; but after death—irrespective of one's attachment to the familiar world—a continued journey becomes a terrible torment, since for the Greeks the soul of an unburied person sets off on a sullen journey, this time aimless and senseless. Without much exaggeration, one can say that Juliusz Słowacki was cast into the same kind of wandering after he had been expelled from Poland. (46)

Słowacki exhibited an acute awareness of his homelessness throughout his entire oriental peregrination. The status of an aimless wanderer sensitized him to the spirit of the times, but it also tired him. Thoughts of rest, even eternal rest, occur in his poems and letters written during the eastern journey. In "God, I Am Full of Sorrow" ("Smutno mi Boże"), a manifesto of emigrant identity composed while he was on board the ship that took him to Alexandria, Słowacki laments his fate:

> Ty będziesz widział moje białe kości
> W straż nie oddane kolumnowym czołom;
> Alem jest jako człowiek, co zazdrości
> Mogił popiołom . . .
> Więc że mieć będę niespokojne łoże,
> Smutno mi Boże! (I, 78)

> You will look upon my white bones,
> Not guarded by a roof over the columns
> But I am a man who is envious
> Of the ashes that have been deposited in vaults . . .
> The thought of an unsettled resting place
> Fills me with sorrow, God.

And yet Słowacki could not extract himself from his internal maze of paradoxes. He seemed to be leaving for Egypt with the hope of escaping the melancholy that had come over him—he longed for change. Or, perhaps, rather than find a burial place for himself, he sought to bury the haunting ghosts of the past: the memories of the failed November Uprising and the pain inflicted by the exile that ripped him away from his home and the people whom he loved, including his mother. The indelible lines from "The Grave of Agamemnon," canto VIII of "A Journey to the Holy Land," confirm this longing:

> Tak więc—to los mój na grobowcach siadać
> I szukać smutków błachych, wiotkich, kruchych.
> To los mój senne królestwa posiadać,
> Nieme mieć harfy i sluchaczów głuchych
> Albo umarłych—i tak pełny wstrętu . . .
> Na koń! chcę słońca, wichru i tętentu! (IV, 76)

> And so I am destined to sit on graves
> and to search for trifling, flimsy, brittle sorrows

> It is my destiny to possess somnambulant kingdoms,
> To have harps that are voiceless and listeners who are deaf
> Or who are dead—and so filled with disgust . . .
> Let's mount our horses! I yearn for the sun, the wind and the
> clatter of a horse's feet!

Polish Romantics personified their homeland as a suffering mother. "In the poetry of the Romantics," Maria Janion informs, "the post-partition fatherland becomes a person of great charisma, endowed with the sanctity of a mother who may be deceased, lethargic, or mortally wounded, a person who needs to be aided instantaneously, and someone for whom the subject has to abandon everything and who must never be forgotten" (11). Janion points out that the domineering motherland sometimes morphed into a specter that tormented the subject, preventing the transfer of emotions elsewhere (12). Słowacki, for his part, was fated to grapple with the ongoing coexistence of two maternal figures: both his actual mother as well as the motherland made claims on his attention and his heart. As he writes in a letter to his mother, Salomea Bécu:

> I can truly call you my mother, because the one in whose service
> I have been enlisted has the right to my life, but not to my heart
> . . . . I sacrificed so much happiness for her, for her I bear lone-
> liness. I have a frown on my forehead from thinking of how to
> feed and how to clothe her, how to spread flowers on her bed. I
> have fulfilled my duties to her, as a daughter ought to, but now
> I am tired of it. I never served you like this, and you love me.[8]

The poet conceived his journey to the East as a flight from feelings associated with both the woman who had given birth to him and the land that had nourished him. The attempted flight was to free him from the profound sadness perpetuated by his separation from both, Salomea Bécu and the other mother. The emotional reliance on his biological mother permeates his passionate and guilt-ridden addresses to her, thereby intensifying the poet's "Antigone's complex."[9]

Słowacki's voyage to Egypt replicated the course of many earlier travelers by culminating in a visit to the pyramids, the world's most ostentatious graves. The poet describes the experience in a letter to his mother:

> The day after my arrival in Cairo I went on a trip to the pyra-
> mids. Both of us traveled on small donkeys, and we seemed

strangely small on these animals next to the huge granite structures. The pyramids did not really impress me with their size. The
Bedouins in white dress arrived from all over, in order to serve as
our guides, and, taking us by our hands, they pulled us through
dark, granite-covered corridors to small rooms, inside the pyramids. Where once there had been two granite coffins, today there
is only one. After leaving the dark pyramids, I started climbing
up the stones to the top, constantly pulled by the hands by two
Arabs. I was at the top of the highest pyramid—a wonderful
view! (13, 295)

The pyramids promise to provide the right setting for depositing his
thoughts of the defeated nation and embalming them with the hope
for a resurrection. In "Conversation with the Pyramids" ("Rozmowa
z piramidami"), the pyramids comfort the subject: they could indeed
shelter those martyred for the national cause, and they do have
room to provide a resting place for the suffering Polish nation. But
they cannot mummify the subject's spirit (I, 76). The graves' disappointing emptiness, already foregrounded in the preceding poems,
amplifies Słowacki's frustration caused by his failure to reinvent
himself in the course of his journey. His disappointment with the
Orient evolves from an Orientalist trope into a trap compelling him
to focus on his own wound.

   In "On the Top of the Pyramids" ("Na szczycie piramid"),
Słowacki notes that he can hear the ticking of a watch and his own
heartbeat:

> Cicho . . . zegarek słyszę idący—i serce . . .
> Czas i życie, Spojrzałem na błękit rozciągły . . . (I, 87)

> Silence . . . I can hear the ticking of a watch—and heart . . .
> Time and life. I looked at the blue of the sky spread wide . . . .

Słowacki's flight from historical time failed. Nor was he able to
embalm his heart. The destiny invoked in "Agamemnon's Tomb"
caught up with him. It prevails when he notices a Polish inscription
on top of the pyramid:

> A tak myśląc, po głazach obłąkane oko
> Padło na jakiś napis—strumień myśli opadł
> Ktoś dwudziesty dziewiąty przypomniał Listopad
> Polskim językiem groby Egipcjanów znacząc
> Czytałem smutny . . . człowiek może pisał płacząc. (I, 88)

And so thinking, my eye, stranded on the rocks,
encountered an inscription—the stream of thoughts died down...
Someone remembered the twenty-ninth of November,
Marking the graves of Egyptians with the Polish language . . .
I was reading saddened . . . the man who left the inscription may
have been crying.

Many European travelers who went to Egypt in the first part
of the nineteenth century either left inscriptions on the pyramids or
at least attempted to do so. Józef Sękowski tended to be critical of
other European travelers to the Orient. But even he succumbed to
the temptation to carve his name into the ageless stone when he visited the pyramids in 1821. He recounts that

> An Arab, as is customary, brought us a small, blunt hammer so
> that we could inscribe our names on the monuments. A desire to
> pass on our names to posterity made us add them to the names
> of numerous bankrupt craftsmen from Cairo, as well as those of
> some eminent personages who had visited the pyramids. (I, 12)

Słowacki reversed the orientalist pattern: when he discovered that
someone had already left a Polish-language inscription, he did not
carve his own. Besides offering a means to stake a claim to immor-
tality, an inscription also provided a way to conquer the foreign and
render it familiar. Contrary to that, the serendipitously discovered
Polish inscription reminded Słowacki of the familiar. He tried to
escape into the Orient's foreignness. But, wherever he went, Poland's
pain and tears went with him. On top of the pyramid, the subject of
his verse reconstituted himself in the same shape in which he had set
out on his journey. As earlier in "God, I am Filled with Sorrow," he
could now concentrate solely on himself and on his own sense of loss.
   Słowacki did leave one inscription in the course of his journey,
but one of a much different type than the conventional name carved
in stone. One of the entries in his travel notebook reads:

> On the Nile—on the 6 of November from Cairo—the ribbon of
> the Nile—palm trees—the moon that rises late—evening—on
> one side the red of the sunset, on the other two vultures on a
> white rock—a hunt on the sand by the river bank—noon—the
> heat of the desert—cranes and storks with a screaming flock are
> landing nearby—an idea from the Wahhabite gospel—**I write my
> name in the sand and another name** [IK]—the killing of two
> doves who were drinking water by the palm village. (11, 186)

Eugeniusz Sawrymowicz juxtaposes this notebook entry with a fragment from canto V of "Beniowski." He thereby links the poet's mother to the repeated act of inscribing her name with a traveler's walking stick (272). The act of writing his mother's name in the desert sand both inverts and seals the experience of deciphering the Polish inscription on the pyramid; if the latter reminds Słowacki of his destiny, the former is synonymous with his surrender to the fate of a Polish exile torn from his subjugated, quasi-colonized homeland. He goes even further by writing his own name next to his mother's, thereby acknowledging his emotional dependence on her. In sharp contrast to a stone carving that will remain impervious to the passage of time, a sand inscription attests to the fatalism inherent in this particular mother-son relationship.

By the time Słowacki reaches Christ's grave, he is overwhelmed by his devotion to both of his mothers. In a letter to Salomea Bécu, he writes: "I spent an entire night all alone in Christ's grave praying for you and for ours" (13, 315). He participates in a symbolic act rife with nationalist undertones, a mass for Poland, during which he also prays for his mother. Before embarking on his return to Italy, his temporary residence, Słowacki spent approximately a month in a monastery in Lebanon. Again, feelings for and thoughts of his mother accompanied him. In a letter to her, he writes:

> If you only knew how in Lebanon, in a monastery high above the clouds, I took out a pack of your letters, how I arranged them, with sadness, according to the dates spanning six years, how I read them, often shedding tears over your fate and mine. (13, 326)

Słowacki's journey to the East did not help him find any radically new solutions to the dilemmas of his spiritual and emotional life. Quite the opposite—it only reinforced his attachment to both his Polish mother and his mother-Poland. As Said writes about Chateaubriand:

> He brought a very heavy load of personal objectives and suppositions to the Orient, unloaded them there, and proceeded thereafter to push people, places, and ideas around in the Orient as if nothing could resist his imperious imagination. (*Orientalism* 171)

Słowacki concentrated on his own "heavy load" born of the inability to overcome the sense of loss that first led him on a journey to the Holy Land. This inherent weakness pushed him to follow the lead of Chateaubriand and Lamartine, the Westerners who had already organized the ideography of the Orient in accordance with their own needs. The situation of Polish writers traveling to the Orient—most notably of Słowacki—was similar to that of Europeanizing South American Creole writers analyzed by Mary Louise Pratt. For this group of writers, she argues, "exile rather than exploration situates the seeing-man and creates the otherness between the seer and the seen. The dynamics of discovery are transculturated into a framework of nostalgia and loss" (183). Słowacki's Egyptian poetry unambiguously posits a subject who insulates himself from the oriental world by falling back on the orientalist cliché. By doing so, the poet is able to indulge in nostalgic remembrance of his own, overbearing exilic losses that will not leave him in peace.

Moreover, Słowacki goes out of his way to situate loss at the center of the two narrative poems composed during his oriental journey, "Anhelli" and "Father of the Plague Stricken" ("Ojciec zadżumionych"). Written in the same monastery in Lebanon where Słowacki cried over the letters from his mother, "Anhelli" presents the other variant of Polish nineteenth-century travel to the East, that is, banishment to Siberia. A Siberian shaman stylized after an Old Testament prophet invites Anhelli, a young Polish exile, to follow him in a painful tour of remembrance of the Poles' national losses. One of the many figures of loss in "Anhelli" is a father who has been sentenced to work in a Siberian mine, presumably for his involvement in the 1830 November Uprising. He survives a mining accident after witnessing the death of his five sons who suffocated when the Russian overseers forbade other laborers to aid them (II, 252). Precisely because of the tragic Polish condition, the fatalistic dynamic expressed by the poet in his sand inscription undergoes a cruel inversion—just as the father must experience the death of his numerous children. The same motif of a father fated to witness the death of his offspring structures the narrative of "Father of the Plague Stricken." An orientalist background does refract these artistically compelling renderings of archetypal loss, but the Orient itself is not part of the picture. The introduction to "Father of the Plague Stricken" records that:

> The history of his [the father's] pain is not without grounding in
> reality: I heard the story from Dr. Steble, whom I would thank
> for the story and for the bread and all his kindness for me, if I
> knew that these words could reach him in the desert. But what
> should this reminiscence, spoken in a strange foreign tongue,
> with a voice whose reach is limited like ripples on the surface of
> the water after a stone has been cast, mean to him? (II, 345)

Dr. Steble was the Italian physician who supervised the quarantine encampment in El Arish on the border between Egypt and Palestine. Słowacki was forced to interrupt his journey to Jerusalem for eight days to spend time in this camp, which provided him with material for his poem. Similarly, the Polish poet used Chateaubriand's and Lamartine's orientalist texts as repositories of ready-made Orientalia. The mediated character of Słowacki's encounter with the East created a context for the metaliterary comments contained in "The Journey to the Holy Land from Naples." But even though Słowacki was capable of using irony to distance himself from available, stereotyped patterns of oriental journeying, the orientalist intertext weights heavily on his orientalist writings. Combined with his omnipresent—indeed, omnipotent—nostalgia for all the things expropriated from him by exile, this dependence on Western European patterns of thinking about the East prevented the writing of an original and complete narrative of his journey.

Il comte Serpentino in the Land of the Bedouins and Beyond

Melancholic mourning prevailed in post-November Polish literature, especially in exilic literature that exerted a profound influence on the way Poles thought about their national community. Nostalgic tears clouded many Polish writers' perception of the countries in which they resided as well as of the ones they chose to visit. Yet by no means did such exclusivity have to become the determining feature of most Polish writers' post-November literary imagination.

One need only turn to the travel writings of Władysław Wężyk to find a heuristically valuable case in point. Wężyk formulated his travel texts while exposed to the exact same cultural and discursive pressures that exerted such a strong influence on so many other Polish writers of his time. But his travel accounts break out of the conven-

Figure 4. Portrait of Władysław Weżyk, painted by Marszałkiewicz. From Jan Bystroń, Polacy, l93.

tional normative boundaries, and they document a quest for alternative travel and narrative modes which could do justice to the novel cultural circumstances surrounding travel from Poland to the East.

Wężyk made his own landing in Egypt and Palestine just three years after Juliusz Słowacki set foot on Egyptian shores. He used Italy as a way station. Once there, a contemporary informs, Wężyk began to refer to himself with a literal Italian translation of his name and title: "Il comte Serpentino della Ruda Granda" (Bystroń 196). From Italy, Wężyk followed the well-established route to Alexandria. He then traveled around Egypt for five months before continuing on by sea from Damietta to Palestine. Over the following year, he traveled extensively in Turkey, Greece, and Italy (Kukulski, *Podróże* 11-12). Like Słowacki, Wężyk first left Poland in the aftermath of the November Uprising. Like so many male teenagers in the Russian partition, he disregarded the advice of his elders and joined the fight that erupted in Warsaw. The unruly youth fled tsarist retaliation and parental authority some time in 1833, only to venture back to Warsaw in 1836. His family boasted good connections with the authorities, thanks to which their impetuous son received a short prison sentence, in spite of his participation in the rising and subsequent close ties to patriotically minded emigrant circles during his initial stay outside of Poland. Nevertheless, his encounter with the tsarist police state's harshness—unmatched anywhere else in the European sphere outside the Ottoman empire—gave Wężyk a taste of the same experiences that embittered generations of Poles under Russian rule and cast a shadow of hopelessness over Polish life in the Russian partition. Yet as Maria Dernałowicz observes, shortly after his return to Warsaw from the East in 1842, Wężyk published an account of his oriental journey devoid of "the burden of the chains of the Romantics' cursed fate" ("Wstęp" 10). Wężyk's position also contrasted with that of other Polish travelers of the time in another important way. His *Travels in the Ancient World* (*Podróże po starożytnym świecie*) attempt to propagate a perspective on the East markedly different from that of his Western European predecessors. Ultimately, however, he failed to see Egypt "with his own eyes," to negotiate a new way of narrating travel to the Orient. This failure demonstrates just how deeply ingrained the orientalist structures were by the time of his journey.

Wężyk divides his *Travels* into two parts: "Egypt—History"(Egipt—historia) and "Egypt—Images" (Egipt—obrazy). Confirming the previously discussed predominance of a binary model of narration in nineteenth-century travel accounts, in the first part Wężyk yields to the imperative to inform his readers about the East. "Egypt—History" parades knowledge borrowed from a wide array of authors, including Herodotus, Strabo, d'Herbelot, Chateaubriand, Volney, Hammer, and Champollion. Wężyk went out of his way to pay homage to the already textualized Orient. This choice led to his subsequent use of the account's next section to narrate his own impressions of Egypt. But this search for his own voice most often produced destabilizing discursive inconsistencies in both parts of *Travels*. As a western commentator, Wężyk is strikingly incongruous in "Egypt—History." Having freed himself from the straightjacket of the textual Orient, in "Egypt—Images" he is still unable to avoid reproducing the patterns of a culturally coded otherness.

In an introductory chapter to Part I, "An Overview of the East," Wężyk presents the Orient in the same terms that, today, have emerged as the favorite targets of Saidian analysis. Wężyk and his contemporaries adhered to an expansive definition of the concept "Orient." They defined it as the region stretching from the Mediterranean, through Persia, India, China all the way to the Caucasus and Constantinople. As he writes, "all of the countries that I have mentioned, and the one I am now approaching more than any of them [Egypt], are barbarian and unhappy" (1842, 11).[9] He proffers a predictable diagnosis:

> The East, the older brother of the West, has become like a child in his old age . . . . Islam, and its stifling rules have made the process of deterioration faster. [The East] looks now like a huge cemetery, with magnificent tombs whose meaning cannot be deciphered by people who live next to them, scattered all around. (6)

Elsewhere he asserts that

> The particular trait of the inhabitant of the East is the excessive effect of temperament on the mind. As a result, all of his actions lack equilibrium, and some of them are so extreme that they impede others. (14)

Wężyk reproduces the commentaries embedded in his predecessors' texts, and he does so in a grotesquely exaggerated manner. But when a definition of the West's relationship with the East is at issue, he exploits the distance afforded him by his nonwesternness. At this point, he diverges from views frequently voiced by Western European travelers and explorers:

> Personal interest has been bringing inhabitants of Europe closer to these once famous, now unlucky shores for some time now.

> Hence, over time, beliefs and customs will transform . . . . But
> this transformation will not take place immediately. All the more
> so, because the brothers from the West, arriving at the other
> shore after a long time, thought only of plundering the corpse
> instead of trying to invigorate the dying man's soul and return-
> ing him to life. (6)

Wężyk goes on to ponder the role the civilized West should play in
the East:

> Instead of applying its intellect to developing steel and steam for
> the sake of broadening its industrial horizons, should the West
> not also pay attention to the large part of the world in need of
> its help? Should it appear before this part of the world with
> chains and with a shovel to dig up the earth's treasures for its
> own profit? (16)

Despite his penchant for reproducing western stereotypes of the
East, Wężyk, himself the "son of a conquered nation," critically evaluates the West's colonial attitude towards the Orient. It is this stark
contrast between generalizing affirmations of European superiority
and critical judgments of Europe's role in the East that generates discursive inconsistency.

Among the several Polish oriental travelers who followed
Mickiewicz to Crimea was Edmund Chojecki, the future translator
of the greatest work of Polish eighteenth-century literary
Orientalism, Jan Potocki's *Saragossa Manuscript*, into Polish
(Potocki, who belonged to one of the greatest Polish magnate fami-
lies, wrote the work in French). In his 1845 account, Chojecki relat-
ed a conversation he overheard on a steamer taking passengers to
Crimea:

> This is what happens when one listens to a female—a short and
> stout man was saying while carrying his fainting wife to their
> quarters—You insisted, Madam, on visiting the East, Wężyk's
> travels have made you lose your mind. You had said that you did
> not know of music sweeter than the storm's wild roar, and now
> you tremble like a wet partridge and you faint. (29)

In the immediate period following the work's publication, Part II
of Wężyk's *Travels* established his reputation as a proverbial oriental traveler. In the first part of the twentieth century, the eminent

Polish philologist and anthropologist Jan Bystroń rediscovered
Władysław Wężyk as a travel writer. Bystroń decided to republish
just the second part of *Travels*. In the same vein, Leszek Kukulski,
the postwar editor and publisher of Wężyk's travel texts, dismissed
the first part as derivative and boring and omitted it from publication (246). Both scholars lavish praise on the text of the account
proper. Bystroń pays homage to Wężyk's travels as "undoubtedly the
best Polish book about Egypt." He offers the following justification
for this distinction:

> This is a travel description written by an author who knows how
> to provide his own distinct and stylistically compelling descrip-
> tion of the country that he assesses as a tourist and as an artist.
> ... The account provides a very engaging reading: Egypt emerges
> here not as a boring country, where you walk around with a
> Baedeker and use every occasion to show off whatever is left of
> your school education, and then quickly move on to banal his-
> toriosophical statements. [Wężyk's Egypt] is not a register of
> Eastern ethnography, surveyed by looking through a hotel win-
> dow, or in the streets of the European districts of Alexandria or
> Cairo; it is something unique, original, fascinating as a painter's
> subject, and something that includes nature, ruins, people. (186-
> 87)

Unencumbered by the burden of citation, Wężyk produced a
fast-paced narrative that delivers a quick succession of images. At
times his prose approximates the poetics of reportage, but, amidst
the rush, he often provides only fragmentary remarks when encoun-
tering other people and visiting various sites. In the aggregate, he
devotes more space to his own impressions of Egypt—as he sees it
through its people—than to descriptions of the famous sites that
other travelers described earlier so many times. He has no fondness
for Alexandria. Yet his comments on the outward signs of the city's
decline differ markedly from Chateaubriand's. "Let us commiserate
with poor Alexandria," Wężyk appeals, and he goes on to bemoan
that

> From the figure of eight-hundred thousand its population has
> come down to thirty thousand. Let us feel sorry; for its remark-
> able robes that can still be glanced here and there are now in tat-
> ters. Alexandria is now trading these robes for cheap European
> dress. (*Podróże* 1957, 53)

Following the visit to Alexandria, Wężyk embarks on his search for "true Arabs." He finds them among a Bedouin encampment in the desert:

> Let us enter the tent of emir Matrud, the leader of twenty-four clans of nomads who commands fifty-thousand people. Matrud is seated among twenty-four chiefs . . . . Their only adornment and distinction—more expensive armor and more prominent scars on their faces. All their faces are beautiful, their gaze honest. They carry themselves proudly. Their gaze makes them appear quick-witted, thoughtful, courageous, dignified. Matrud is seated in the center. His face and figure are the least Bedouin. A young man of twenty-four, pale, slender, with a physiognomy that is quite European.—"Greetings, Matrud. We come to your tent to dine with you, to rest after the weary journey, and to bless your arms, your family, and your herds."—"God be with you, Franks. Welcome to our midst." Matrud leads us to the tent where he usually receives guests. There we sit down comfortably, on carpets spread on the ground. Let us now talk with his wives and his sisters who, with their faces uncovered, with a bold and intelligent gaze, do not shy away from us, as the dim-witted Turkish women would. They do not cover their noses and mouths with sheets. (53-54)

Wężyk admires the Bedouin's egalitarianism and simple lifestyle. Invited to share a meal, he savors the food. But the descriptions' exalted tone betrays his penchant for romanticizing the Bedouins. When depicting his stay in the desert, he can scarcely restrain his excitement:

> It is so nice to be with you, brothers Bedouins! With you it is so nice, Bedouin sisters! Had we no fathers and mothers, no friends and no country, we would stay with you and share your battles and your feasts! (58)

Wężyk eschews a factual account of his Bedouin interlude. Instead, his description borrows from and in turn perpetuates the myth of a free and noble Bedouin. Matrud's European countenance facilitates the Polish traveler's quest for self-definition as the mythic Other. The myth, as previously noted, had its origins in eighteenth-century Europe. As Naomi Shepherd explains:

> The mystique of Bedouin gallantry had been current, particularly in France, ever since Laurent d'Arvieux, Louis XVI's commercial

envoy to the Levant in the eighteenth century, had been hos-
pitably received by a friendly sheik on Mount Carmel in 1718;
Gibbon, in the famous fiftieth chapter of *Decline and Fall*, had
perpetuated the myth and the British diplomat Terrick
Hamilton's translation of the Arabic epic Antar, the picaresque
tale of the bastard son of an Arabian prince, who in translation
emerged possessed of a combination of Herculean strength and
Arthurian chivalry, had reinforced it. (28-29)

In Polish tradition, the myth of the free Arab found a real-life
embodiment in the person of Wacław Seweryn Rzewuski, paternal
uncle of the siblings Karolina Sobańska and Henryk Rzewuski.[10] In
1817, Rzewuski traveled to the Orient to purchase horses. He developed an absolute fascination with the desert's nomadic inhabitants
and their way of life. He adopted their customs, and—according to
his own testimony—became the emir of several Bedouin tribes. In a
sign of how various Orientalisms went hand in hand in this period,
prior to becoming a Bedouin, Rzewuski contributed to the development of oriental scholarship by publishing Hammer's *Fundgruben
des Orientes* (Bystroń 90-110). Inspired by Rzewuski's unusual personality, Mickiewicz wrote "Farys," one of his two quasidahs.
Cyprian Kamil Norwid, one of the leading figures of Polish nineteenth-century literature, was Wężyk's close friend as well as his
travel companion in his journeys around Poland. Norwid provided
testimony about Wężyk's fascination with the Polish emir. "My dear-
ly departed Władysław Wężyk," he records, "intended to explain the
life and personality of emir Wacław, but he himself was too much
like him, almost as if they had served under the same banner" (qtd.
in Dernałowicz 5, 10).

Wężyk's few critical readers emphasize his relative independence
from contemporary literary fashions (Bystroń; Kukulski; Piwińska;
Dernałowicz). Yet, in addition to Rzewuski's noble Orientalism, the
conventions of sentimental travel seem to have influenced the form
of Wężyk's account. Wężyk's exalted description of the Bedouins
reveals a literary inspiration. Throughout his journey, sentimental-
ism colored the Polish writer's reaction to places and his interactions
with people. Finally, his general comments about travel bear a telling
resemblance to similar passages in Laurence Sterne's *Sentimental
Journey*. Sterne influenced Wężyk's criticisms of other oriental travelers as well as his self-fashioning as a traveler. Wężyk's account of
his travels in Upper Egypt includes the author's insights into the

═══ 178 ═══

Copie d'une lettre de M. le comte Rzewuski,

à MM. les collaborateurs aux Mines de l'Orient.

Messieurs!

Séparé de vous par des distances lointaines et par des difficultés, qui mettent de si grandes entraves à notre commerce épistolaire, je vous prie de m'excuser si je ne vous écris pas à chacun en particulier, pour vous remercier d'avoir contribué jusqu'à présent par vos savans travaux à donner à cet ouvrage la réputation dont il jouit. Je vous prie de les continuer pour l'avancement des études orientales, auxquelles je me suis voué particulièrement.

Elles vous auront autant d'obligation que moi, de ce que vous soutenez la suite de cette publication, et de ce que vous nourrissez, au milieu des orages politiques, qui obscurcissent l'horizon de l'Europe, la flamme de ce foyer sacré, où se réunissent les lumières des orientalistes de toutes les nations, sans autre intérêt que celui de contribuer à la propagation des connoissances, et sans autre but que l'amour de la vérité. En des temps plus tranquilles je me flatte de pouvoir vous donner plus souvent de mes nouvelles, et de me concerter avec vous plus activement sur le bien des études orientales. En attendant, je vous prie d'adresser vos envois, comme jusqu'à présent, à Vienne, où les *Mines* continuent de se publier avec la rapidité que permettent les circonstances, et qui ne sera jamais égale à l'impatience avec laquelle je voudrois recevoir les cahiers enrichis de vos intéressans mémoires.

J'ai l'honneur d'être avec la plus parfaite estime et considération,

Messieurs,

Kremieniec, ce ⅓ avril 1813.   Votre très-humble et très-obéissant serviteur

Venceslas S. Rzewuski.

Figure 5. The text of Wacław Rzewuski's letter to the contributors of *Fundgruben des Orients,* one of the most influential orientalist publications of the first part of the nineteenth century, edited by Joseph von Hammer and funded by Rzewuski. *Fundgruben des Orients.* Vol. 3 (1813). 178.

ways people of different professional, social, and national backgrounds travel in the East (142-46). According to Bystroń, the
classification provides the "best proof of Wężyk's keen sense of
observation" (192). But to a reader familiar with the literary travel
topos this particular digression evokes Sterne's literary voyage, published nearly a century prior to Wężyk's account. In his "Preface in
the Desobligeant," Sterne divides "the whole circle of travelers" into
several categories (81-82). This typology served to identify and
stamp all the things the author did not like in his contemporaries'
unreflective, mechanical approach to the then-popular Grand Tour.
Sterne elaborates on the same subject elsewhere in the *Journey:*

> The learned Smelfungus traveled from Boulogne to Paris—from
> Paris to Rome—and so on—but he set out with the spleen and
> jaundice, and every object he pass'd by was discoloured or dis-
> torted—He wrote an account of them, but 'twas nothing but the
> account of his miserable feelings . . . .
>
> I popp'd upon Smelfungus again in Turin, in his return
> home; and a sad tale of sorrowful adventures had he to tell,
> "wherein he spoke of moving accidents by flood and field, and
> of the cannibals which each other eat: the Antropophagi"—he
> had been flea'd alive, and bedevil'd, and used worse than St.
> Bartholomew, at every stage he had come at—I'll tell it, cried
> Smelfungus, to the world. You had better tell it, said I, to your
> physician. Mundungus made the whole tour without one gener-
> ous connection or pleasurable anecdote to tell of; but he had
> travell'd straight on looking neither to his right hand or his left,
> lest Love or Pity should seduce him out of his road. (116-19)

"Lord save us from memoirs and heroic rhapsodies of famous people and travelers, of whom even the French have had enough!"
Wężyk intones in the first part of his *Travels.* The Polish writer's own
version of the traveler typology follows the lead of Sterne's Yorick in
that it criticizes those who remain centered on themselves in the
course of their journeys. Wężyk pokes fun at people who complain
about the inconveniences of travel, poor lodgings, and terrible food,
and who engage in philistine bickering over prices. He ridicules
those who appear bored by everything they see when they travel, but
who later produce exaggerated accounts of their journeys.

The traits castigated by Wężyk were probably just as common
among European travelers who visited the Middle East in the nineteenth century as they had been among Englishmen touring Europe

in the previous century. Amidst the ever-more stifling conventions of nineteenth-century oriental travel, Wężyk's reliance on the impressionistic, sentimental tradition promised to produce a refreshing effect. It may also have helped him avoid straying into the subjects then consuming his compatriots. Significantly, his classification of oriental travelers refrained from any mention whatsoever of Polish voyagers. When he encounters an elderly Polish emigrant, Michał z Kęczek Kęczkowski, a nobleman-turned-tailor in Cairo, he gives him a sentimental pat on the shoulder and he rushes on, unfettered by the type of soul searching that a mere Polish inscription provoked in Słowacki (86-87).

Contrary to Słowacki, whose travel letters and poems devoted to his 1836 journey place the Arabs in the background to serve as mere props, Wężyk was ready to absorb local culture. It fascinated him. Cairo dazzled him. En route to Upper Egypt, he listened attentively to the stories he heard along the way. He watched a spontaneously organized theatrical performance in which his fellow Arab travelers dramatized their relationships with other cultures. Wężyk tries to involve the reader in his account by addressing him directly. He takes the reader by the hand; first-person plural and second-person singular verbs set the tone of his narrative.

But Wężyk distorted some of the elements of sentimental travel in curious and disquieting ways. This habit undermined his apparent openness towards the native inhabitants of the areas he visited. Mary Louise Pratt points out that sentimentalist travel narratives set in the contact zone often contained stories of interracial romance and conjugal love that eroticized cross-cultural encounters. These idealized images of cultural harmony served the legitimization of imperial rule. They masked the real-life institution of colonial sexual exploitation,

> whereby European men on assignment to the colonies bought local women from their families to serve as sexual and domestic partners for the duration of their stay. In Africa and the Caribbean, and probably elsewhere, such arrangements could be officially sanctioned by formal ceremonies of pseudo-marriage . . . (Pratt 95-96)

Erotic undercurrents are apparent in Wężyk's sensuous description of Egypt. He hints at the illicit pleasures available to the European visitor, including sex with minors of both genders. At first, he discreetly abstains from this type of interaction with the orientals. But, finally, in his characteristically excessive manner, instead of follow-ing the sentimental paradigm of cross-racial romance Wężyk goes straight to the source, that is, he provides a detailed description of the institution of fake colonial marriages. There is no indication that he does so to unmask the exploitative character of Europeans' inter-actions with the natives. Quite to the contrary, Wężyk's description of this practice and his unabashed praise for its many practical advantages raise the suspicion that he is relaying firsthand informa-tion to the reader. As he writes:

> Perhaps you would like to get married my friend? . . . Oh, you probably think that it's the same as back home, that you have to become saddled for ages! Here you can get married for a month or two, for a year, for any period of time that you like. (113)

He further explains that he does not advocate buying a slave. "What I mean is a real wife. A Christian who will be given to you by her own parents, and they will not feel that they have been dis-honored by you at all." A bizarre and a detailed guide to sexual exploitation under the pretense of marriage ensues. "You first have to reveal your intentions to a suitable Levantine matron," he advis-es. "You will describe to her exactly the goddess of your dreams, her eyes, her hair, her age, her height, her complexion. And then you just fold your arms, close your eyes, and you wait until this dream mate-rializes . . . and at a good price" (114). He describes how the matron approaches a Coptic family and tenders a marriage offer to the par-ents of a fourteen-year-old virgin: "My principal fancies a freshly hatched chicken" (115). Next comes the signing of the marriage con-tract followed by the actual wedding ceremony. Wężyk even proffers advice on the way the wife should be handled:

> She ought to remember that your servants should be loyal and that they should not steal. Dinner should be served at a set hour. Fruit should be ripe, water fresh, everything inexpensive! When you come back home after your morning stroll, she should expect you by the doorstep with a copper basin in her hands, wash your feet, fill and light your pipe, and during the time you have your breakfast or dine, she should stand behind you with her hands crossed, or sit at your feet and fan off flies. (120)

The East becomes a realm for the fulfillment of sexual fantasies and the affirmation of male dominance. All rules of moral conduct

are conveniently suspended here. Even though Wężyk appears to
have shed the orientalist skin in the first part of his *Travels*, ultimately, his attitude towards the East is encoded in the old, familiar
terms of European supremacy.[11] Though he ostensibly identifies himself as a traveler by opposing the dominant conventions, inconsistencies mar his account. They destabilize his narrative and prevent
him from creating an alternative to the established modes of narrating travel and representing cross-cultural encounters.

In *Travels in the Ancient World*, Wężyk deals only with his stay
in Egypt. He later published two fragmentary accounts of his visits
to Palestine and to Greece. An account of his journey to the Holy
Land appeared in a periodical publication under the title "The
Words' Original Meaning: A Travel Adventure."[12] Jan Bystroń, who
dedicates a chapter of his monograph to Wężyk, does not make any
references to the text of the pilgrimage account. Leszek Kukulski dismisses it as a text of little literary merit, arguing that

> the traveler who in Egypt spontaneously reacted to every new
> sight or event, and measured them according to the intensity of
> his impressions, behaves differently here: he prepares himself
> for certain experiences, organizes them consciously, but at the
> same time the literary quality of their description diminishes.
> (254)

Yet, it is finally here, in the pilgrimage text, that Wężyk found a for-
mula that allowed him to narrate oriental travel in an original way.
The account of his pilgrimage to the Holy Land differs from the
dynamic and colorful description of his travels in Egypt. It is much
shorter and a lot sketchier in form. Wężyk refrains from addressing
the reader directly. A description of the sea voyage to Jaffa begins the
account. The journey takes five days, during which the narrator feels
completely alienated from the other passengers, "twenty-six people
of the poorer class, foreign to me by virtue of their different nation-
alities, outlooks, languages and customs" (190). His scrutiny of the
"Orientals" concludes with a confirmation of European superiority:
"Their thoughts are chaotic like the thoughts of children" (192).
This atmosphere induces him to reflect upon the purpose of life: "I
was deep in thought about the purpose of my journey, life's journey,
the heavens' journey, the journey of time" (191). In keeping with the
pilgrimage tradition, Wężyk becomes highly introspective. He closes
his eyes and rummages through his memory:

> Abandoning the famous Alexanders, Caesars, Saladines, Richards, my soul entered the abode of its own heart with its most secret places, and there it looked at its reflection as if in a pail, where, similar to goldfish, memories swim. Not in personal memories did it search for its own reflection, but in recollections of those thoughts which had been the first to nourish it, until it became used to a different fare. (192)

As the account's title foreshadows, the notion of pilgrimage as a return to a point of origin, back to some long-lost simplicity, to "the word's primeval meaning," resonates throughout Wężyk's account.

It is not the introspection itself, but the way in which Wężyk manages to recapture the "word's primeval meaning" that sets him apart from many other pilgrims who produced written accounts of their journeys. According to the account, at the sea journey's onset the author secures a place for himself in the lifeboat, a step calculated to assure a more comfortable sea passage. When he goes to get a drink of water, another traveler settles down in his place.

> "This is just what I need"—I thought to myself, and since something like this had not yet happened to me, I frowned and—with the humanity of a Westerner—I put my hand, casually, on the handle of my gun. I was ready to scream at the navigator to remind him of the conditions of our contract. The guest to my quarters spoke before I had a chance to do so. Calmly he uttered these words: "I am a Christian . . . I am a little weak." Everybody's eyes turned towards the two of us, and everything, including the sea—which now looked at the dark mountains of Judea—became silent. In this portentous moment I could finally comprehend the primeval power of the word. Without saying anything, I pointed with my eyes towards my berth and I looked at him until he comfortably positioned himself there. I stepped into the lifeboat and sat down—on the other side of my "comfort." In silence I passed a flask filled with Rhodes wine which was attached to my belt to my new companion. It was already getting dark, still I could see how the Muslims looked at us with more respect, as if they were saying to themselves: "After all, that Issa [Jesus] of theirs did teach some practical things." (196)

Wężyk resolves to travel to the Holy Land in comfort. Yet the circumstances of the sea passage, related in a humorous, good-natured way, force him to renounce comfort and reconsider the meaning of his pilgrimage. Jonathan Sumption defines the practices and the aims of medieval pilgrimage in the following terms:

> By inflicting severe physical hardship on the pilgrim, it satisfied a
> desire for the remission of his sins, and opened up to him the
> prospect of the "second baptism." By showing him the places
> associated with Christ and the saints, it gave him a more person-
> al, more literal understanding of his faith. (114)

Wężyk's behavior during the confrontation with his fellow traveler
is inspired by precisely the type of attitude Sumption's study
describes. The humbling experience on the boat sets the tone for
Wężyk's entire account.

Once he has set foot in Jaffa, the Eastern Christian travel companion assures Wężyk of his gratitude. In the following chapter,
Wężyk describes how, after several days, he arrived in Bethlehem
from Jerusalem. Upon leaving the church housing the Chapel of the
Manger, he noticed a group of people in eastern dress. One of them
approached him. This was his acquaintance from the boat, who now
invited Wężyk to his home and introduced him to his family. Later
the man and his son guided Wężyk on his tours around the area.

The Bible functions as a universal subtext for all Holy Land pilgrimages. Unlike other authors, Wężyk does not confront the biblical account with the story's original setting. He does not map the
Holy Land, and he does not quote the Bible to recall the events
described in the New Testament. Rather, he tells simple stories reminiscent of biblical parables. At the same time, his narration remains
natural; the biblical stylization is not obtrusive. What makes
Wężyk's text interesting, however, are the ways his account diverges
from traditional pilgrimage accounts.

Wężyk's pilgrimage does not culminate with the description of
the author's visit to Jerusalem and to the Holy Sepulcher. He relates
a conversation with the monks who tend the Chapel of the Manger.
They ask about the places he has visited in the Holy Land, especially Jerusalem. In response, he says:

> I asked them not to take me for an Englishman. So they asked
> me whether I had visited the Redeemer's Sepulcher. I told them
> that I had not done so yet, as I intended to visit all the memo-
> rable places in order, and only then, after having fulfilled the
> duties of a Christian, would I kneel down at the Holy Sepulcher.
> (203-4)

Wężyk distances himself from the conventions governing the genre
of pilgrimage accounts by mentioning Jerusalem and the Holy

Sepulcher only in passing. The focus of his description shifts to the sea passage and to his Bethlehem visit.

Two moments of particular importance take the place of a description of a visit to Christ's tomb. The first one comes when Wężyk removes his hand from the handle of his gun and welcomes the stranger to his place in the life boat. The second turning point arrives with the sighting of the stranger at the entrance to the church containing the Chapel of the Manger. The traveler is reborn as a Christian when he gives up his place for another. Christ's actual birthplace then provides a convenient background—and nothing more—for fully grasping a new, more literal understanding of his faith. When the companion from the sea passage approaches Wężyk to welcome him to Bethlehem, this worldview is confirmed.

Standing at Christ's birthplace, Wężyk comes to grasp what it means to be a Christian. The necessary element of this process is the presence of another human being, a biblical neighbor. By including the Eastern Christian in the picture and, furthermore, presenting him as a necessary part of the equation, Wężyk escapes the excessive egocentrism and ethnocentrism evident in most Jerusalem pilgrimage accounts. In spite of the unconventional structure of both the journey and the account itself, Wężyk accomplishes the ultimate goal of Catholic pilgrimage. His text leaves the reader with the impression that the author's journey to the Holy Land did indeed effect a spiritual renewal.

Wężyk's travel accounts met with a lukewarm reception from the critics (Kukulski 250-53). Like Mickiewicz before him, Wężyk received no encouragement to continue his endeavours in the oriental field. His *Travels* remain an archive of the author's attempts to narrate oriental travel from a different, non-Western European perspective. To a certain extent, Wężyk affirms a native tradition of travel to the Orient that stretches even beyond Rzewuski and Potocki and extends back to the sixteenth-century pilgrimage of Krzysztof Radziwłł "Sierotka." No one followed the path Wężyk charted with his travel prose, so uneven in its form and content, often oscillating between the extremes of imitation and spontaneous expression, between assertions of western superiority and openness towards others. The exilic lamentations of other Polish writers, including Słowacki, overwhelmed his chosen option of traveling free from the emotional burden of national losses.

Apart from depending on Western oriental voyages for inspiration, Słowacki also drew on the then-available versions of

Radziwiłł's pilgrimage account as a source. Not long after the trip to the East, he wrote two prose fragments imitating the language of sixteenth-century Poland, "Preliminary to Radziwiłł Sierotka's Journey to the Holy Land" (Preliminaria peregrynacji do Ziemi Świętej J.O. Księcia Radziwiłła Sierotki); and "Easter Breakfast at Radziwiłł Sierotka's" (Święcone u J.O. Księcia Radziwiłła Sierotki). These stylistically remarkable texts make it clear that Słowacki did not see himself as a continuator of a specifically Polish tradition of oriental travel. Both provide ample proof that Słowacki was critical of the Sarmatian cultural heritage and—unfortunately—that he was unwilling to appreciate Radziwiłł Sierotka's accomplishments as a traveler and as a writer. Słowacki's Sierotka emerges as a backwards monstrosity: a strong tendency to luxuriate and overconsume demonstrate his attachment to the extravagant, profligate lifestyle of the Polish nobility, whose debauchery rose in inverse proportion to the Commonwealth's decline. His arrogance is boundless, his mental abilities limited. In both texts, Słowacki exposes and condemns the selfish excesses of the old noble Poland, implicitly blaming it for precipitating the country's demise. This attitude towards Radziwiłł's text is consistent with Słowacki's worldview as it took shape in the aftermath of his oriental journey: his oriental poetry and his letters project a subject structured primarily by the losses sustained by the country with which he identifies.

Neither Słowacki nor Wężyk succeeded in producing a narrative of oriental travel that approximated the accomplishment of Mickiewicz's *Sonnets*. That being said, a comparison of their very different oriental texts produces a comprehensive picture of the varied intellectual traditions, influences, and often contradictory tendencies that animated nineteenth-century Polish literature in the wake of the failed uprising of November 1830.

NOTES

1. Up to now, the orientalist scholar Jan Reychman is the only author of a book-length study of nineteenth-century Polish oriental journeys (*Podróżnicy*). Stanisław Burkot has provided the best overview of Polish nineteenth-century oriental travel literature in his book on Polish travel literature of that period. Erazm Kuźma's 1980 monograph attempts to analyze Polish Orientalism alongside western and Russian literary phenomena. Ryszard Przybylski's study of Juliusz Słowacki's journey to the East, published along with an anthology of

the poet's oriental texts, offers one of the most comprehensive and interesting analyses of Polish oriental travel literature produced so far.

2. Juliusz Słowacki mocked wallenrodism in his narrative poem "Beniowski," charging that this approach to the Polish predicament "introduced a method into treason" (III, 43).

3. The announcement was appended to Chodźko's *Le drogman*.

4. A large number of Polish officers under the leadership of general Henryk Dembiński joined the Egyptian army. Russian diplomatic intervention forced them to abandon this venture.

5. Czajkowski worked to convince Slavs living under Ottoman rule to seek the political support of France instead of Russia. He agitated for Turkey's involvement in a war against Russia during the Spring of the Nations. After his conversion to Islam, he fought in the Crimean war. Following France's military defeat by Prussia in 1871, Czajkowski went over to the Russians. He perceived a unified Germany to be the greatest threat to Polishness (Lewak 155-59). As a successful fiction writer, whose novels were translated into several languages, including French and German, Czajkowski represented native Polish literary Orientalism. His novels were often set on the eastern outskirts of the Commonwealth and relied heavily on Cossack folklore.

6. While the literary output of Słowacki's voyage is disappointing, in some respects, the journey itself proved to be a critical turning point in the poet's literary career. Ryszard Przybylski asserts that it is important "to think of this pilgrimage as preparation for a great spiritual turning point, which was soon going to manifest itself fully in the great poetry of [Słowacki's] mystic period. This poetry, a phenomenon entirely exceptional and unique, amazes due to both its wisdom and its artistry" (73).

7. This as well as all the remaining volume and page references given in the text pertain to Juliusz Słowacki's *Dzieła*. Wrocław: Ossolineum, 1952. All of the translations are mine.

8. This particular letter, signed "Zosia," was not included in the 1952 edition of Słowacki's works. The grammatical form of the verbs used in the original is feminine (*Dzieła wybrane* 6, 318).

9. In one of the letters from his journey, Słowacki addresses the following questions to his mother: "Why am I throwing myself into this unknown world with such desperate eagerness? . . . Do you think that I want to further distance myself from you?" (*Dzieła wybrane*, 13, 292).

10. All of the citations that pertain to the first part of Wężyk's *Travels* indicate pages in the 1842 edition. The material cited from the second part ("Egypt—Images") comes from the 1957 version edited by Leszek Kukulski.

11. Wacław Seweryn Rzewuski was the first cousin of Karolina's and Henryk's father, Adam Rzewuski (Ślisz 13-15).

12. Published originally in *Pielgrzym*, vol. 1 (1843): 320-340, this text was also included in Kukulski's edition of *Travels*.

CHAPTER 3

Empire in the Background: Russian Oriental Travel from Crimea to the Holy Land

When Juliusz Słowacki ridiculed the tendency to collapse many different areas into one exotic, all-inclusive concept of the proverbial Orient, he responded to a literary and cultural reality. Ever since Mickiewicz introduced the Crimean peninsula to Polish literature as the "Orient in miniature," the Polish popular imagination viewed Egypt and Palestine as interchangeable with Crimea. In lieu of going to Egypt, a Polish nobleman could treat his wife to a *voyage orientale* by taking her on a journey to the much more accessible Crimean peninsula. At the same time, although religious pilgrimages were common, even for Catholic clergy travel to holy sites provided an occasion to experience the differences of the Orient.

Józef Drohojowski was a Cracow monk whose 1812 pilgrimage account inaugurated the writing of Polish oriental travelogues in the nineteenth century. He offered a straightforward testimony about his journey's more-than-religious character. "A traveler," he states, "needs a goal: my first objective was to visit Palestine, that is, the Holy Land; the second—to get to know things that are of interest. To achieve both, I needed two companions: the first one was piety; the second curiosity" ("Introduction," no page numbers). Throughout the nineteenth century, Poles traveled to the Orient in search of both spiritual edification and intellectual enrichment. The thrill of experiencing the Orient's exciting otherness provided an additional bonus. The pious, the curious, the grieving, and the politically engaged: Polish nineteenth-century travelers wore many hats that were often interchangeable amidst the composite and increasingly conventionalized oriental setting that also changed to match the roles the travelers assumed.

In sharp contrast to the relatively unsystematized Polish mode of oriental travel, Russian nineteenth-century travel to the region followed a clear, teleological geographic and ideological progression. Descriptions of travels to Crimea and the Caucasus were the first oriental voyages to attract the Russian readership's attention. These initial travels either followed in the wake of or occurred alongside Russian imperialism's military conquest of these areas (Layton 5). The popularity of Holy Land pilgrimages among Russia's social elite did not ensue until about a decade later. The first literary fruits of journeys to Crimea and the Caucasus catalyzed the era of imperial Russian literary oriental mythmaking. These Russian romantic oriental tales borrowed from the language of western literary Orientalism (Greenleaf 114-38). Notwithstanding the emergence of a textual imperial tradition in Russian writing, an alternative mode of relating to the Orient best described as anti-conquest also made its presence felt in both the literary and critical works of the time. As Susan Layton so trenchantly notes, "Russian literature does indeed run a gamut between underwriting and resisting the Caucasian conquest: writers were sovereign in their textual domains but wielded their representational authority to different ends" (9). In the 1820s, then, the southeastern borderlands of the newly expanded and still-expanding Russian Empire provided a setting in which Russian imperial authority was either asserted or questioned.

Widely read accounts of Russian Holy Land pilgrimages started to appear in the 1830s. These nineteenth-century Russian pilgrimages differ notably from the earlier Russian oriental journeys as well as from their Polish counterparts. The authors' emphasis on the journey's religious purpose gives them a more homogeneous character. Even though Holy Land pilgrims traveled to areas far removed from the Russian Empire, their texts uniformly promoted the type of exclusive, religion-based nationalism that, at the time, began to reassert itself as a dominant current within Russian culture. A diminishing reliance on western models of oriental travel went hand in hand with a growing assertion of the superior character of Orthodox Russian traditions. This geographical progression, from Crimea and the Caucasus to the Holy Land, tracked a peculiarly Russian ideologization of culture. The writings of two authors and prominent cultural adjudicators, Andrei Nikolaevich Murav'ev and Petr Viazemskii, provide useful sources for tracing this process.

Andrei Nikolaevich Murav'ev: The Making of a Russian Chateaubriand

Поведай: набожной рукою
Кто в этот край тебя занес?
Грустил он часто над тобою?
Хранишь ты след горючих слез?

Иль, божьей рати лучший воин,
Он был, с безоблачным челом,
Как ты, всегда небес достоин
Перед людьми и божеством.

М. Ю. Лермонтов, "Ветка Палестины"

Say thou: whose pious hand has brought you to this land? Was
he often overcome with sadness when looking at you? Do you
shroud traces of anguished tears?

Or, was he, the best soldier in God's retinue, with a clear forehead, like you, always worthy of heavens, in the eyes of people
and of deity.

M. Iu. Lermontov, "Palm of Palestine"

It is a well-known fact of literary history that Mikhail
Lermontov wrote the poem "The Palm of Palestine" ("Vetka
Palestiny") after he saw the collection of objects, including pilgrims'
palms, Andrei Nikolaevich Murav'ev brought back from his 1830
Holy Land pilgrimage.[1] Murav'ev's name is also linked to Pushkin's
"Journey to Arzrum at the Time of the 1829 Military Campaign"
("Puteshestvie v Arzrum vo vremia pokhoda 1829 goda"). He is one
of two poets Pushkin mentions in the account's introduction:

> As for the poets in the Turkish campaign, I knew only of A. S.
> Khomyakov and A. N. Murav'ev. Both were in Count Dybich's
> army. The former wrote some lyric poems at the time; the latter
> reflected upon his journey to the Holy Land, which had pro-
> duced such a strong impression. (11)

Murav'ev's name is also associated with Pushkin's unfinished review
of the writer-pilgrim's *Journey to the Holy Places of Palestine*
(*Puteshestvie ko sviatym mestam Palestiny*).

At the beginning of his professional career, Murav'ev tried to advance into Russia's literary pantheon. He did eventually succeed in carving out a perfect niche for himself within Russia's nineteenth-century literary culture, but not as a poet. Instead, he established himself as a well-known and respected writer of religious prose. The fact that, today, the reading public's awareness of Murav'ev does not extend beyond the level of the footnote is an irony of fate.

The restrictive, highly politicized, anti-religious cultural atmosphere during Soviet times predictably sentenced to near oblivion the poet and writer whose main claim to literary fame was his *Journey to the Holy Places in 1830*. The only serious reexamination of Murav'ev's place in Russian letters during the first part of the nineteenth century took place as the Soviet Union was collapsing, in V. E. Vatsuro's 1989 article on the genesis of Pushkin's epigrammatic poem "From the Anthology" ("Iz antologii"). Thanks to the Orthodox Church's highly positive assessment of Murav'ev's work, the post-Soviet era has witnessed the publication of several of his works. In fact, history may extract Murav'ev from obscurity. The introductions to Murav'ev's republished works boast a nearly hagiographic tone that holds forth the prospect that he may still earn resurrection as a prominent figure in Russia's cultural traditions. N. A. Khokhlova's recently published monograph signals a renewed interest in Murav'ev the writer. This author reasserts Murav'ev's position as a literary figure while underscoring the particular importance of *Journey*. Khokhlova engages in a systematic and valuable investigation of the circumstances of Murav'ev's life and his literary career. She bases her study on both published and unpublished archival materials. But her analysis fails to venture beyond the parameters of the literary reputation Murav'ev established for himself while he was still alive. Khokhlova does not deal with issues relating to Russia's policies towards the southeastern borderlands and the East in general. Nor does she discuss the elite's attitudes towards imperial expansion. The imperialist connotations of Murav'ev's writing remain outside the scope of Khoklova's analysis.

As alluded to previously, Andrei Nikolaevich Murav'ev authored the first widely read Russian nineteenth-century description of a pilgrimage to the Holy Land. Though he is now remembered chiefly for his pilgrimages and works on church history, at the beginning of his literary career, Murav'ev's desire to join the company of Russia's premier poets drove his literary activity. In 1827, he published a collection of poems under the title *Tauris (Tavrida)*. This small volume included an eponymous longer poem. "Tavrida" marked Murav'ev's first foray into the field of literary oriental travel.

Evgenii Baratynskii reviewed Murav'ev's poetry volume for *Moscow Telegraph (Moskovskii telegraf)*. The senior poet discerned little merit in the presumptuous upstart's work. Baratynskii made this negative assessment despite his stated intent to proffer constructive criticism only. His review evaluates the young poet's account of Tauris in the following manner:

> "Tavrida" bears all the signs of being the work of a beginner. It is a poor creation, or better still, let us say that it is not a creation at all. It is a rhetorical diffusion of two lines from Pushkin's "B.F." ["Bakhchisaraiskii Fontan"]: "Where have the khans concealed themselves? Where's the harem? Everything is empty all around, everything's dejection . . . ."
>
> If we add that in Mr. Murav'ev's poem there isn't a single stanza, from beginning to end, written in good verse, its merit will not be too great. . . . But even if we don't see any art in it, we can still see some potential. The descriptions, which are not very accurate, are at times quite vivid, and the badly crafted lines do occasionally breathe of some sort of anxiety that is reminiscent of inspiration. (326)

Murav'ev, in other words, failed in his heartfelt attempt to follow in what proved to be Pushkin's hallowed footsteps. Indeed, precisely those works by Pushkin that were inspired by his travels in the South, including Crimea, solidified the master poet's literary reputation. The "young poet" Murav'ev considered the review to be unjustly severe. It left him so discouraged that, according to his own testimony, he resolved to abandon poetry altogether. In *Acquaintance with Russian Poets (Znakomstvo s russkimi poetami)*, Murav'ev supplied an autobiographic account that contains the following version of events:

> In the winter of 1826, I published a collection of my poems describing the southern shore of the Crimea under one title— *Tauris*. It was a really bitter experience for a writer's self-esteem, when, in the spring, while in the country, I read in one of the Moscow journals a critical analysis of my book, which was not only fairly condescending, but, as it seemed to me then, a bit severe. My friend, the poet Baratynskii, was the author of this anonymous critique . . . , a serious blow for a young writer at the

very beginning of his literary career, and one that made me turn
to prose. (44)

In addition to Baratynskii, A. S. Pushkin and S. A. Sobolevskii
also openly criticized Murav'ev's poetry. V. E. Vatsuro scrutinizes the
background and the dynamic of these three writers' utterances concerning Murav'ev and concludes that, by downgrading Murav'ev as
a poet, they wished to reassert a hierarchy of literary merit. A blow
no less severe than Batatynskii's review came in the form of Pushkin's
"Epigram: From the Anthology" ("Epigramma: Iz antologii"). It was
said that Murav'ev accidentaly broke the hand of a plaster statue of
Apollo displayed in Princess Zinaida Volkonska's residence. He then
covered the base of the statue with spontaneously composed verses
(Vatsuro 222). Pushkin exploited this incident, characteristic of
Murav'ev's attempts to fashion himself as a poet, to mock and undermine the image Murav'ev so desperately wanted to create for himself. Pushkin's epigram ridicules Murav'ev's rivalry with the
Belvedere Apollo by dubbing him the Belvedere Mitrofan. One could
hardly think of a more derogatory epithet for a young poet of that
time. Mitrofan, the title character of Denis Fonvizin's play *The
Minor*, was a well-known caricature, a dull-witted youngster predes-
tined to failure. The embarrassing analogy stuck to Murav'ev. In an
epigram written in the 1840s, Sobolevskii thumbed his nose at
Murav'ev's career within the church hierarchy by referring to him as
the vain Mitrofan who made an investment by giving his talent to
Christ at high interest (qtd. in Vatsuro 235). For his part, Baratynskii
focused his criticism of *Tavrida* on Murav'ev's alleged stylistic weak-
nesses. He pointed out the Pushkinian subtext as a way of commenting on what he saw as the poor quality of Murav'ev's literary
adventure in Crimea. Baratynskii dismissed Murav'ev as nothing
more than a poor imitator in the increasingly popular field of
Russian literary Orientalism.

To foreground "Tavrida's" ideological ramifications, it may be
useful to broaden the field of its intertextual references to include
Mickiewicz's "Crimean Sonnets." The Polish poet's *Sonnets* came
out in December of 1826. Contrary to Murav'ev's contention,
Tavrida did not appear in 1826, but at the beginning 1827.
Regardless of whether or not Murav'ev knew of "Crimean Sonnets"
when he was putting the finishing touches on "Tavrida," the proximity of the two texts' origins begs for a juxtaposition.

Like Mickiewicz, Murav'ev visited Crimea in the momentous year 1825, shortly before the ill-fated Decembrist conspiracy against the tsar reached is denouement. In a memoir written at the time, Murav'ev notes, "Finally, in August of 1825 I fulfilled my burning desire: I saw Crimea and I became a poet, like a painter who upon seeing a painting of Raphael exclaimed, 'I am a painter!'" (Vatsuro 226) A portion of Murav'ev's Crimean journey took place in the company of Aleksandr Griboedov, who was already the celebrated author of *Woe from Wit* (Gore ot uma, Khokhlova 46-47). Griboedov's correspondence from Crimea laments the tiresome company of the admirers of his talent. With the latter in mind, he records that, "if you are on your way to visit famous ashes and stones, you are better off to leave the living behind" (Griboedov III, 177-79). Having just resolved to ascend to the ranks of Russia's great poets, Murav'ev presents himself as a likely candidate for membership in the group of Griboedov's overbearing admirers. Vatsuro discerns in this posture a characteristic feature of Murav'ev's psychology: the close similarity between his own creative ideas of this period and some of the literary projects Griboedov himself was pondering (226). Griboedov most likely knew Mickiewicz from St. Petersburg, and he may even have met with the Pole while in Crimea, at the estate of Gustav Olizar (Gomolicki 81). Murav'ev may thus either have encountered Mickiewicz or heard of the Polish poet during his Crimean voyage.

Mickiewicz's and Murav'ev's paths most certainly intersected in the Moscow salon of Princess Zinaida Volkonska. According to his own testimony, Murav'ev frequently visited the salon after his fall 1826 return to Moscow. Vatsuro points out that Volkonska's literary interests and efforts inspired two poems contained in Murav'ev's 1827 collection (232). At the beginning of 1827, Petr Viazemskii introduced Mickiewicz to Zinaida Volkonska, and the princess soon became a devoted supporter of the Polish poet's literary efforts. The Mickiewicz-Volkonska Moscow acquaintance subsequently evolved into a close, life-long friendship (Gomolicki; Mucha 13-33).

Volkonska and Viazemskii espoused unanimous support for Mickiewicz. In April 1827, Viazemskii's enthusiastic review of the "Crimean Sonnets" appeared in the seventh volume of *Moscow Telegraph*, together with a prose translation of the Polish poet's work. The review made a discernible impact as a conspicuously large number of translations into Russian followed. Baratynskii published his thinly veiled condemnation of *Tavrida* just one month earlier. As Murav'ev tried to come to terms with the highly critical reception of his own poetic travel account, Mickiewicz's sonnet cycle was one of the most talked about oriental works among the Russian literary elite.

Murav'ev subdivided his "Tavrida" into twelve parts with the following titles, all of which refer to place names: "Tavrida," "Chatyr-Dag," "Bakchi-Sarai," "Razvaliny Korsuni," "Georgievskoi monastyr'," "Balaklava," "Merdven'," "Alupka," "Ornanda," "Ialta," "Aiu-Dag," and "Kuchuk-Lambat." In addition, he organized the entire poem into 107 eight-line stanzas. This structure emphasizes the continuous character of his utterance. The poem's peculiar, rigid structure, with the titled and numbered subdivisions, bears no resemblance whatso-ever to Pushkin's narrative poems. Rather, "Tavrida's" formal features evoke parallels to Mickiewicz's "Crimean Sonnets," which are likewise identified with Roman numerals and titles. Murav'ev did not compose sonnets, but the visual effect produced by the poem's formal organization bears a striking resemblance to Mickiewicz.[2] If the Crimean setting and the two works' form create a common ground between the two cycles, the manner in which Murav'ev speaks about Crimea differs from the Pole's representational prac-tices. Mickiewicz meandered through orientalist texts in search of his own way of relating to the oriental Other. Murav'ev's "Tavrida," on the other hand, operates firmly within Orientalism's imperialist context. Quotes from two discrete parts of "Tavrida," "Chatyr-Dag," and "Bakhchi-sarai," illustrate Murav'ev's relationship with the Orient.

XIV

Луна на высоты эфира
Идет в уединенный путь,
Как одинокий странник мира,
Кому отрады уж не льют
Мечты обманчивыя жизни, -
Разорвала все узы смерт,
И удаленьем от отчизны
Из сердца грусть он хочет стерть.

Бакчи-Сарай

XV

Пустынный двор Бакчи-Сарая
Унылой озарен луной,
Розвалин друг, она, играя,
Скользит по келье гробовой,

Где грозных и надменных Ханов
Давно забытый тлееть прах,
Где воля дремлющих тиранов
Уж не закон - в немых гробах!

XVI
Изчезла слава сильных ханов!
Дворец их пуст, гарема нет,
Там только слышен шум фонтанов, -
Луны непостоянный свет
На стеклах расписных играет,
И по узорчатым полам
Широкий луч ея блуждает,
Как бледный дух по облакам.
(...)

XIX
За все отмстила вам Россия -
Орды губителных Татар!
Вы язвы нанесли живыя,
На вас обрушился удар;
В крови вы злато добывали,
Огнями пролагали след,
И на главу свою сзывали
Отмщение грядущих лет!
(*Tavrida* 12)

XIV

The moon is going on a solitary journey
to ethereal heights
Like the world's lone wanderer
Who can no longer find delight in life's deceitful dreams
Death has severed all ties
And by going away from the fatherland,
he wants to erase the sorrow from his heart.

Bakchi-Sarai
XV

The deserted castle of Bakhchisarai
A weary moon engulfs in light
She [the moon], who is a friend to ruins, playfully slides on a
grave cell
Where the long forgotten ashes of the frightful and haughty
Khans molder
Where the will of slumbering tyrants is no longer the law—in
the silent graves!

XVI

The glory of the mighty Khans has passed
Their palace is empty, the harem is gone

One can only hear the murmur of the fountains
The moon's unstable light is playing on the colored glass
And on the patterned floors
Its broad ray roams
Like a pale ghost in the clouds.
(. . .)

XIX
Russia has taken her revenge on you—
Rampant Tatar hordes!
You had inflicted live sores
Now the blow has turned on you
You acquired gold in bloody strife
Your footsteps were marked in fire,
And thus you were bringing upon yourself
The revenge of future years.

Roman Koropeckyj interprets the favorable reception of Mickiewicz's "Crimean Sonnets" in Russian literary circles as proof that the Polish poet coded the Orient in terms that appealed to the Russians' growing imperial sentiments (661). The echoing of Mickiewicz in Murav'ev may at first appear to confirm Koropeckyj's suggestion that Mickiewicz wrote the "Crimean Sonnets" with a Russian reading public in mind. Yet precisely the superficial similarities between the "Crimean Sonnets" and "Tavrida" emphasize the substantive difference between the Crimean cycle's cultural dialogism and "Tavrida's" imperial fashioning. Murav'ev and Mickiewicz wrote about the same territory in two entirely disparate ways. Even though the Russian conquest of Crimea took place four decades prior to his tour, Murav'ev sentenced the Tatar Khans to complete oblivion. In the fragment excerpted above, the light of the moon strays into Tatar graves, and Murav'ev's persona, who becomes one with the moon, triumphantly confirms that the Khans, Russia's long-time foes, are indeed defeated, dead, and forever gone. The logic of Murav'ev's poem establishes Russia as a rightful avenger of the suffering inflicted on her people by the Tatars in centuries past. Since the Tatars were ruthless tyrants, Russia had every right to obliterate the domain of the Khans.

In a turn that distinguishes Russian nineteenth-century imperialism from its Western European counterpart, Murav'ev transforms conquest into an act of self-defense and, morally, a just punishment for aggression. "Tavrida" legitimizes imperial conquest and the

ensuing appropriation and exploitation. "Tavrida" provides a peculiar rhetorical sequel to Pushkin's "Fountain of Bakhchisarai."
According to Monika Greenleaf, in "Fountain," Pushkin asks about
the fate of the khans and the harem, "but then dismisses his own
question." "He was never interested in the history itself," concludes
Greenleaf, "which is why he diverged so freely from its factual basis.
In the conclusion of the poem Pushkin encourages his reader to view
his story as Byron's readers viewed his Turkish Tales, as an allegori-
cal representation of the poet's otherwise hidden and unspeakable
psychic underworld" (134). Murav'ev interpreted Pushkin's question quite literally, and his "Tavrida" provides an answer to it: since
the Tatars inflicted harm upon holy Mother Russia, the Russians
dealt them a deadly blow. Oddly enough, later in his career, Pushkin
embraced the same discursive strategy in his verses celebrating the
defeat of the Poles' 1830 November Uprising.

Seymour Becker argues that in the nineteenth century Russia
adopted "the collective wisdom of Europe vis-à-vis the Orient,"
according to which the East was "the realm of despotism and slav-
ery instead of freedom, of emotion instead of reason, of stifling con-
formity and unbridled indulgence instead of self-controlled modera-
tion . . . , of stagnation and poverty instead of purposeful action"
(48-49). Murav'ev's scrutiny of Crimea in "Tavrida" follows the
borrowed western pattern: he adopts the air of European superiority vis-à-vis the South. But he integrates this attitude within a "defen-
sive and compensatory" rendition of Russian nationalism, the same
kind of nationalism that, according to Becker, characterizes
Karamzin's influential *History of the Russian State* that belongs
roughly to the same period of Russian letters (Becker 49). The
dialectic evident in the quoted fragment from "Tavrida" reflects the
movement from the recycled, ornamental Romanticism of moonlit
ruins towards a pronouncement of integral nationalism.

Why did Murav'ev's politically correct narrative of Tauris—as
the Russians renamed Crimea in the aftermath of its annexation—
fail to meet with a favorable reception? Why did Mickiewicz's
"Crimean Sonnets" overshadow it? After all, the story of a Pole and
a Tatar trekking the Crimea together, remembering their dead and
experimenting with alternative modes of attaining freedom, presents
a paradigm dangerously close to exploding the project of Russian
imperialism. But Mickiewicz was a much better poet, and people
such as Sobolevskii, Viazemskii, and Pushkin were quick to notice

this fact. Additionally, a positive response to *The Sonnets* may have helped alleviate some of the anti-conquest anxieties experienced by the liberal-minded portion of the Russian proto-intelligentsia. Meanwhile, for Murav'ev, the failed "Tavrida" served as a prelude to a successful discursive annexation of the biblical East in his *Journey to the Holy Places in 1830* (*Puteshestvie ko sviatym mestam v 1830 godu*). This account of his pilgrimage to the holy sites of Palestine and Egypt in 1830 presents Murav'ev's lasting, if now largely unknown contribution to the genre of oriental travel writing. The work's eight editions offer best proof of Murav'ev's impact on Russian nineteenth-century readers (Ponomarev 15).

In a eulogy published in the *Russian Archive* (*Russkii arkhiv*) an acquaintance remembered that even as a young boy Murav'ev cherished dreams of travel to the East, which "strongly attracted his imagination as the cradle of Christianity and the scene of the crusades" (Putiata 357). But like other insights into Murav'ev's biography, this one may also be apocryphal. What we know for sure is that following his participation in the war with Turkey and after the signing of the peace treaty in Adrianopole in 1829, Murav'ev left the army of General Dybich to become a pilgrim.

According to Orthodox tradition, pilgrimage to the Holy Land is an act of preparation for one's own death. Glenn Bowman observes that Orthodox pilgrims "come to the Holy Land in old age to prepare themselves for a good death and for their subsequent assumption into the redeemed world promised by Jesus" (108). The case of Andrei Murav'ev does not conform to this rule. Not only did he travel to Palestine as a relatively young man. His pilgrimage proved to be a truly liminal experience that spawned a new beginning. It thrust him into the public limelight as a writer, and it opened the door to a successful government career. Upon completing his pilgrimage account, Murav'ev presented his work to Tsar Nicholas I, who granted him a high-ranking job with the Holy Synod. He later worked in the Asiatic Department of the Ministry of Foreign Affairs.

Vatsuro documents that Nikolai Polevoi, the editor of *Moscow Telegraph*, belonged to the few figures on the Moscow cultural scene who appreciated Murav'ev's early literary work (228-29). Soon after the publication of *Journey*, Polevoi pronounced Murav'ev's pilgrimage account a major literary and cultural event. In a lengthy two-part review published in the *Moscow Telegraph,* Polevoi identifies the uniqueness of Murav'ev's book:

> It rarely happens that you will not find news about Russian pil-
> grims leaving for Jerusalem. But what can they, mostly old men and
> women, people of lower social standing and without education, tell
> us? Faith alone leads them, and they are often forced to support
> themselves by asking for alms along the way. Jerusalem still remains
> especially interesting for us because of how rare *Russian*, and in
> general *new* accounts of its present situation are. (572)

In contrast to the bulk of Russian pilgrims, uneducated old men
and women of the lower classes who, from the elites' perspective,
inhabited a realm of their own and who could not contribute to an
educated Russian's knowledge of holy places, Murav'ev's account
has a lot to offer. Polevoi explains that

> He visited holy places and he describes them as a poet, as an
> enlightened observer, and as a Christian. To this let us add the
> freshness of the information and delightful newness of descrip-
> tions. If we also say that the author was able to balance the nar-
> ration concerning himself and the description of that which has
> not yet been observed by others concerning Jerusalem topogra-
> phy; if we relate to the readers that, although Jerusalem remains
> the main object of the book, the author also describes his journey
> to Jerusalem and back from Jerusalem, they will undoubtedly
> agree that we want to draw their attention to a book that
> deserves to be noticed. To this book's credit, we note that the
> author occupies the reader not with himself, but with what he
> has seen. He describes what he himself saw and noticed. He does
> not compile his account from excerpts [of other accounts]. After
> Chateaubriand, who has become for Russian readers of the high-
> er classes the same as Grigorovich has been for the lower, you
> can read the new description of travel for your instruction, and
> with interest. (528)

In a note, Polevoi points out that Chateaubriand's *Itinéraire de
Paris à Jérusalem* was translated into Russian twice. Even though he
never again mentions Chateaubriand, Polevoi's unstated goal is to
convince his readers that, from a Russian perspective, Murav'ev's
text is equal if not superior to the famous Frenchman's account.
Nikolai Nadezhdin uses his review of Murav'ev's text to make
explicitly the same point:

> Now, as we are still waiting to see the fruits of [Lamartine's] trav-
> els, we can display for Europe our Russian traveler's depictions—
> ones that, we have to confess, we would not trade for those

authored by Chateaubriand. The distinguishing trait of our traveler is his Russian, passionate feeling that pours out of the depth
of his soul, saturated by true piety. (251)

Murav'ev's sojourn to Palestine began roughly at the same time
and place where Pushkin's second oriental journey ended—in the
southeastern theater of war, around the time of the signing of the
Treaty of Adrianopole. In a fragmentary review of Murav'ev's pilgrimage account that remained unpublished during Pushkin's life,
the great poet admits that he read the account "with affection and
involuntary envy." He emphasizes that Murav'ev traveled to the
Holy Land neither in order to find colors for his poetry nor to
relieve his boredom. Rather, Murav'ev traveled there as a Christian:
"He visited the holy places as a believer, as a humble Christian, as a
simple bearer of the cross who desired to turn into dust in front of
the grave of Christ the Savior" (*Polnoe sobranie sochinenii* 7, 262).

Monika Greenleaf's astute commentary detects in Pushkin's
review both sympathy and irony. For Pushkin, Murav'ev's account
represented a "straightforward model of travel writing, unhindered
by any awareness of the clichés of its own discourse" (Greenleaf 47).
Indeed, for the most part, the heavy load of Western European sub-
texts does not burden Murav'ev's *Journey*. Yet there is no reason to
believe that he was unaware of the discourse of western Orientalism.
Murav'ev chooses to suppress the western textual Orient in his
account to recreate an alternative, native Russian, pre-1800s textual tradition. Pushkin's brief characterization of Murav'ev's *Journey*
emphasizes one of the text's most important aspects, no matter
whether Pushkin intended the commentary to be serious, or whether
he was yet again poking fun at the "young author." The review
stresses the overtly Orthodox Christian character of the text. In contrast to Polevoi, whose critique foregrounds elements of "enlightened commentary," Pushkin correctly highlights the one aspect of
Murav'ev's text that most clearly distinguished it from Western
European travelogues. Murav'ev's comments concerning the current
state of political affairs in the East, including his thinly veiled suggestions that Russia should play a more prominent role in oriental
affairs, follow from the firm footing he gains by identifying himself
as an Orthodox pilgrim.

In the third and most complete edition of *Journey* (1835),
Murav'ev begins his account by providing a fairly thorough

overview of earlier Russian pilgrimages to the Holy Land. He provides extensive quotes from Igumen Daniil's twelfth-century pilgrimage, thereby introducing this text into print two years before the
publication of its full version. In fact, Murav'ev begins his account
with a two-page quote from the introduction to Daniil's narrative,
which opens with the words:

> Behold, I, the unworthy abbot Daniel of the Russian land, least
> of all monks, humbled by many sins and lacking in any good
> deed, urged by my own imagination and impatience, conceived a
> desire to see the Holy City of Jerusalem and the Promised Land.
> (Wilkinson 120)

Scholarly interest does not motivate the extensive quotes from
Daniil. Murav'ev's primary intent is to make his readers aware of his
medieval predecessor's existence and to draw their attention to
Daniil's pious accomplishments. The Old Russian source endows
Murav'ev's account with native Russian patrimony. Since he posi-
tions himself as a continuator of a veritable Russian tradition, he
conveniently dissociates himself from Western European discourses.
Murav'ev makes his choice of lineage quite explicit:

> I would consider myself blessed, if repeating the words of his
> [Daniil's] modest prayer ensured that I could visit the holy places
> in a similarly humble spirit. (IX)

Murav'ev then presents an analysis of all major Russian pilgrimages
up until the 1820s that includes the accounts of Saint Evfrosinia,
Stefan Novgorodets (1349), Zosima (1420), Vassily Gost'
Moskovskii (1466), and several others. Interestingly, Murav'ev's
interpretation identifies as the most remarkable those Russian
descriptions of travel to the Holy Land that were produced in the
eighteenth-century, that is, at a time when Western Europe was
embracing the rational doctrines of the Enlightenment. European
Catholic pilgrimages almost completely ceased at that point. As
Naomi Shepherd observes:

> By Napoleon's time the tradition of Catholic pilgrimage was
> moribund. Only a handful of Europeans were to be seen in
> Jerusalem during Easter Week, vastly outnumbered by pilgrims
> from the Eastern Churches. (13)

Murav'ev identifies the account of Vasilii Barskii as the most noteworthy of all Russian pilgrimages. Barskii embarked on a twenty-four year journey to the holy places of Europe, Asia, and Africa in 1723. Murav'ev praises Barskii for the great precision of his description, especially in the detailed account he gives of all "the most notable Greek shrines, all church holidays and the condition of the clergy, and in general all that pertains to 'pravoslavie'" (LXXVIII). He sees him as by far the most pious of all the travelers of "recent times":

> What ardent feeling of faith accompanies him in his journey, what selflessness and trust in overcoming all obstacles. Praising Christ, he visits all the places of Christ's works, without knowing whether he will have food for the following day, and he falls asleep peacefully among danger, suffers blows and curses and receives them happily, as a true pilgrim would . . . (LXXIX)

If Daniil was the father of all Russian pilgrims, Barskii, son of a Kiev merchant, became a role model for Murav'ev, who himself was reared within the traditions of the post-Petrine Russian aristocracy. Murav'ev's analysis of Barskii's account provides insights into his own attitudes. He fashions himself as a pious traveler who concentrates on providing an accurate description of the Holy Land. He is especially sensitive to issues pertaining to the "Greeks" and Orthodox Christian control over the Holy Land's shrines and other sanctuaries.

Murav'ev's *Journey* delivers a meticulous description of the locations and present condition of the holy places. He informs his reader, for example, that fifty broad stone steps lead down to the grotto of Gethsemane, which the empress Helena, mother of Constantine, determined to be the burial place of Mary, and that

> In a small niche on the right side, attached to the wall, are the graves of the parents of the Holy Virgin, on the left across from them, carved in stone is a narrow grave of Joseph . . . . In its depth the grotto contains its main holy place, the grave of the Mother of God . . . . There, across from the main entrance is an elevated stone plate, covered by another, marble one, and covered with candles; a multitude of lanterns shine over it. This is the main altar, where the Greeks and Armenians celebrate the liturgy every day; this is the grave of the Mother of God, or to be more exact the grave stone, for a while illuminated with the

virgin burden of her ashes, since the Apostles did not entrust the
chaste body to the earth, but enclosed it inside the grave room
and laid it on the stone, where Apostle Thomas vainly looked for
it three days afterwards, as he was late for the funeral. (I, 242-
43)

The first volume of Murav'ev's pilgrimage account culminates
with a description of his visit to the Holy Sepulcher. He relates the
great emotional intensity of his encounter with the place where
"rested the body not of some mortal intermediary, and not of an
angel, but of the God who suffered for us himself" (I, 256).
Orthodox pilgrimages have traditionally had a different temporal
organization than Catholic pilgrimages. For the Orthodox, the stay
in Jerusalem has always coincided with the observances of the Holy
Week. The pilgrim's main goal is not just to visit the Holy Sepulcher
but to be present in Jerusalem during Easter observances (Bowman
111). The *Journey's* second volume centerpieces a detailed account
of Holy Week observances. This structural device accentuates once
more Murav'ev's identification with the Orthodox tradition.

Murav'ev exerted unquestionable influence on the reawakening
of the genre of pious traveling among the Russian elites. His contemporary, Avraam Sergeevich Norov, traveled to the Holy Land in
1834.[3] As Norov states in the introduction to his account: "I am

Figure 6: A lithograph panorama of Jerusalem reproduced in Avram Norov's
Puteshestvie po Sviatoi Zemle v 1835 godu (Saint Petersburg, 1838), part I, page
not numbered.

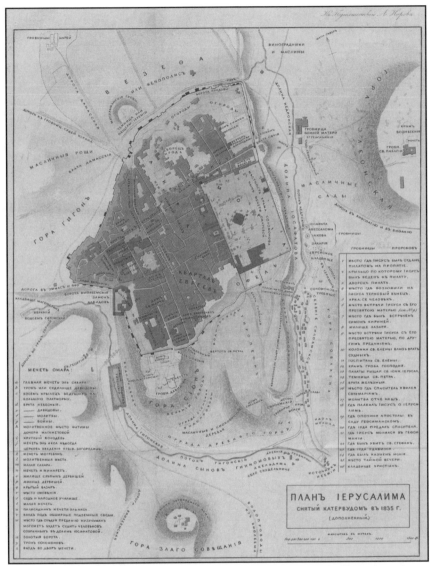

Figure 7: Plan of Jerusalem reproduced in Avraam Norov's *Puteshestvie po Sviatoi Zemle,* appended to part I.

addressing readers whose familiarity with Palestine is much greater—the beautiful pages of Mr. Murav'ev's book have brought the Holy Land closer to them. These pages certainly moved many hearts to the plight of the Jerusalem Church, struggling under the yoke [sic]" (ii). Norov's reputation as a Holy Land pilgrim possibly helped his career within government service; this was certainly the case with Murav'ev. Norov, a writer and esteemed Orientalist, eventually occupied the prominent post of Minister of National Education. Like Murav'ev's account, Norov's *Journey in the Holy Land in the Year 1835* (*Puteshestvie po Sviatoi Zemle v 1835 godu*) went through several printings. Czech and German translations provided further evidence of Norov's popularity (Ponomarev 16). Most important, a meticulously accurate description of Palestine's holy places meant that Norov's account of his 1835 Holy Land pilgrimage tread openly in Murav'ev's footsteps.

At first, Norov's pilgrimage description appears to refrain from underscoring the journey's specifically Russian character. For one thing, the author does not shirk from referencing Western European texts; the account begins by paraphrasing the opening verses of Dante's *Divine Comedy*; among the foreign sources it quotes is Chateaubriand.[4] But Norov also grants a prominent place to Daniil in his pilgrimage text. In the account's second edition, the author concedes that Igumen Daniil has already correctly located all the Holy Land sites he describes (Ponomarev 16).

Norov's reverent attitude towards Daniil stood in opposition to the common western practice of discrediting the accounts of one's predecessors. Moreover, Norov's heavy reliance on biblical quotes underscored both the religious character of his journey and his adherence to the native Russian tradition of travel. George P. Majeska points out that Daniil's text, the prototype of all later Russian pilgrimage accounts, incorporates numerous Old Church Slavonic quotes from the scriptures. "This literary device," Majeska records, "raises such moments of religious feeling to a higher plane by drawing on the connotations of the liturgical language of the Church in Russia" (7). Norov's account reasserts this important aspect of Russian pilgrimage writing.

Behind Norov's journey stood the desire to see the places where the Savior fulfilled the mystery of mankind's redemption. The account's main purpose is to provide an accurate description of these places. Norov's comment on the illustrations reproduced along with the account characterizes his understanding of the role of a religious travel writer:

> The locations of the most holy events of the Old and New Testaments were depicted from nature, with as much assiduity as

possible; no artistic ornaments that did not exist in the places depicted were allowed in these illustrations. (Norov iii)

Norov's narrative focuses on exact descriptions of the holy places he visited. Just like Murav'ev, Norov had an awareness of the importance of cultivating a specifically Orthodox way of traveling in the Holy Land. The two writers' focus on the holy places is no less strict in form and no less religious in character than the travel notes of the monk Anikita, in lay life Count S. A. Shirinskii-Shikhmatov, who ventured to the Holy Land in the years 1834-36.

These accounts' specificty resides in the way Murav'ev, Norov, and Anikita conceived the relationship between the prototype and the image, or, specifically, between a location marked by the presence of the body of Christ and the words used to describe it. In this

Figure 8: The icon "Not by Human Hand" reproduced in Avraam Norov's *Puteshestvie po Sviatoi Zemle,* part II, between pages 172 and 173.

sense, both the perception of the Holy Land they communicate and the descriptions they provide in their texts share a lot with the spiritual contemplation of icons propagated by Orthodox Christianity. According to Pavel Florenskii, icons fulfill a function linked to remembrance:

> Over and over, the proponents of icons refer to the icon's power to remind: the Holy Fathers of the Seventh Ecumenical Council say, "the icons remind those who pray of the icons' prototypes and, through gazing upon the icons, the believers lift up their minds from the images to the prototypes." (70)

But if the notion of returning to the origin and of remembering the prototypes unites the Catholic and Orthodox experiences of Palestine, the key difference between the two categories of pilgrimages lies in Florenskii's elaboration of the link between the icon and the prototype. He underscores the "ontological connection between icon and prototype." Without this connection, "the honor given to icons—given because of the ancient teaching that, in doing such honor, the believer ascends from image to proto-image—this ascending, this ancient Church belief, becomes something absolutely incomprehensible" (70).[5] The story of the first icon illustrates this special link that runs from the prototype—the body—to a holy site—marked by the body—to the icon. According to Orthodox tradition, the first icon was made when, on his death bed, king Abgar of Osroene (Edessa) sent a message to Jesus, begging him to visit and to cure him. As Leonid Ouspensky explains,

> the Edessa image would be an impression of the face of the Saviour on a piece of linen, which Christ had pressed to His face and sent to the envoy of Abgar. Thus, the first images of Christ, the "mandilion" and its two miraculous reimpressions on bricks—the "keramidia"—would have been documents "made without hands," direct, and, so to speak, material testimonies of the Incarnation of the Word.[6] (69)

The Holy Land boasts an abundance of imprints that bear witness to God's Incarnation. The very existence of these imprints provides the underlying principle of iconography. Glenn Bowman's study of Orthodox pilgrimage leads him to conclude that "perhaps the one thing that makes the Holy Land more sacred than the other sacra experienced in the life of a Greek Orthodox person is that it is the most realistic icon, or representation, of the spiritual truths expressed in all Orthodox religious forms" (110). When Norov describes the location of the alleged imprint of Christ's right foot, he does so with great accuracy, because he verbally depicts a site whose status is synonymous with the status of a holy icon:

> At the rostrum of the first alcove, which is to the right, [there is] a footprint of one human foot on a simple stone; at the rostrum of the other one—footprints of two feet. The first single foot is the imprint of Jesus, moved here from the heights of the Eleon Mount where the second Divine imprint remained. The two other footprints were left on this earth by, as the Muslims say, the Holy Virgin Mary. I fell to my knees and I kissed the two sacred places that are now, oh great sorrow, in the hands of the infidels. (I, 220)

Like Norov's response to these footprints, a pilgrim had to afford great reverence to all the other places in Palestine associated with the presence of Jesus, Mary, and other figures from the Gospels.

In the texts narrating their pious travels, both Murav'ev and Norov act simultaneously as devout pilgrims who prayed by contemplating the icons or holy imprints, of the Holy Land, and icon painters. Both the icon and a pilgrim's written account function as vehicles for transmitting the message of incarnation.[7] And both provide conduits towards a communion with God. Thus, Murav'ev, Norov and other nineteenth-century Russian pilgrims continued the tradition of what could be described as liturgical travel initiated by Daniil.[8] Their texts' emphasis on locating the proper sites and on providing detailed descriptions, as well as on establishing the Russian lineage of pilgrimage writing may be explained by placing them in the framework of the traditions of Orthodox icon painting. As Florenskii asserts:

> In the depths of Christian antiquity there is rooted the understanding that the icon is something not subject to arbitrary change . . . . The many icon-painting authentications, both verbal and visual, testify to the stability of the traditional practice; and their essential terms and concepts flow down into the very depths of Christian antiquity . . . . Thus we can understand the deliberate warning to the icon painter repeated many times in the authentications: anyone who ignores the Holy Tradition and begins to fashion icons according to his own thinking will be condemned to eternal torment. (78-79)

Russian Orthodox pilgrims endowed the Holy Land with a status comparable to that of an icon. Consequently, they expected to approach the area with appropriate veneration. And this is precisely the point where religion and politics began to intersect. Throughout his account, Murav'ev expresses alarm at the condition of the holy sites. His tone becomes most emphatic towards the end of the *Journey*:

> He who has never gone to Jerusalem as a pilgrim cannot clearly imagine the destitute condition of its sanctuary. If you have been there, and prayed—amongst the shame and profanation—on the sepulcher of the Savior to whom you are entirely devoted, if along with the tears of redemption, you vainly shed tears of sorrow, only then can you comprehend Europe's indifference to [the fate of] this founding stone of her salvation. I don't have the crusades in mind, and not a new offensive of the West against the East; the days when blood was spilled have passed, the time of international agreements came, and western countries abandoned Jerusalem at the time when Russia, which has been chosen by Providence to crush Islam, has so sternly moved towards its high vocation. She alone can alleviate the lot of the Holy City. (II, 132)

Murav'ev endowed Russia with the fulfillment of a political as well as a civilizing mission in the East made all the more urgent by his belief that oriental pollution had infected the local Orthodox Christians' ranks. While in Palestine, Murav'ev displayed open hostility and condescension towards all segments of the local population, including the Orthodox Arabs. The *Journey* devotes a large part of the description of the observances of the Holy Week to comments on the wild, unruly Orthodox Arabs and the curious and, in Murav'ev's opinion, repugnant ways in which they celebrate Easter. On Good Friday, for example:

> The holy doors were open for the evening observances, and, following the clergy, a loud crowd of believers invaded the church. They were of the Greek creed, but most of them were half-wild Arabs, those who lived scattered in the mountains of Palestine or came from beyond the Jordan and the Dead Sea, where they merely preserved the name of Christians, while living surrounded by wild Bedouins. Believers of this type filled the church, to the shame of Orthodoxy. (II, 112)

The noisy Orthodox Easter observances of the time irritated western, and especially Protestant visitors to Jerusalem. Shepherd quotes some western descriptions of the Orthodox ceremonies, and she concludes that: "Such reports created deep concern in the West over the custody of the Holy Places by the Eastern churches and contributed, among other things, to the rise of violent anti-Russian feeling in the mid-century" (33). Convinced that strength could be found in numbers, Norov takes the side of the Orthodox believers, supporting them in a confrontation with the Muslim guards at the Holy Sepulcher. Murav'ev complains often about the "Greeks'" insufficient presence in the administration of the holy sites. Yet he wants to see the Arabs reformed to the ways of the "motherland." He thus identifies Russia as the one and only guardian of the true faith. His description of the daybreak service in the church of the Holy Sepulcher provides a clear indication of his views:

> But this great daybreak service, which in the Orthodox mother-land is an impressive funeral celebration, did not affect my soul as I had hoped it would, in its original setting, where it was once not just a memory, but the event itself. Its great rites were polluted with disorderly choirs and the insensitivity of the rude crowd. (II, 118)

As a covert imperialist doctrinarian, Murav'ev distinguishes himself by developing yet another line of argumentation in support of Russian intervention in the East. Russia may be morally obligated to expand its custody to the Holy Land because everybody there expects her to do just that, and the *Journey* does relate the views of some local groups and individuals who would welcome Russian expansionism. Murav'ev also occasionally finds himself forced, as he states, to dismiss alleged rumors of Russia's plans to assume a dominant role in the East, as in the following fragment:

> The clergy, while asking me about the conditions of the Adrianopole peace treaty wanted to know whether we negotiated anything to the advantage of the Holy Sepulcher. Strange and ridiculous rumors spread in the city concerning my arrival. People were saying that I was the commander of a strong force, which had been sent to conquer the Holy City and that 10,000 Russians would follow me from Arzrum, or would anchor their ships at Akra . . . . The main source of these speculations was the quite widespread fear of the word Russian, augmented by the glory of our victories over the Porte. (I, 237)

These rumors of direct Russian involvement in the affairs of the East are not, according to the author, met with fear, but with joy or, at worst, with resignation by local Christians and Muslims alike. Polevoi proudly quotes several such cases in his *Telegraph* review of the *Journey*: the Muslim administrator of Jerusalem understands that everything around him is in the future going to belong to the Russians, and he asks for lenient treatment (531); a Christian Arab asks Murav'ev not if but when the Russian tsar is going to bring freedom to the Holy Land (533); in Ghaza, the traveler is surrounded by Christian Arabs who ask him about the conditions of the peace with Turkey and who proclaim that the Holy Land awaits liberation by the Russians (223). Even more noteworthy, the Jerusalem administrator, who traces his origin to Sukhum-Kale in Abhasia, "expresses joy at seeing a Russian" when he learns that his homeland already finds itself under Russian rule (532). And in Rama, a monk shows Murav'ev a twelfth-century prophecy about the taking of Constantinople by the Russians (223).[9]

According to the terms of the Treaty of Adrianopole, Turkey granted Russia access to the Danube and ceded additional territory on the Black Sea. The peace additionally compelled Turkey to open the Dardanelles to all commercial vessels, to grant autonomy to Serbia, to promise autonomy to Greece, and to consent to the Russian occupation of Moldavia and Walachia. Russia's successful assault on the Ottoman presence in the Balkans enhanced the tsarist state's international position. As the first step towards Russia's political expansion in the East, Adrianopole provided a suitable background for Murav'ev's innuendoes and retracted statements. Considering the political dimension of his *Journey*, it is not at all surprising that the account won official sanction. In addition to asserting Russia's place as the bulwark of modern Christendom, the pious traveler acknowledged her position as a major power broker in the Eastern question. Murav'ev's religiously colored statements of imperial greatness fit the political atmosphere of the reign of Tsar Nicholas I. Moreover, Nikolai Polevoi's enthusiastic review of the *Journey* indicates that these imperial sentiments likely met with the approval of Russia's non-official readership as well. Murav'ev's journey to the origins of Christianity and Russianness intersected with the emergence of a new quality in the intellectual portrait of post-Petrine Russia.[10]

Prince Viazemskii Travels to Jerusalem

Там краски светлыя Евангельской картины
Еще не стерлися под давкою веков,
Там в почву врезан след Божественных шагов,
Там чуешь в воздухе Евангельския речи,

Там с смутным трепетом ждешь и боишься встречи,
Как тут-же некогда, дорогой в Еммаус,
Внезапно братьями был встречен Иисус.

Князь Вяземский, "Памяти Авраама Сергеевича Норова."

The bright colors of the New Testament picture
Have not yet faded due to the pressure of time there.
There, the imprint of Divine steps has been pressed into the soil,
The Gospels fill the air there.

With an anxious trepidation you await and fear the encounter
Similar to the brothers' sudden meeting with Jesus, once upon
the time, in the same place, along the way to Emmaus.

Prince Viazemskii, "In Memory of Avraam Norov."

Even the reformist Decembrists espoused openly expansionist views about Russia's imperial policies along the southeastern borderlands (Becker 51). Speaking about the epilogue of Pushkin's "Prisoner of the Caucasus," Susan Layton perceives a possible influence of one of the Decembrists' leaders, Pavel Pestel, behind the poem's chauvinistic tone:

> Along with other Decembrist adherents to the Enlightenement idea of progress, Pestel regarded Russia as a backward, retrograde force vis-à-vis Europe. In relation to Asia, though, the semi-Europeanized homeland was granted the "western" role. This outlook made Russian imperialism in the orient fully compatible with a program for radical reform and modernization at home. (Layton 102)

If the challengers to the tsarist status quo incorporated orientalist patterns of thinking into their ideas for a better Russia, did any room exist for alternative ways of constructing Russia's national identity? One might be hard pressed to find nineteenth-century texts

expressing open opposition to Russia's imperial expansion, especially into the oriental borderlands. However, a practice of representing
otherness described by Mary Louise Pratt as "anti-conquest" did
inflect many literary and critical texts of the 1820s.

"Anti-conquest" does not denote opposition to imperial expansion. Rather, Pratt coins the term to encompass the "strategies of representation" that allow representatives of the dominant culture to
"secure their innocence in the same moment as they assert European
hegemony" (7). One of Russia's prominent literary-cultural figures
with a documented record of anti-conquest sentiments was Petr
Viazemskii. Viazemskii produced official and unofficial critiques of
Pushkin's narrative poems, and he reviewed and translated
Mickiewicz's "Crimean Sonnets." He thus participated in the first
phase of Russian literary Orientalism as a commentator/mediator,
not as a writer. Susan Layton incorporates a quote from a letter
Viazemskii wrote to Aleksander Turgenev into her reading of "The
Prisoner." Harsh words targeted at Russian cultural discourse's
engagement in the Caucasian conquest counterbalance Viazemskii's
public praise for Pushkin's Caucasian poetry:

> I am sorry that Pushkin bloodied the last lines of his tale. What
> kind of a hero is Kotliarevsky or Ermolov? What is so good
> about his "leaving a trail of black contagion to deal a death blow
> to the tribes?" That sort of notoriety makes your blood run cold
> and your hair stand on end. If we were bringing enlightenment
> to the tribes, then there would be something to sing about.
> Poetry is not the ally of butchers. The political life may need
> them, and then history must judge whether their acts were justi-
> fied or not. But a poet's anthems should never glorify slaughter.[11]
> (qtd. in Layton 107)

Significantly, Viazemskii does not call the conquest itself into question. Rather, he rejects the incorporation of the military campaign's
unseemly reality into a literary work. Viazemskii protests a fellow
writer's representational practices. That being said, he still speaks
about the Caucasian tribes from the superior position of a participant in a culture entitled to some sort of civilizing intervention.
Although Viazemskii's unofficial criticism of "The Prisoner" did not
break out of the general frame of imperial discourse, the position he
articulated did not denote a straightforward promotion of conquest.
As Layton points out, Viazemskii "withheld approval of the con-

quest, punctured the state's self-image as an agent of enlightenment and conveyed revulsion for the pacifiers' blood-curdling deeds" (107-8).

Roman Koropeckyj's interpretation of Mickiewicz's "Crimean Sonnets" through the prism of their reception in Russia presents Viazemskii as a mouthpiece of Russian imperial ideology (Koropeckyj 663). Yet, such characterization does not do justice to Viazemskii's overt criticism of the political status quo in the early years of his literary-critical career. During his service in Warsaw from 1817 to 1821, his oppositionist views inclined him to empathize with the Poles' plight under Russian occupation. He paid the price for his free thinking when his superiors terminated his government employment and ordered him back to Russia, where he was subsequently banned from occupying any government post until 1830 (Łużny 5-8). The warm welcome Viazemskii extended to Mickiewicz's *Sonnets* constituted an act of revindication on behalf of the Polish poet, not an imperial appropriation. To the extent that such identification was possible in a text subjected to official censorship, Viazemskii portrays Mickiewicz as a great poet and as a political exile:

> Here we have an unusual and delightful phenomenon. A wonderful creation of foreign poetry, a work of one of the foremost poets of Poland, printed in Moscow, where, most likely, there are no more than ten readers capable of appreciating its value. This work passed from the printers to the book sellers incognito, not honored by periodicals, without being announced by the critics, in a manner similar to a distinguished traveler who avoids the tributes of curiosity and the public displays of vanity because of his own sense of dignity. (326)

Mickiewicz is a dignified foreigner now barred from contact with his natural readership because of his exile—at the hands of tsarist officialdom, to read between the lines. The Pole is the antithesis of someone like Murav'ev, a native Russian poet busy cultivating his image in order to promote his own poetry. Viazemskii, an authoritative Russian critic, gives high marks to Mickiewicz's poetic travelogue without ever mentioning Murav'ev's *Tavrida*. He classifies Mickiewicz's dialogic Crimean poetry as a significant literary and cultural event.[12] By way of contrast, he allows Murav'ev's cries of imperial glory to die down and vanish. Viazemskii's anti-conquest stance manifests itself in his suggestions that Russian readers might benefit from learning Polish, as "study of the Polish language might complement the study of the native tongue" (327).

Viazemskii's attitude conflicted with the colonizer's usual practice of trying to render the colonized speechless. Later, in the wake of the failed 1863 January Uprising, Russia banned the Polish language from the offices and schools in the Polish lands that belonged to the Russian Empire. These policies confirmed the colonizing power's propensity to silence the colonized either by depriving them of their own language or by designating their native toungue as substandard. Viazemskii's review of the "Crimean Sonnets" placed him in opposition to such Russian colonial practices. Viazemskii's political views evolved following the wave of revolutionary movements that swept across Europe in 1848. The successive deaths of three of his children, in 1835, 1840, and 1849, contributed to a spiritual crisis. In June 1849, Viazemskii left his estate in Ostafevo to embark on his Holy Land pilgrimage. As he records in his notes, published as *Journey to the East* (*Puteshestvie na Vostok*):

> Had I not been swept by the wave of sorrow, I probably would never have gone anywhere. My travels, so far always marked by death, find their fitting finale in my journey to the Holy Sepulcher, the grave that makes it possible to reconcile with all the other graves. (71)

Viazemskii's little-known travel notes, first published after the author's death in 1883, document an ideological shift. In them, the writer affirms his great sensitivity to the dialectics of the literary process. His pilgrimage account demonstrates that he was also aware of the new tendencies that emerged within Russian culture along with the rebirth of the genre of pilgrimage writing. Yet, even though he no longer adhered to the liberal creed of his youth, Viazemskii remained inclined to question Russia's dominant imperial discourse on the occasion of his oriental journey. His *Journey* interrogates the type of travel writing that Murav'ev and Norov promulgated.

In 1848, Viazemskii published a monograph on Denis Fonvizin. The analysis of Fonvizin's travel letters provides him with an opportunity to make some observations about traveling Russians and about travel in general:

> For a curious and observing mind, travel is a type of practical learning. You return home enriched by new insights, new experiences and, so to speak, reshaped by the influence of diverse impressions. But to accomplish this, one needs a cosmopolitan mind, capable of functioning in unfamiliar circumstances, within a foreign element. Minds that are firmly established, and that have, due to their originality and independence, become one-sided, when moved to a climate foreign to them, do not draw anything from the new sources . . . . They do not develop, but quite to the contrary, they loose their freshness and power, like a relocated plant which needs native soil in order to bloom and to bear fruit. (*Fon-Vizin* 116)

For Viazemskii, Fonvizin the traveler belongs to the category of "minds that are . . . firmly established." Outfitted with a perennial awareness of his Russianness, Fonvizin often felt out of place when he was abroad. He was hence prone to judge everything foreign unfavorably. Viazemskii draws on an anecdote to characterize further this type of attitude: while passing through a German city, a certain traveler saw a red-haired woman beating a boy in an inn. In response, he inscribed in his travel notes: "Here all the women are red-haired and evil" (125). Viazemskii's philosophy of travel stemmed from the Enlightenment, and, in keeping with the latter's precepts, his analysis implies that he is on the side of the cosmopolitan-minded travelers.

In the pilgrimage notes jotted down just two years after the publication of the Fonvizin monograph, Viazemskii revisits his earlier comments on the subject of travel.[13] He argues that

> When you are nearing the end of your earthly existence and you think about the inevitable journey into the land of the fathers, any voyage, unless undertaken with the special goal of benefiting science, serves only the purpose of gratifying a vain whimsy, unproductive curiosity. Only the journey to the Holy Land can provide an exception to this rule. Jerusalem is like a stop on the road to the great rest. This is a preparatory rite for the solemn migration. (70)

Even though Viazemskii's account differs significantly from Murav'ev's and Norov's, the religious character of his *Journey* still determines its form and substance. Undiluted adherence to the intersection of Russianness and Orthodoxy strongly color the impressions and messages delivered by the author to his readers.

Viazemskii begins his pilgrimage account on July 15, the feast of Saint Vladimir, a day of celebration for both the Orthodox Church and for Russia:

> By uniting himself and the Russian nation with Orthodoxy, Vladimir had shown Russia her path . . . . All of our affairs, all that constitutes our national identity, our spiritual, moral and political strength, all of our successes and advances, all purifying and seminal ordeals, through which Providence has led us along a path of struggles, sacrifices, victory and glory, all of this stems from the eminent and holy bath, in which Vladimir immersed the young Russia, along with himself. Our spiritual sustenance and our patriotic upbringing began and took shape thanks to him. He determined our place in the history of humanity. Events of our distant past, and of recent history, current circumstances, and no doubt also future developments, have been and will continue to be linked together because of our union with the Orthodox Church . . . . A lot has changed and a lot may still change in the particulars of our national existence; but the key to Russia's destiny and her fate rests primarily in the holiness of her Orthodox faith. (1-2)

Just like other Orthodox pilgrims, Viazemskii made the journey in time to participate in the Holy Week observances (30).

At the same time, Viazemskii fortuitously uses a work posthumously titled *Journey to the East* to give expression to his enlightened skepticism, which comes to the fore in the doubts he now enunciates about the enterprise of travel writing in general:

> there is nothing more boring and senseless than the writing or dictating of one's own travelogue. I am always amazed by the craft of people who publish books of their own travels. My impressions are never productive, and I really do not know how to present them. A traveler has to be a bit of a charlatan. (29)

This statement is bereft of hypocrisy. Viazemskii's account was, regretfully, not meant for publication. His private notebook allowed him to expand on the view expressed above. In it, he engages in a polemic with the travel-writing practices of his Russian predecessors, especially the ones who built their careers on published accounts of their pilgrimages. The tone of Viazemskii's account differs defiantly from the texts of Murav'ev and Norov. He takes them to task for the way they looked at the Holy Land, and his view of the current political situation again puts him at odds with the politically correct line. Viazemskii counters the exalted manner of Murav'ev's narration with the casual tone of his own account, as his own reportage deflates the usually celebrated approach to Jerusalem:

> I openly confess and regret that no holy emotions moved me as I was entering Jerusalem. The body overcame the spirit. Apart from exhaustion due to a twelve-hour horseback ride along a difficult route and to the heat, I did not feel anything. I only sensed the need to lie down and rest. But beneath my window there reigned noise and confusion caused by several thousand believers. And this only intensified my agitation. (41)

In his notes from Palestine, Viazemskii repeatedly questions the attempts to pinpoint the precise locations of biblical sites. He underscores that the visitor's respect for the holy places should not depend on whether or not it is possible to ascertain beyond doubt the "authenticity" of a given place. (40). The Gospels, he maintains, do not offer precise descriptions of localities. Instead, the text of the New Testament contains detailed descriptions of events, actions, and words (43). Norov's description of the site of an imprint of Christ's right foot preserved in the mosque of Omar elicits the following reaction:

> It ought to suffice that there is no doubt concerning the main, general locations .... And the additional sources of information, cited by travelers who try allegedly to strengthen the holiness and truth of the Gospels, are not only redundant, but harmful rather than beneficial. Why summon superstition where faith can unite with the truthfulness of conviction .... There is no doubt that present-day Jerusalem stands in the same place where the ancient one did; that the main surroundings mentioned in the Gospels are the same. All this is obvious, and, consequently, the main setting of the events described in the Gospels is right in front of us. One does not need to know anything beyond all that is either stated in the Gospels, or described there. Robinson's refutations, and Norov's supplementary proofs are equally vain and worthless. After the natural and man-made disasters to which Jerusalem has been subjected, just a few stones remain from the old city, and even they may have been moved from their original place to another location. (43-44)

Responding no doubt to Murav'ev's laments about the Russian Orthodox church's insufficient presence in the Holy Land, Viazemskii's *Journey* blames the Russians themselves, not the rival Christian churches, for the paucity of Orthodox churches, schools, hospitals, hostels, and monasteries (46). As an Orthodox Christian, he wants Russia's "Christian voice" to be heard "in the land from where the Christian faith has come to us" (47). But he again differs with Murav'ev and Norov when addressing Turkish rule over the Holy Land. The militant hostility dividing the various Christian churches of Jerusalem makes Turkish political dominance "needed and remedial." Viazemskii notes that

> At least the outward, visible order between the churches is main-
> tained by the Turks. Without them they would be in constant
> struggle and would destroy one another. In the event of conflicts,
> the local pasha acts as the peacemaker between the churches.
> The name and the might of Mahomet secure, if not the love, then
> at least some modicum of consent and mutual tolerance between
> the children of Christ. (44-45)

Viazemskii's stance on Constantinople reveals his penchant to stay within the general bounds of imperial discourse while questioning the particulars of Russia's imperial ambitions. He counters the nationalist cries demanding the reconquest of the historical center of Eastern Christianity by asserting that the time has not yet come: "A fortuitous, violent, and premature expulsion of the Turks would be useless and destructive rather than beneficial" (45).

Turning his attention to the politics of the Holy Land, Viazemskii strives to keep Murav'ev's compensatory nationalism at bay while still articulating a specifically Russian position. As a pilgrim, Viazemskii, finds himself closer to the western side of the intra-Christian dividing line. Unlike other Orthodox pilgrims, he regards the Holy Land as a location that generates symbols. The account notes that the Holy Land impresses him above all as a symbol of faith: the Holy Land presents "an abbreviated biography of the Savior in a place marked by the great events of his life, accomplished by him for each of us . . . . for eternity" (54). Not surprisingly, Viazemskii values Chateaubriand's account more than any others:

> The graves of the Kings, or of the Judges, or God knows who they
> were. Chateaubriand describes them well and accurately. In gen-

eral his travelogue is still considered to provide probably the best guide to Jerusalem by both lay people and by clergy. In his case also a Frenchman often sticks out from underneath the pilgrim's robe, but his self-adoration, if not the bragging and false pride, are in his case more measured than in the accounts that followed. (63)

In general, although Viazemskii polemicizes with the two earlier Russian accounts, this argument does not help him reconcile the contradictions of his own account. Viazemskii's opinion of Turkey, for example, appears at first to concur with Murav'ev's views. Turkish rule is "senseless and lifeless," and Turkey is a land that bears "the signs of barrenness, disease and decay" and that "needs greater care and industriousness" (15, 17). Yet while he asserts that "both the people and nature of Turkey are lifeless, as if influenced by the pernicious spirit of Islam," two pages back he concludes that some of the Turkish customs are in fact similar to customs of the Russian "narod" (18). The similarities he perceives between Turkey and Russia confirm in his view the profound character of eastern influences upon Russia. Nor is Viazemskii consistent as a pilgrim. Although he opposes the way in which other Russian pilgrims have sought to map the Holy Land, he dutifully describes the location of the well where the Virgin Mary used to draw water and the place where the tree from which the cross was made grew (50-51).

The contradictory tendencies within Viazemskii's Holy Land travel notes suggest that, as a representative of a certain socio-cultural formation, Jerusalem pilgrimage represented for him a transitory stage. Throughout his career as a writer and literary critic, Viazemskii maintained an awareness of the existence of a certain literary process. As he writes in the introduction to his collected works,

> the words: past, present, future have a conventional and figurative meaning. Everything present was once future, and this future is going to turn into the past. Something old may remain on the side and appear forgotten; but this does not yet prove that it has aged; it has just gone out of circulation . . . but the demand for it may reappear. (*Polnoe sobranie sochinenii* I, i)

The pilgrimage illustrates this ongoing process of change: as a writer Viazemskii intuitively adhered to the western ideas that permeated the Russian intellectual elites earlier in the century. As a pilgrim offering an account of the Holy Land, he endeavors to speak with the voice of a Russian Orthodox believer convinced of the "life-giving and redeeming" power of the Russian church (3). And by the 1840s pilgrimages were once again ensconced in Russian cultural life. Ponomarev writes about Viazemskii:

> On his way back from Palestine, Odessa and Moscow welcomed him with festive dinners, where he was celebrated not only as a writer, but also a man privy to the highest expression of Russian national life—the expression of religious feeling. (Ponomarev 19)

Peter Weisensel analyzes Russian self-identification as manifested in descriptions of the Ottoman Empire in the first half of the 19th century.[14] He maintains that religion was not particularly important to travelers from the service cohort who visited the Orient during this period. He also notes an increased presence of secular attitudes that "began to erode the definition of peoples on religious grounds" (70-71). In his concluding remarks, Weisensel states that:

> nevertheless, the reappearance of the pilgrim account and discovery of "new" holy places, such as Hagia Sophia and Mount Athos, in writings by bureaucrat-pilgrims, amounted to a persistence of old Russia in the midst of the rush towards Europe. For all its "Europeanness" this cohort evidently had not lost all its "Russianness" in the end. (80)

This study's reading of the pilgrimage literature of the same period gives rise to the conclusion that not only did the service cohort maintain its Russianness at the time - it also reasserted its allegiance to Russia and to Orthodoxy in no uncertain terms. Just as Chateaubriand rediscovered Christianity for Western Europe, Murav'ev's text reflects a rediscovery of Orthodoxy by the Russian elites. Old Russia does not linger in the nineteenth-century travel accounts, but it resurfaces as a crucial element of Russian identity.

The great success of Murav'ev's pilgrimage account suggests that by the end of the third decade of the nineteenth century Russian culture reached a phase of being "firmly established," to borrow Viazemskii's term. It no longer needed to look for ways to reaffirm its Europeanness. Viazemskii's account demonstrates that by the middle of the century Orthodoxy entered into the world view of Russia's educated elites. Nineteenth-century pilgrimage accounts prove conclusively that a greater emphasis on Russian specificity began to manifest itself towards the end of the 1820s. The oriental journey served the purpose of asserting the Russianness—not the Europeanness—of imperial Russian culture.

In the introduction to his *Itineraire* Chateaubriand emphatically proclaims:

> The church of the Holy Sepulcher no longer exists; it was totally destroyed by fire since my return from Judea. I am, I may say, the last traveler by whom it was visited, and, for the same reason, I shall be its last historian. (*Travels* 28)

A passage from Avraam Norov's account may be taken for the Russians' reply:

> The church of the Holy Sepulcher belongs mainly to three nations: the Greeks, the Latins and the Armenians . . . . One thing cannot be contested: the rights of the Greeks should be greater than the rights of other nations; they are the ones who erected the Church in antiquity—and the Greeks alone raised it from the ashes after the last fire in 1810. (143)

For Norov, the concept "nation" corresponds to that of "denomination." Because he sees the Russians as the modern-day Greeks, the reconstruction of the church after the fire may be interpreted as a metaphor of Russian culture. After the rebuilding of the church, the Russians, now identifying themselves as heirs to the Byzantine tradition, no longer needed to rely on Chateaubriand's story of the Holy Sepulcher. They could rewrite this story so as to satisfy the growing feelings of a specific national-religious identity.

A comparison of Polish and Russian nineteenth-century pilgrimage accounts demonstrates both the texts' similarities and differences. Such a comparison offers a window into the cultural contexts in which Polish and Russian authors operated. For the Catholic Poles, the Holy Land functioned as a destination that held forth the promise of spiritual renewal. An Orthodox Russian traveler, on the other hand, had a predisposition to treat pilgrimage as an opportunity for self-purification before death. Russian pilgrimages were more ritualized than their Polish counterparts. Widely divergent theological and, indeed, metaphysical presuppositions affected the categories underlying travel literature. Within the Polish context, the

Holy Land was an area that generated symbols, as in the case of both Słowacki and Wężyk. The types of symbols invoked depended, to some extent, on the author's reliance on the ideas of other Western European travelers. For the Poles, the nineteenth century was a period of protracted national grief defined by their state's dismemberment and the failure of the two major national uprisings of November 1830 and January 1863. A Polish pilgrim's ability to identify himself independently of foreign influences as well as of his own national experiences determined his ability to establish a dialogical relationship with the Holy Land.

For Russian pilgrims, the Holy Land and Christianity existed in a metonymic relationship; the Holy Land functioned as an icon, providing a link to Christ himself. The predominance of Eastern Orthodox elements in nineteenth-century Russian pilgrimage accounts reflects Russia's growing independence from Western European ideas and trends. Russian literary encounters with the Holy Land do not recapitulate a European search for the center; rather, they attest to a return to what the intellectual elites were beginning to perceive as the center of Russianness.

Notes

1. Murav'ev described Lermontov's visit in his memoir. Here, as elsewhere, he did not prove to be the most accurate source of information. Lermonov scholars have questioned the dating of the event he described (Vatsuro 223).
2. N. A. Khokhlova also notes the formal similarities between Mickiewicz's "Crimean Sonnets" and Murav'ev's "Tavrida." She maintains that "there are no grounds to talk about their [the "Sonnets'"] direct influence on [Murav'ev's] collection" (70). Indeed, the short interval of approximately two months separating the publication of the two poetic cycles seems to preclude such influence. Murav'ev may have become aware of Mickiewicz's ideas for the cycle during the time both of them were touring Crimea, but this, at present, would be a purely speculative argument. Khokhlova points out that Murav'ev did not know Polish. But other Russian poets who read Mickiewicz, including Pushkin, did not know the language either.
3. S. S. Landa determines that Norov spent some time in Odessa back in 1825, soon after his return from his journey to the holy places. But according to other sources, Norov's first journey to the Holy Land occurred in 1834. As an interesting aside, it is worth mentioning that Norov must have become acquainted with Mickiewicz shortly before the Polish poet's departure from the port city for Moscow. Landa's article includes the text of a letter Norov wrote to Prince Petr Viazemskii, introducing "Professor Mickiewicz, a man of great genius and

a profoundly sensitive soul," and asking the prince to acquaint Mickiewicz with his circle (242).

4. Norov notes in the introduction to his account that he made references to other travelers accounts only in the cases when their descriptions of the holy places he visited corresponded to biblical passages (iv).

5. Annemarie Weyl Carr, who has researched the role of icons in middle Byzantine pilgrimage, comes to some illuminating conclusions. During the period that she examined, Carr notes, icons served, first of all, as markers that identified a sacred person or place. Pilgrims venerated the relics icons marked, not the icons themselves. "Second," continues Carr, "icons served to disseminate the saint from the site of her or his tomb or relic. For the pilgrim, this often took the form of a remembrance, as in the tokens that pilgrims took with them. Once again, such remembrances could often in themselves serve as potent objects, saving their owner from the vicissitudes of life or of the journey. But they were enabled in this by their contact—the pilgrim's actual contact, or the tokens' implicit contact—with the saint's presence at the pilgrimage site from which they were brought. Along with tokens, painted panels—and eventually engraved prints—served a similar purpose" (82-82).

6. Within the Catholic and Protestant traditions, another legend, that of Veronica, superseded the King Abgar story. According to the legend, when he fell under the weight of the cross on his way to Golgotha, St. Veronica wiped Christ's face, which left an imprint on the cloth. This version of the Veronica legend dates back to the fourteenth century. "There is no evidence that this event was part of a popular belief in earlier times, and it was not pictured in art, so far as is known, before the 14th century" (*New Catholic Encyclopedia* vol. 14: 625). The Gospels do not mention Veronica. Nor is she listed among the first Christian martyrs.

7. Daniel Sahas points out that "the word for Scripture in Greek (Graphe) means both 'writing' and 'painting'; in the Greek Orthodox mind there is no separation, no division, between these two forms of communication, let alone abrogation of each other" (14). A similar attitude had to engender the descriptive character of Russian pilgrimage accounts.

8. George Majeska provides an illuminating insight into Russian pilgrimage accounts' icon-like stature. "Well into modern times," asserts Majeska, "the simpler folk continued to regard these works as testimonies to God's grace. They were sometimes copied by hand even in the nineteenth century, and the popular editions of the last century were purchased in large numbers not so much for their antiquarian interest as for their pious content" (6).

9. Boris Fonkich notes that "already in the first half of the sixteenth century emerged the idea regarding Russia as the liberator of the Christian East from the Turkish Yoke" (440). The same author mentions Murav'ev as one of the authors who made important contributions to the history of Russia's ties to the Christian East (446).

10. Nadezhdin concludes his review of Murav'ev's book with the following assertion: "Briefly put, *Journey to the Holy Places* presents a journey of an enlightened Russian Christian, and consequently a new phenomenon, non-existent until now, in all respects, and thus of interest to all" (253).

11. D. P. Ivinskii observes that censorship as well as personal considerations prevented Viazemskii from including his criticism of the epilogue to "Prisoner of the Caucasus" in the published review (59).

12. The long list of Russian poets who translated selections from Mickiewicz's *Sonnets* includes, in addition to Viazemskii, I. I. Dmitriev, I. I. Kozlov, M. Iu. Lermontov, A. A. Maikov, N. V. Berg, A. A. Fet, V. G. Benediktov, and many others (Landa). Viazemskii's review greatly contributed to the sequence's popularity in Russia.

13. According to Guenther Wytrzens, Viazemskii started working on the Fonvizin monograph in 1823 and finished it in 1832.

14. Peter Weisensel, along with Theofanis Stavrou, contributed greatly to the study of Russian oriental travel by compiling an annotated bibliography of Russian travel accounts, *Russian Travelers to the Christian East from the Twelfth to the Twentieth Century.* This bibliography provides an indispensable guide to Russian oriental travel narratives.

CHAPTER 4

Aleksandr Pushkin's Caucasian Cycle: From the Orient Back to Russia

Aleksandr Sergeevich Pushkin traveled to the southeastern outskirts of the Russian Empire twice in his lifetime: once forcibly, in 1820, as punishment for what the tsarist authorities deemed his subversive verses; and a second time voluntarily and without official permission in 1829. Scholars have thoroughly investigated the circumstances of the two southern episodes in Pushkin's life and their significance for the evolution of his literary career. But not all of these journeys' literary fruits have garnered the attention they deserve. Up to now, discussion of Pushkin's second trip to the Caucasus has focused almost entirely on the prose account of the journey published in the first issue of Pushkin's own journal, *The Contemporary* (*Sovremennik*). The account appeared in 1835, six years after the trip, under the title "Journey to Arzrum at the Time of the 1829 Campaign" ("Puteshestvie v Arzrum vo vremia pokhoda 1829 goda"). The poetry of Pushkin's second southern sojourn has received much less attention. For the 1832 edition of his poetry, Pushkin grouped several of the poems he wrote three years before in the Caucasus into a cycle. Interpreted as a travelogue, the Caucasian cycle's text provides an alternative record of the Russian poet's oriental journey.

In her analysis of "Journey to Arzrum," Monika Greenleaf explains both the personal and literary parameters of Pushkin's second journey to the South. "Willfully tearing through the net of restrictions that had tightened around his professional and personal life," she tells us, "Pushkin bolted" (140). The liminal character of the ensuing travel experience went hand in hand with Pushkin's sought-after disengagement from Russia and his official existence there. But the desired border crossing remained elusive. Greenleaf notes that the published account communicates "no faith in the traveler's ability to negotiate his way—sexually, monetarily, sentimentally, or verbally—around the various borders that divide cultures, classes, and genders" (142). As presented in the 1836 account, the trip to the South did not enable Pushkin to free himself from the pressures of his life in Russia. But the text of "Journey to Arzrum" did allow him to "disengage himself from Orientalist discourse, both professional and poetic, and clear a space for his own journey in the overpopulated space of literary travel" (147). Greenleaf shows how Pushkin's "Journey" inverts and questions the conventions of Romantic oriental travel that his very own southern poems of the early 1820s had been so instrumental in embedding in Russian literature.

The concept of the border figures prominently in another recent analysis of Pushkin's 1829 Caucasian venture. Yuri Druzhnikov's search for the "real Pushkin," one unencumbered by the myths in the Russian and Soviet renditions of the poet's biography, leads him to conclude that Pushkin conceived his journey to the Russo-Turkish theater of war as a way of fleeing Russia via the Black Sea (431). Druzhnikov gleans his evidence from the following facts: the amount of planning that must have gone into the preparation of the unauthorized trip; the circumstances of Pushkin's departure from Moscow; the restraint the poet demonstrated in his contacts with people whom he encountered along the way; and Pushkin's narration of these encounters. Although the prose account of the journey does not address the true motives of the poet's voyage, Druzhnikov perceives a striking lack of sincerity in Pushkin's declarations of loyalty to the state and patriotism (434). The "Journey's" affirmation of Russia's expansion therefore renders Pushkin's position as a writer and a participant in the campaign morally ambiguous. At the same time, the Arzrum text reflects "Pushkin's own vacillation throughout the journey" (435).

Focusing on the one passage whose sincerity makes it stand out, Druzhnikov highlights Pushkin's recounting of the excitement he feels when crossing what he thinks is Russia's border:

> "Here's the Arpachai," the Cossack told me. Arpachai! Our border! . . . I galloped toward the river with an indescribable feeling. Never before had I seen a foreign land. There was something mysterious about the border for me; from childhood, travel has always been my favorite dream. For many years, I had led a nomadic life, wandering through the South, then the North, but I never before broke free of Russia's immense border. I rode hap-

pily into the cherished river, and the good stallion carried me to
the Turkish shore. (qtd. in Druzhnikov 421)

But the border crossing turns out to be yet another illusion; the
opposite bank of the Arpachai is already under Russian control.
Pushkin was fated never to make good on his desire to get out of
Russia. Druzhnikov speculates about the reasons why the poet did
not go through with the planned escape. On several occasions, the
Caucasian journey brought him face to face with death. Among
other things, Pushkin crossed paths with the escort carrying the
remains of Aleksandr Griboedov, who had been killed in Persia, and
he also learned of the death of his friend Ivan Burtsov, who was mortally wounded while on a reconnaissance mission. In addition, while
he was in Arzrum Pushkin learned that the plague was stalking the
area (426-431).

Both interpretations of Pushkin's second southern episode
emphasize the "Journey's" theme of a yearned-for and subsequently
frustrated border crossing. It is noteworthy that Pushkin's poetic
travelogue of his 1829 journey does not intimate a wish to flee from
present circumstances by crossing the physical border of the Russian
Empire. The metaphor of the "chasm of life" does loom over the
poetic travelogue's central part, and the cycle as a whole generates a
sense that the journey fails to provide a release from an existential
entrapment. On occasion, the inbetweenness of physical passage and
the dispassionate perspective of an observer provide Pushkin with
attractive venues for nurturing a sense of dejection and for main-
taining a comfortable distance between the subject of his poetry and
the two endpoints of his journey's trajectory: imperial and
Europeanized Saint Petersburg, and the conquered Caucasus. The
Caucasian poetic cycle confirms that Pushkin attempted to use his
revisitation of the Caucasus as an opportunity to position himself on
the threshold, both emotionally and in relation to the- powers-that-be.

But the cycle's resolution goes further than the text of "Journey
to Arzrum." In the poetic travelogue, the frustrated crossing of the
Russian border brings Pushkin back to Russia. The Caucasian
cycle's text does not feature the Europeanized Russian metropolis as
the point of arrival. Instead, Pushkin's oriental journey brings him
back to the idea of Russia as a reconstructed mythic periphery, as a
space between the East and the West. Like the "Journey's" frustrated
crossing into the territories beyond Russia's imperial reach, in the

Caucasian cycle the poet's arrival in a space demarcated by another river, the Don, heralds his return to the native realm. Moreover, the prose account's description of the border-crossing fiasco that prevented Pushkin's exit from Russia does not determine the character of his return as it is presented in the poetic cycle. The poet's return depicted in the 1829 cycle has all the trappings of a longed-for reunion. The voyage's resolution comes closer to fulfilling the role of a "rite of passage."[1] This new paradigm at once inverts the earlier Pushkinian mode of voyage to the South and confirms the general pattern of travel, in which the more-or-less fixed place of the traveler's origin operates as the travel narrative's primary reference point. Although there is no textual evidence suggesting that Pushkin conceived the Caucasian poems as a polemic with Mickiewicz's "Crimean Sonnets," the Russian poet's cycle nevertheless does reverse the Pole's journey towards otherness.

The Cycle

N. V. Izmailov first highlighted Pushkin's tendency to organize his poetic utterances in the form of poetic cycles as an important principle governing the poetry written from the spring of 1829 to the poet's death. After 1830, Pushkin displayed a marked tendency to group poems according to shared ideas and subjects and not according to their form. In his study, Izmailov refers to the 1832 edition of Pushkin's poems, *Aleksandr Pushkin Poems. Part Three* (*Stikhotvorenia Aleksandra Pushkina. Tret'ia chast'*). The poet did not arrange the texts published in this edition chronologically. Instead, he put them in thematic groups. The poems of the Caucasian cycle open the volume. In light of their common, unifying biographical and thematic factors, Izmailov argues that

> this cycle may indeed be referred to as the "Caucasian Cycle"— a cycle in the true sense of the word, more worthy of this classification than any of the other thematic series, not counting "Imitations of the Koran" ("Podrazhania Koranu") and "Songs of the Western Slavs" ("Piesni zapadnikh slavian)," which have a different background and a different character. (Izmailov 219)

According to Izmailov, the cycle begins with "The Caucasus" ("Kavkaz"), followed by "The Avalanche" ("Obval"), "Monastery at the Kazbek" ("Monastyr' na Kazbeke"), "Delibash," "The Peaks of Georgia" ("Na kholmakh Gruzii"), "From Hafez" ("Iz Gafiza"), and "The Don" ("Don"). In Izmailov's view, "Oleg's Shield" ("Olegov shchit") closes the cycle, even though he provides possible reasons why this poem can be placed outside of the travel cycle proper. Written in September 1829, it is the last of the eight Caucasian poems Pushkin composed. The August 1829 Treaty of Adrianopole provided the immediate context for the writing of "Oleg's Shield" and thematically linked the poem to the subject of the Arzrum campaign. Adrianopole sealed Russia's victory over Turkey, so it may seem logical that Pushkin used a historiosophical note to conclude a travel narrative that coincided with the military campaign. But, within the entire cycle, "Oleg's Shield" functions more as an afterthought than as a vital part of the travelogue. Another objection to the inclusion of "Oleg's Shield" in the cycle composed in 1829 arises from Pushkin's decision not to make it part of the cycle when he planned a future edition of his poems.[2]

For the 1836 edition of his poetry, Pushkin intended to combine the Caucasian poems into a formally separated whole titled "Poems Composed During a Journey (1829)" ("Stikhi sochinennye vo vremia puteshestvia (1829)"). As with Mickiewicz's "Crimean Sonnets," the motif of a journey delivered the crucial principle for the poems' organization. In the projected edition, the order of the poems and the content of the cycle were to differ from the earlier version. Pushkin intended to begin the cycle with "Travel Laments" ("Dorozhnye zhaloby"), followed by "To the Kalmyk Girl" ("Kalmychke"), "The Peaks of Georgia," "Monastery at the Kazbek," "Avalanche," "The Caucasus," "From Hafez," "Delibash," and "The Don" (Izmailov 223). Because Pushkin released it closer in time to the actual journey, the 1832 edition of his poetry stands at the center of this study.

A comparison between Pushkin's Caucasian cycle and Mickiewicz's "Crimean Sonnets" reveals that, as a unit, Pushkin's travel poems do not have the same degree of formal coherence as Mickiewicz's Crimean cycle. The cycle's 1832 version lacks the kind of structural framework that Mickiewicz's work exhibits in its title, epigraph, dedication, and notes. In contrast to the "Crimean Sonnets," Pushkin's poems display considerable variations of length, with the longest, "Avalanche," measuring thirty lines, and the shortest, "The Peaks of Georgia," eight lines; the remaining poems count

24, 11, 16, and 12 lines respectively. In addition, the poems of the cycle boast an impressive variety of metric patterns. Three of them are written in a four-foot trochee, a meter that was gaining prominence in Pushkin's poetry at the time; three are iambic; and one is a four-foot amphibrach. These formal discrepancies may in part explain why even academic editions of Pushkin's collected works do not list the Caucasian poems as a cycle, but merely mention the author's intention to arrange them cyclically. The poems have not functioned as a single text, not even to the extent to which the "Crimean Sonnets" have.

What, then, substantiates an analysis of the poems as a lyric cycle? In his convincing theory of lyric cycles, David Sloane argues that

> the individual poem, like the word in a coherent utterance, belongs to a syntactic sequence that allocates meaning to its component parts. Just as the context of an utterance actualizes certain of the word's semes [semantic markers], the context of a cycle actualizes those features of the poem that are relevant to the dynamics of the whole. (23)

Pushkin's consistent effort to organize several of the poems of his second southern journey into a cycle provides sufficient proof that he perceived them as a unit. The unit's meaning arises not only from the sum of the individual poems, but also from the texts' interaction with one other. When the grouped poems chronicle the experiences of travel, the internal dynamic of a lyric cycle becomes more tangible and apposite for the understanding of its constituent parts. Pushkin's Caucasian poems belong to this category of cycles, no less than Mickiewicz's *Sonnets*.

The Journey

The first of Mickiewicz's sonnets, "The Akerman Steppes," and the first poem of Pushkin's Caucasian cycle, "The Caucasus," are both poetic travelogues, but they differ in the way they organize space. Pushkin confronts the reader with a perspective completely different from if not diametrically opposed to "The Akerman Steppes." As the first line of his first sonnet indicates, Mickiewicz begins his journey by crossing the flat expanses of the steppe: "I sailed onto the expanses of the dry ocean." In Pushkin's case, the cycle's first poem features his subject looking down on Caucasian scenery:

Кавказ подо мною. Один в вышине
Стою над снегами у края стремнины:
Орел, с отдаленной поднявшись вершины,
Парит неподвижно со мной наравне. (3.1, 196)

The Caucasus stretches **underneath** [emphasis IK] me. Alone in
   the heights,
I am standing above the snow, at the edge of a precipice.
An eagle, having risen from a faraway summit,
Hovers, motionlessly, as if we were equal.

In Mickiewicz's "Crimean Sonnets," the horizontality of perspective established by the first two sonnets, "The Akerman Steppes" and "The Silence at Sea," gradually subsides. In "The Tempest" ("Burza"), the sea then becomes stormy during the crossing. Following the sea voyage, the Pilgrim finds himself at the foot of a mountain. In the final poem, *The Sonnets'* persona leans against a rock atop mount Aiudagh and looks down at the sea. In contrast, the beginning of his poetic travelogue sees Pushkin's subject standing on a Caucasian mountaintop, gazing down and scrutinizing the area that stretches below him. In crude, topographical terms, Mickiewicz's point of arrival marks the beginning of Pushkin's poetic cycle. "The Caucasus" foreshadows the direction of Pushkin's journey in the remaining part of the cycle. With his back turned towards the breathtaking mountain peaks, Pushkin's persona travels downward.

The second poem of Pushkin's cycle, "The Avalanche," transforms the visual plunge of "The Caucasus" into the subject's physical descent, signaled by the mountain heights' and the eagles' changed position vis-à-vis the traveler:

И надо мной кричат орлы,
И ропщет бор,
И блещут средь волнистой мглы
Вершины гор. (3.1, 197)

And **above me** [emphasis IK] eagles cry,
And the forest murmurs,

And in the fog spawned by the waves
The mountain tops glisten.

"The Monastery at the Kazbek" gives the next indication of a continuing downward movement. From this vantage point, Pushkin's
subject gazes towards the Kazbek and expresses a wish to overcome
the distance separating him from the mountain and the monastery
on its slope. The ongoing descent frustrates the fulfillment of this
longing. Having traversed the Georgian highlands, the poet
arrives—in the cycle's last poem—at the bank of the river Don. If the
Caucasian cycle documents a journey, then it is not a voyage to the
peaks of the Caucasus; rather, it is a return from the mountainous
borderlands to the familiarity of the plains. The direction of the
journey documented by the cycle captures the character of Pushkin's
encounter with the South. From the Caucasus, he proceeds down
towards where the Don floats. He transits from Asia to Europe.

The visual dominance over the scenery in "The Caucasus" signals the persona's mastery over the landscape that stretches down
beneath him. Unlike Mickiewicz, in Pushkin's case the physical ele-
vation has no connection to the overpowering enthrallment of the
natural sublime. The specifically Russian linkage of imperial politics
and poetry that Harsha Ram identifies and labels the "imperial sublime" best describes the situation:

> The vertical terror of lyric afflatus is resolved in a compensatory
> and transformative identification with the horizontal stretch of
> Russian might. An experience of poetic inspiration is thus pre-
> sented as analogous to the political power it then describes:
> impersonal, absolute, a vision that soars to embrace the expand-
> ing realm. (5)

In "The Caucasus," such a perspective has clear political connotations. Already in the opening line, "Kavkaz podo mnoiu" ("The
Caucasus stretches underneath me"), the Russian poet endows himself with a privileged position vis-à-vis the conquered Caucasus. He
maintains this vista through most of the poem. In the second stanza,
Pushkin's subject, armed with an all-seeing eye, scrutinizes the
descending layers of mountain scenery. From the clouds, down
through the waterfalls and shrubs, he is able to discern even such
minutiae as moss on the ground, a deer, and birds. This extraordi-
nary, nearly superhuman perceptiveness strengthens the impression

of the viewer's privileged status. It also suggests that the poem's landscape is—at least partly—reconstructed. The subject of "The Caucusus" has traveled the paths down below, and he is now able to revisit them and lay bare all that would normally be hidden from sight. The Caucasus harbors no mysteries for the visitor's penetrating gaze. In fact, the first part of the poem contains such a statement of *veni, vidi, vici* that its subject could be identified with General Aleksei Petrovich Ermolov, the ruthless conqueror of the Caucasus, as he was presented in the popularly reproduced 1825 portrait by D. Dou. A native Caucasian coat draped over his Russian uniform, poised on a mountain top and turned sideways, Emolov proudly surveys the surroundings.

Certain lexical features of "The Caucusus" as well as the visual descent's organization reveal a relevant intertextual dimension in Pushkin's revisitation of the subjugated region. In her discussion of Pushkin's use of "The Prisoner of the Caucasus" to invent the literary Caucasus for the Russian national imagination, Katya Hokanson observes that Pushkin

> placed himself in the company of Zhukovskii and Voeikov by describing Caucasian scenery. Pushkin proclaimed, in effect, that to describe Caucasian scenery was already something of a tradition in Russian poetry. (339)

Hokanson refers to Pushkin's notes to "The Prisoner of the Caucasus" in which the poet credits Zhukovskii with "some delightful lines" describing the Caucasus. Pushkin augments this statement with lengthy fragments from Zhukovskii's "To Voeikov: A Letter" ("K Voeikovu. Poslanie"), and from Derzhavin's ode "To Zubov" ("K Zubovu"). In "To Voieikov," Zhukovskii's landscape description shifts from the cliffs and waterfalls down through the level of rich mountain fauna, towards the animals and human settlements, creating a pattern that Pushkin repeats in "The Caucasus." Zhukovskii had never even set foot in the Caucasus. That he provided a blueprint for Pushkin's scrutiny of the area in the 1829 poem suggests that Pushkin approached this second southern journey to the Caucasus with that same sense of cultural continuity that he first conjured in the early 1820s. This same tendency to create and preserve a native textual tradition similarly free from the influences of western oriental discourse motivated Andrei Murav'ev's choice of intertextual lineage in his Holy Land pilgrimage account.

In the first two stanzas, Pushkin's subject looks down on the Caucasus. Like Voeikov in Zhukovsky's poem, he does so in a manner that allows him to assert his superiority and control over the foreign terrain. But a distinctly different tone surfaces in the poem's final lines. At the end of the third and penultimate stanza, the subject's focus shifts towards the ferocious current of the Terek. The river is like a caged, angry young animal. The sight of prey induces the animal to try to escape his confinement. Imprisoned by the cliffs, deprived of its freedom, the river-turned-animal struggles hopelessly against the confining banks. The Terek's vivid struggle grows to overshadow all other landscape elements in Pushkin's text.

In the larger text of Pushkin's cycle, as well as in the whole of his Arzrum text and in the texts of other nineteenth-century Russian authors who wrote about the Caucasus, the Terek metonymically represents the entire area through which it flows. In an unpublished version of the last stanza of "The Causasus," Pushkin clearly spells out this metonymy. He draws a comparison between the Terek and the Caucasus and its inhabitants:

> Так буйную вопьность законы теснят
> Так дикое племя (под) властью тоскует
> Так ныне безмолвный Кавказ негодует
> Так чуждые силы его тяготят . . . (3.2, 792)

> That's how the laws oppress untamed freedom
> That's how the wild tribe suffers under the ruling power
> That's how the speechless Caucasus shows its indignation
> That's how foreign powers trample over him . . .

Had Pushkin not omitted it, the last stanza's admission of Russia's imperial ruthlessness would have counteracted the imperial connotations of the perspective he adopts at the poem's outset. The focus on the forceful occupation of the Caucasus represents a potential anti-conquest gesture by Pushkin. Ultimately, however, the published version features the poet's own autobiography, not the author's suppressed anti-conquest sympathies, as the element that undermines the hegemonic scrutiny of the Caucasus. The omission of the subversive fragment cited above from the poem's final version brings the identification of the self with the river Terek into focus. The first stanza's image of the lone man standing at the edge of a precipice sways towards the image of the river struggling against the cliffs confining it to its established course. Looking down towards the river, the "I" from the poem's first stanza must situate himself in relation to the metaphor of captivity arising out of the juxtaposition of two images: that of the mountain river and that of a wild animal chafing against its imprisonment. The cycle's second poem, "The Avalanche," develops this association further.

In fact, the persona's identification with the river becomes even stronger at this point. From the onset of the text, Pushkin's subject has a perspective identical to that of the river. From within the mist of the Terek's splashing waves, the persona looks up at the murmuring forest, the flying eagles, and the glistening mountain peaks ranging far above. Pushkin immerses himself and the reader in the waters of the Terek by beginning the poem with an image of the river splashing on the rocks that form its embankments. This initial contact with the powerful natural element draws both the subject and the reader to follow the river's tumultuous course.

In "The Avalanche," a mass of snow has fallen onto the Terek and obstructed its course even more. The snowy block forces the river underground. At the same time, life goes on as usual along a road that crosses the Terek's established course, as travelers intersect the river's stubborn flow. Pushkin juxtaposes the point of view of the angry river, forced into submission in the penultimate stanza, with the view of the road that now traverses the Terek's flow in the poem's last stanza.

The Orient appealed to the Romantic imagination as a realm of uninhibited freedom that promised an alternative to the rational, regulated Europe. By focusing on the Terek's vain attempts to free itself from the cliffs' stifling embrace, Pushkin subverts this orientalist topos; the Caucasus becomes transformed into a metaphor of captivity. Except for the intertextual tradition of identifying the Terek with the Caucasus, nothing in the text of "The Avalanche" suggests that the metaphor carries broader political connotations. The poem does not present an explicit commentary on Russia's imperial policies in the South. Just as in the previous poem, "The Caucasus," the identification of the river with the subject of Pushkin's poetry comes into focus. The Terek's predicament speaks of the impossibility of transcending both the culturally determined and the psychological boundaries of the self. As Monika Greenleaf argues, the "Journey to Arzrum" inverts the paradigm of Pushkin's first oriental sojourn:

> In the early 1820's Pushkin had used the place of his enforced
> exile to incarnate the Romantic trope of imprisonment as spiri-
> tual freedom . . . . Turning the tables on the space of imprison-
> ment, the poet converted his central image of captivity into cap-
> tivation—a punning emblem of his inventive freedom. In 1829
> the situation was reversed. (140)

The Caucasian cycle documents this reversal's overpowering character. Instead of unbounded freedom, the high mountains of the
Caucasus offer images of bondage. The manner in which Pushkin
describes the mountainous landscape ran counter to nineteenth-century conventions of writing about high mountains.

The anaphoric repetitions of "и" ("and") throughout "The
Avalanche" emphasize the linear aspect of language. Pushkin uses
this device to mark the landscape's winding lines: the course of the
river, the path of the avalanche, and the snowy passage over the
Terek. Even though the poem is set in the Caucasus, it is nearly
bereft of the vertical lines normally associated with either a visual or
a literary representation of this mountainous landscape. Throughout
the entire cycle, Pushkin privileges horizontal lines—a choice prominently featured in the river's flow over the verticality of the mountains. Of the seven poems that make up the Caucasian cycle, only
one—"The Monastery at the Kazbek"—foregrounds the high mountains as the landscape's dominant element. The image of the river, foregrounded in the cycle's first poem and dominant in its second poem,
disappears from sight in the following two poems. But it does reap-
pear: first, in "On the Peaks of Georgia" as the quietly flowing Aragva;
and then in the cycle's last poem as the longed-for sign of homecoming, the river Don.

The rocky but not very steep mountains of Crimea appear
insignificant in comparison to the much higher and steeper cliffs of
the Caucasus. As Griboedov remarks about Crimea: ". . . here
nature—compared to the Caucasus—looks diminished. There are no
such granite cliffs; no snow-covered peaks of Elbrus and Kazbek; no
ferocious rivers, like the Terek and the Aragva. The soul does not
faint upon seeing the bottomless precipices" (III, 176). And yet
mountain peaks dominate the landscape of Mickiewicz's "Crimean
Sonnets." The Polish poet builds his metaphors around the notion of
a physical ascent that grows to represent a spiritual journey towards
the discovery of the source of all creation, the Romantic Absolute in
nature. In contrast, Pushkin, who had a chance to experience both

Crimea and the Caucasus, deemphasizes the vertical aspect of the mountainous Caucasian scenery. The rivers' familiarity overpowers the "mountain gloom and mountain glory." The rivers determine Pushkin's path on his mental map of the Caucasus, and the horizontal lines they trace through the the landscape become dominant. The spatial destination of the poet's journey, the flatlands of the Don delta, determines his perception of the Caucasus.

Susan Layton points out that in Pushkin's "Prisoner of the Caucasus" the river becomes more than just a geographical divider: "fraught with symbolic significance as the end of Russian space, the geographically imprecise river . . . has the thrilling connotation of civilization's last outpost" (93). In his Caucasian cycle, Pushkin manifests the same tendency to transform rivers into markers of symbolic spaces. Although he does equivocate some in his identification of the Terek with the South, Pushkin draws nearer to a metaphoric representation of the self in the image of the river. But in the cycle's last poem the river Don marks the beginning of Russian space and thereby becomes an indubitable symbol of a return home.

The Negative Pleasures of Passage: Sublimity and Nostalgia

The third poem of Pushkin's cycle, "The Monastery at the Kazbek," illustrates the poet's temptation to view the high mountains of the Caucasus in exactly the same terms in which Mickiewicz looks at the Crimean peaks: as gateways to the transcendental order. Even though the traveler appears to continue his descent from the physical position that he occupies in "The Caucasus," his progress briefly halts when he glances at the mountain and the monastery. The movement downward, towards the horizontality of the river's flow, so strongly suggested by the previous two poems, clashes with a desire to rise up to the monastery. Why did the grandiose vista of the "The Caucasus" fail to produce a similar effect on the viewer?

In his investigation of the psychology of the sublime, Edmund Burke, the author of one of the principal modern formulations of the sublime, identifies "greatness of dimension" and "vastness of extent" as a "a powerful cause of the sublime" (72). But Burke talks about other circumstances of experiencing the sublime that are notably missing in "The Caucasus." In developing his conception of sublimity, which he associates with the experience of astonishment and terror, he stipulates that obscurity and surprise belong to its necessary elements. Pushkin assures dominance over the Caucasian scenery to the subject whose voice is heard in "The Caucasus." He may be standing at the edge of a cliff, but, rather than evoking the threat of disintegration, a glance into the precipice reassures him of his power. In addition, the visual clarity in "The Caucasus" reveals everything to the systematic scrutiny of the traveler's eye. Since the penetrating gaze uncovers all, nothing is left to the imagination, and the possibility of discovering the sublime in nature vanishes.

In contrast to "The Caucasus," in "Monastery at the Kazbek" Pushkin lets the view of the mountain both surprise and overpower him. He thereby acknowledges the possibility that the contemplation of mountain nature can evoke a spiritual experience. He is able to glimpse the promise of a transformed and liberated self because he lets the mountain rule the scenery. At the same time, he withdraws from the position of seeing and therefore of knowing all. The view of Kazbek awakens a wish to escape to the faraway ridge of the pure sublime. This wish, however, remains contained in the conditional mode of Pushkin's utterance: "Tuda b, skazav prosti ushchel'iu,// Podniat'sia k vol'noi vyshine!" (There [I'd like], after saying farewell to the ravine// to ascend to the free height!). As long as the ravine holds the persona within its walls, the potential for transformation glimpsed in the view of the mountain may go unrealized.

Pushkin's attraction to the imagery associated with confinement returns to haunt him in "Monastery at the Kazbek." The poem's second stanza seems to divide the world between the desired "free height" (vol'naia vyshina) and the place now occupied by Pushkin's subject: the restraining chasm, the "ravine" (ushchel'e). Pushkin contrasts the envisioned liberating ascent with the reality of confinement to the "ravine." Earlier variants of the poem, preserved in the poet's notes, confirm the metaphor of a divided world. Here, instead of "ushchel'e," Pushkin uses the phrase "zemli ushchel'e" (the earthly ravine) (3.2, 794).

The juxtaposition of the mountaintop with the ravine assumes even more striking proportions in light of an unpublished poetic fragment in which Pushkin intimates that, transported to the Caucasus, he finds a "new home" in the image of the ravine. The fragment's imagery continues the association of the Caucasus with confinement, with limitations on the ability to see clearly and to catch a glimpse of the realm of the sublime.

> Страшно и скучно.
> Здесь новоселье,
> Путь и ночлег.
> Тесно и душно.
> В диком ущелье --
> Тучи да снег.
>
> Небо чуть видно,
> Как из тюрьмы.
> Ветер шумит.
> (Солнцу обидно) (3.1, 203)

> It's frightening and morose.
> Here a new dwelling,
> the road and a place to sleep.
> Narrow and suffocating.
> In the wild gorge—
> Clouds and snow.
>
> The sky barely visible,
> As from a prison.
> The wind is blowing.
> (The sun is ashamed)

In "The Monastery at the Kazbek," just one place on Pushkin's Caucasian itinerary, the limited perspective of the ravine speaks, on the one hand, of the poet's conception of the self as limited and enmeshed by the circumstances of his life. On the other hand, the image of the ravine provides an indication of the desublimating way in which the poet perceives the Caucasus; he demythologizes an area associated with inspiring sublime feelings.

"The Monastery at the Kazbek" gives expression to a feeling of nostalgia born of the awareness that the poet is leaving the realm of the Romantic sublime behind him. Significantly, it is the only poem of the 1829 cycle written in the four-foot iamb that, until shortly before Pushkin's journey to Arzrum, was the poet's meter of choice. Pushkin uses a meter that he was gradually overcoming in favor of the more epic-sounding trochees to express purely lyrical longing. In the cycle's unpublished 1835 version, "To the Kalmyk Girl" and "On the Hills of Georgia" precede "Monastery at the Kazbek," which

"The Avalanche" follows. Pushkin wrote "To the Kalmyk Girl," one of the two poems absent from the cycle's earlier version, in the same meter as "The Monastery at the Kazbek." "On the Hills of Georgia" and "The Avalanche" are also iambic. With the exception of the introductory "Travel Laments," the poems in the first part of the nine-poem cycle have a distinctly iambic beat, whereas the cycle's second part is purely trochaic. In the second variant of Pushkin's "Verses Composed During a Journey," the passage from the Caucasus to Russia coincides with a journey through meters that takes the poet from iambs to trochees. This dialectic of meters corresponds to the overcoming of the Romantic search for sublimity. Pushkin's poetry guided numerous poets, including Mickiewicz, in their quests towards the ruptures produced by the mixture of oriental exoticism and mountain nature. And yet the master's own 1829 cycle charts a path back to the familiar.

In the course of his travels in the South, Pushkin directed himself towards Russia. His poetry does not put a lot of emphasis on the encounter with the Caucasus. In fact, the Caucasian poems never go much beyond the transformation of the foreign landscape into a metaphor of the self. This preoccupation with the self comes to the fore in the cycle's fifth poem, "On the Hills of Georgia." A meditation inspired by a foreign landscape redirects the poet's thoughts towards the absence of the woman whom he has loved. Pushkin expresses the pain of loss and separation in a way that reveals his attachment's ambivalence. The poem provides another illustration of the paradoxes inherent to Pushkin's movement within a cultural and an emotional space during a journey that simultaneously takes him away from and back to Russia.

In the "Crimean Sonnets" Mickiewicz's determination to push onward with his journey allows him to overcome the grief caused by the separation from his homeland. His impressions of the foreign territory fill the emotional vacuum created by the loss of the native realm. Mickiewicz's progress corresponds to the Freudian paradigm: "when the work of mourning is completed the ego becomes free and uninhibited again" (Freud 154). Since the process of substitution is gradual, at times the memories of the life that the poet left behind resurface. But they are never strong enough to stop Mickiewicz's progress altogether.

In Pushkin's cycle, the night-time, fog-enshrouded hills of Georgia and the flow of the Aragva form a perfect background for the poet's elegiac reminiscences. The lyrical subject mourns his detachment from the object of his desire. He becomes so engaged in this process that he loses all interest in the surrounding world. The lexical series "sadness—sorrow—dejection" (grust'—pechal'—unyni'e) at the center of this eight-line poem determines the mood. The consuming memories transform the loved one's physical absence into an emotional omnipresence: "pechal' moia polna toboiu, // Toboi, odnoi toboi . . . ." (You fill my sorrow, // you, only you . . ."). Like Freud's unsuccessful mourner, Pushkin's persona slips into melancholia. He is unable to detach his libido from the lost object, and he shows no interest in finding a substitute for his frustrated desire. However, the placement of the three main semantic signals leads the reader to question whether Pushkin's persona truly longs to be reunited with the loved one. The oxymoronic merger of sadness and lightheartedness in the expressions "I am sad and happy; my sorrow is joyous" (Mne grustno i legko; pechal' moia svetla) suggests a certain emotional ambivalence. The process of mourning triggered by the separation from the love object satisfies the subject emotionally, instead of causing him distress. Moreover, this situation — "Unyn'ia moego//Nichto ne muchit, ne trevozhit" (Nothing disturbs my distress) proves to be revitalizing for the self—"I serdtse **vnov'** [emphasis IK] gorit i liubit" (And the heart **again** is on fire and it loves again). The memories that cause pain provide a convenient pretext for generating the condition of a comfortable dejection.

The stubborn clinging to the memories of the past reveals a compulsion to repeat that overrides the pleasure principle. The phrase "toboi odnoi toboi" (you, only you) exemplifies such repetition. In her analysis of Pushkin's elegies, Monika Greenleaf follows the Lacanian tradition of associating language with the social order. She contends that "by expressing his idiosyncratic pain in socially intelligible and binding language, the elegiac poet in fact reintegrates his radically and even destructively solitary experience into the community" (90). In his Georgian elegy, Pushkin uses the genre's repetitive language to delay reintegration into society. The elegiac mode of expression corresponds to a desire to prolong the state of physical detachment and emotional suspension in which the poet finds himself in the course of his journey. The elegy provides Pushkin with an alternative to the positive sublime that briefly appears on the horizon in "The Monastery at the Kazbek." "On the Hills of Georgia" brings the sublime's negative version to life. Harold Bloom, for whom the literary sublime "seems always a negative Sublime," expounds that Freud's revised account of anxiety is precisely at one with the poetic Sublime, for anxiety

> is finally seen as a technique for mastering anteriority by remembering rather than repeating the past. By showing us that anxiety is a mode of expectation, closely resembling desire, Freud allows us to understand why poetry, which loves love, also seems to love anxiety. Literary and human romance both are exposed as being anxious quests that could not bear to be cured of their anxieties, even if such cures were possible. (549)

For Pushkin, the elegy becomes a sort of textual *purgatorio* that brings to mind Thomas Weiskel's notion of the "egotistic sublime," a concept that sees "the myth (or plot) of memory . . . not a[s a] problem, but [as] an answer" (143).

"On the Hills of Georgia" speaks of the gratification Pushkin derives from the travel-induced detachment that allows him to maintain a safe distance between himself and his place of origin, the ultimate destination. By the same token, the motions of passage determine Pushkin's attitude towards the physical and cultural territory he traverses during his journey on the periphery of the Arzrum campaign.

Pushkin, Hafez, and the Question of Russia's Imperial Expansion

Ewa Thompson reads "Journey to Arzrum" as an utterance of an unrepenting bard of Russian imperialism. "Pushkin was not an observer but a participant in the war, and the refreshment course he took at Arzrum clearly met with his approval," Thompson asserts (61). The Caucasian poetic cycle sheds a different light on Pushkin's view of the military campaign, and it casts doubt on the accuracy of Thompson's interpretation. To begin with, the first sounds of battle are not heard until the cycle's fifth poem. Second, neither "Delibash" nor the following "From Hafez," the only two poems that mention the fighting, provide any evidence of Pushkin's purported warmongering sentiments. Pushkin's detached attitude towards the events he describes in these two texts demands a serious look at the hypothesis about his military zeal. At the same time, a close reading of the

two poems demonstrates the increasing complexity of the consequences of Pushkin's detachment. Both the content and the form of
the poems, in particular the oriental stylization of "From Hafez,"
present interesting material for a consideration of Pushkin's view of
Russia's imperial politics, and, more generally, of his relationship
with oriental otherness.

In the 1832 edition of Pushkin's poetry, "Delibash" stands at the
cycle's center. It is the fourth of the seven poems, and it consists of
four stanzas. *Delibash* is a Turkish word that may denote either a
hat worn by a Turkish soldier or the soldier himself. The poem's first
stanza reads like a brief report from the battlefield. Two hostile
camps face each other. The narrator of the poem identifies with one
of them by referring to it as "our camp." As one side moves closer, a
red Delibash comes into view:

> Перестрелка за холмами;
> Смотрит лагерь их и наш;
> На холме пред казаками
> Вьется красный делибаш. (3.1, 199)

> A skirmish over the hills;
> Our camp and theirs are on guard
> On a hill in front of the Cossacks
> Hovers a red delibash.

Pushkin's subject becomes involved when he addresses representatives of first one side in the second stanza, and then of the other
side in the third stanza. These warnings have a dispassionate tone,
although in both cases the speaker points out that the conflict is a
dangerous gamble that threatens the lives of those doing the actual
fighting. Pushkin's persona sides neither with the Delibash nor the
Cossack. In fact, lacking any extra textual information, the reader
finds himself unable to determine which one of the two participants
in the duel comes from "our" camp, and who represents the enemy.
Siniavskii observes that

> the dramatic poet—Pushkin demanded—must be impartial, like
> fate. But that's true only within the boundaries of the whole
> work . . . but while the action is going on, he is partial at every
> step and takes care by turns now of one, now of the other side,
> so that we don't always know whom we are supposed to prefer.
> (Tertz 79)

Pushkin grammatically excludes himself from the division of territory between the two rival forces, "our" and "their" camp. Not a single verb in the entire poem suggests the speaker's identification with the "my" (we). Second-person singular verbs—"ne suisia k lave" (do not approach the column), "ne rvisia k boiu" (don't rush into battle), etc.—convey warnings both to the Delibash and the Cossack. After these warnings, the narrator switches to the descriptive and distancing third-person plural. The second-person plural "posmotrite" (look) emphasizes that from the narrator's point of view the described event has more in common with a spectacle than with a military conflict in which he participates.

Despite the gravity of the life-threatening situation, the narrator's warnings reveal a light-hearted quality:

> Эй, казак! Не рвися к бою:
> Делибаш на всем скаку
> Срежет саблею кривою
> С плеч удалую башку. (3.1, 199)

> Hey, Cossack! Do not rush into battle:
> Delibash will cut off
> From your neck
> Your bold head with his scimitar.

The same tone of mocking aloofness dominates the poem's final stanza, which mirrors the first one. Again, Pushkin provides a dispassionate account from the field of battle.

The description of the confrontation between the Delibash and the Cossack sounds more like a report from a wrestling contest than an account of a serious military campaign. The battle becomes an oriental spectacle. Pushkin, a western traveler, reserves for himself the role of a spectator. Without a hint of pathos, he describes both the Delibash's death, "Delibash uzhe na pike" (The Delibash already pierced by a lance), and the Cossack's death, briefly noted in the phrase "a kazak bez golovy" (and the Cossack without his head). The poet relegates the contest between the Russian and Ottoman Empires to the status of a senseless military duel as he remains on the sidelines of the conflict.

The middle stanzas establish an equilibrium between the Delibash and the Cossack that appears to shift slightly in the Turk's favor when the poem's title is taken into account. But *delibash* functions as a motif as much as it does a personal name. The noun consists of two lexemes; "deli" may mean mad, insane, crazy, foolish, rash, wild, "violently addicted to," or "mad on"; and "bash" denotes a head (Hony 33, 77). The Turkish "deli-bash" is synonymous with the Russian "udalaia bashka" (daring, bold head), the phrase that describes the Cossack. In fact, the Russian word *bashka* is a Turkish borrowing. Both participants of the duel are indeed "violently addicted to" fighting. They both make the mistake of equating the imperial conflict with a contest of bravery, and they pay for the mistake with their lives: the Cossack literally loses his "bold head" and the Delibash is pierced by his adversary's lance. Siniavskii asks the following about "Delibash":

> But from which vantage point is Pushkin looking? From both sides at the same time, from their camp and ours? Or perhaps from above, from the side, from some third point of view, equally distant from "them" and from "us"? (Tertz 79)

Lacking sympathy for either one of the fighters, the "Delibash" narrator responds to both of their deaths with indifference. He remains nothing more than a bystander, an amused spectator, a Westerner who happens to come upon the spectacle of male bravery while traveling in the Orient. Pushkin looks at the conflict as an exotic, male form of entertainment devoid of nationalistic undertones. Half way through the poetic account of the journey officially intended to enable his participation in the military campaign against Turkey, Pushkin subverts the expectations of those of his readers who were prone to identify the Cossack as a soldier fighting on the side of the Russian "my" (we). The formalist critic Iurii Tynianov comments on this subversive aspect of "Delibash" in his article on "Journey to Arzrum." Tynianov concludes that the prose account, joined by the poems "Delibash" and "From Hafez," convey criticism of Russia's military campaign in the South. These texts originated, he argues, as Pushkin's polemic with the conservative critics Bulgarin and Nadezhdin and their expectation that the poet sing praises of Russia's military forces and their commanders. Meaning to disappoint, instead of an ode Pushkin provided a "generic battle scene" in "Delibash" (Tynianov 195).

"From Hafez" develops the same antimilitarist theme, only in an entirely different form. Pushkin translates his message here into the form of an oriental stylization. All critical editions of Pushkin's works note that "From Hafez" is not a translation from the Persian poet Hafez, while crediting the Russian poet's text with various degrees of resemblance to the oriental original. An analysis of the form and the substance of Pushkin's imitation against the background of Hafez's poetry helps to determine the nature of its relationship to the original. Did this cultural impersonation bring Pushkin any closer to breaking the established conventions of oriental travel?

The growth of orientalist interests around the turn of the nineteenth century turned Hafez, a fourteenth-century Persian poet, into a widely translated and well-known figure in Europe.[3] The first full translation of his "Divan" was the German version published by Josef von Hammer in 1813. Despite its many flaws, Hammer's translation brought Hafez to the attention of cultured Europe. Goethe received a copy of Hammer's book early in 1814. The poetry so impressed the German master that he soon began to work on poems praising and emulating Hafez. These poems later comprised Goethe's famous *West-Eastern Divan* (*West-Oestlicher Divan*).

In an 1856 article, Savel'ev surveys the development of Russian Orientalism and points out that "Arab and Persian literatures were only studied [in Russia] to the extent to which their historic texts referred to the history of the Mongols, Tatars, or Russia itself" (28). The political character of Russian scholarly Orientalism dictated this specific focus. Thanks to Western anthologies and scholarship, however, the Russian reading public was familiar with most of the major representatives of Middle Eastern literatures. Periodicals published translations of Arab and Persian texts, usually from Western languages, but occasionally from the originals as well.[4] Hafez's voice did not reach Pushkin via Russia's shared border with Persia. Instead, it bounced off western letters before attracting his attention. The full text of Pushkin's "From Hafez" best demonstrates specific formal and thematic features of the poet's choices in stylization.

Из Гафиза
(Лагерь при Евфрате)

Не пленяйся бранной славой,
О красавец молодой!
Не бросайся в бой кровавый
С карабахскую толпой!

Знаю, смерть тебя не встретит:
Азраил, среди мечей,
Красоту твою заметит—
И пощада будет ей!
Но боюсь: среди сражений
Ты утратишь навсегда
Скромность робкую движений,
Прелесть неги и стыда! (13.1, 163)

From Hafez
(Encampment by the Euphrates)

Do not let yourself be captivated with martial glory
Oh beautiful young man.
Do not throw yourself into the bloody battle
with the Karabakh crowd.
I know that death will not meet you:
Azrael among the swords
will notice your beauty,
And it will be spared.
But I am afraid: among the battle
You will forever lose
The shy timidity of your movements
The charming sweet bliss and abashment.

Like the orientalizing "Delibash" discussed earlier, Pushkin wrote the six rhyming couplets of "From Hafez" in the four-foot trochee. Russian literature learned of this meter already in the eighteenth century, when it was primarily associated with light, Anacreontic poetry. In the nineteenth century, the four-foot trochee grew to be used for folk stylization and in genres such as the ballad. Through stylization, the four-foot trochee came to be associated with longer epic forms. According to M. L. Gasparov, "association with the ballad (along with classic antiquity, as in Pushkin's "Prozerpina") suggested the use of the four-foot trochee also for exotic (in particular Eastern) subjects" (115). The character of von Hammer's translation led Western European as well as Russian literati to refer to Hafez as the "Persian Anacreon." Pushkin's use of the four-foot trochee united the Anacreontic connotations of earlier Russian literary tradition with the nineteenth-century genre of oriental stylization.

The basic unit of versification in Persian poetry comparable to the European line is the *bayt*. Each bayt is split into two hemistichs. All bayts of the *ghazal* are united by a monorhyme, which may sometimes involve half of the syllables in the bayt. Semantically, the bayts are often comparable to stanzas, as a single bayt may develop a separate theme. An 1815 issue of *Vestnik Evropy* (*The Herald of Europe*), a leading Russian intellectual publication at the time, contains an article by Jourdain devoted to Persian language and literature that may very well have provided Pushkin with information on the subject. This Russian translation from the French explains that

> the ghazal is a type of poem, similar to the ode and song. It differs from the casedegh, in that it cannot be shorter that five couplets, and longer than thirteen. ... In the ghazal each of the couplets contains a whole concept; one can move from one subject to another, present one thought separately from another. A lack of order contributes most to the beauty of the ghazal; in this sense it is very much like our ode. (nr 82. 1815, 120)

Pushkin's imitation of Hafez consists of six couplets that, visually, may correspond to bayts. However, a closer reading of the poem reveals that semantically "From Hafez" is divided further into three separate parts. Each of the parts consists of three couplets, and, like a single bayt in Persian poetry, each couplet develops into a separate theme. The themes that Pushkin introduces into his ghazal do not deviate from the usual repertoire of Persian poetry.[5]

The first part of "From Hafez" admonishes the beautiful youth not to succumb to the lures of military glory. The following two fragments from ghazals by Hafez illustrate the extent to which Pushkin approximates the Persian poet:

> Be not deceived, our days are short and few.
> The seeming lures of this encircling dome
> Are hued with fraud, delusions, lies.
> O cherish now this precious hour, be fair and good to friends.
> Our hour is brief beneath the glaring sun. (Nakosteen 57)

> The lusts of this deceiving world are like those stormy seas,
> the greed for shining gems beneath the waves
> May lure our souls - but mark!
> This lure for gain may lead to pain in fatal storms.
> Beware! a thousand pearls are worth as naught
> If whirled and tossed, the divers soul is lost
> Within the oceans subtle self. (107)

In the second part of "From Hafez," the poet speaks from the perspective of a "wise man," a prophet whose knowledge extends into the future and who knows that the young man will not perish in battle. This speaker reveals that the warrior will avoid an encounter with death. Azrael, in Muslim theology the angel who stands by the side of the dying and separates the soul from the body, will take note of the youth's beauty and spare him (although such liberation might still denote physical death). Pushkin alludes to the prognostic value of Hafez's verse. Continuing the pattern established in his earlier orientalizing poetry, "Prophet" ("Prorok") and "Imitations of the Koran" ("Podrazhania Koranu"), Pushkin's poet becomes a living prophet.

In the poem's third part, the poet expresses concern that, even though his life is not at risk, participation in the military conflict jeopardizes the young man's beauty. The experience of battle will deprive him of the bashfulness of movements and of his sensuous, timid charm. In an earlier version of "From Hafez," preserved in Pushkin's notes, the adjective "devstvennykh" ("virgin-like") qualifies the noun "dvizhenia" ("movements") (13.2, 736). This textual clue emphasizes a difference between the virility of the Caucasian mountaineers of Pushkin's earlier southern narrative poems and the effeminate character of the addressee of "From Hafez." This part of the poem echoes Hafez. Many of his ghazals address or contain a reference to a young man, a friend, "the true beloved." Hafez's poetic cosmos revolves around the beauty of the beloved (Schimmel 225). Full of sensuous expressions, these lines of Hafez's poetry have been interpreted as a veiled reference to Divinity, as panegyrics in which the true addressee is transformed into the beloved, and finally—quite literally—as a hedonistic call to enjoy life.

In the Persian ghazal, the monorhyme constitutes one of the means of assuring the entire ghazal's unity. Early European Orientalists often overlooked this element of the poetic genre (witness the above quoted fragment from Jourdain which "credits" the ghazal with a "lack of order" in the development of its themes).[6] I. S. Braginskii identifies the influence of Eastern monorhyme in the rhyming pattern of Pushkin's 1823 poem "Freedom's Desert Advocate" ("Svobody seiatel' pustynnyi") (121). "From Hafez" appears to lack a monorhyme. However, just as Pushkin does not render bayts as lines, he does not render the monorhyme simply as a European end-rhyme. He appears to define it more broadly. As indicated earlier, the Persian ghazal may have an extensive monorhyme that may involve a word or even a phrase. In "From Hafez," a thematic element, the physical beauty of the addressee— "krasavets molodoi" (the beautiful youth)—unifies the poem in a way comparable to the monorhyme's function in the ghazal: "Krasavets molodoi" of the first part is echoed by "krasota tvoia" (your beauty) of the second part. The third part spells out the "krasota" (beauty) as: "skromnost robkaia dvizhenii, prelest' negi i styda." (the shy timidity of movements, the charming sweet bliss and abashment). Despite the oft-repeated and mistaken claim of a lack of unity in the Persian ghazal in general, and in the poetry of the master of this genre, Hafez, in particular, Pushkin perfectly comprehends and captures the form of this poetry, which is divided into separate bayts, yet ultimately united by the monorhyme. Each of the three parts of his poem develops a separate theme, but the repetition of the object's attributes also unites them.

Monika Greenleaf addresses the subject of Pushkin's attitude towards oriental literatures. She quotes a fragment from Pushkin's letter to P. A. Viazemskii in which the former discusses his "Fountain of Bakhchisaray":

> The Eastern style was a model for me, insofar as it is possible for us rational cold Europeans. A propos again, do you know why I dislike Moore? Because he is excessively Eastern. He imitates childishly and in an ugly manner the childishness and ugliness of Saadi, Hafiz, and Mohammed. A European, even in the rapture of Oriental splendor, must preserve the taste and eye of a European. That is why Byron is charming in *The Giaour, The Bride of Abydos*, etc. (qtd. in Greenleaf 117)

A comparison of Pushkin's "From Hafez" and Mickiewicz's "Crimean Sonnets" demonstrates that the Russian's imitation is free of ostensible oriental stylization in both its vocabulary and its imagery. Oriental words—*Allah, diwy, dżamidy, izan, harem*—dot Mickiewicz's cycle. The "Crimean Sonnets" sparkle with oriental metaphors. Mickiewicz refers to the harem of skies, the caravan of stars. He makes the shy evening sky blush, and he compares the night to an oriental woman who caresses him while he is falling asleep. On the other hand, Pushkin introduces only one oriental word and cultural concept into his poem: the Muslim name of the angel Azrael. Not only is "From Hafez" free of bright oriental metaphors, it is almost entirely free of any metaphors.

V. Eberman observes that Pushkin transmitted some of the ideas present in Hafez's poetry to Russia, but that he did so without providing any indication of eastern form and poetic devices (113). Yet a careful reading of the poems demonstrates that despite a lack of dazzling oriental adornments Pushkin managed to create an impressive imitation of certain formal as well as semantic qualities of the Hafezan ghazal, a conspicuous feat for someone who attached the adjectives childlike and monstrous to the names of Saadi, Hafez and Mohammed. What, then, was the Russian poet's relationship to Hafez's text? Russian and Soviet critical tradition offers one way to interpret this relationship; contemporary western criticism presents an alternative perspective. In his famed "Pushkin speech," Dostoevskii asserts that

> there has never been a poet with this kind of universal sensitivity that we find in Pushkin. And it is not just the ability to emulate other cultures which comes into play, but its amazing profundity, the ability to transform one's own spirit into the spirit of foreign nations, an ability to transform oneself almost completely, and therefore a miraculous ability, as nowhere, not in any poet of the whole world has this phenomenon ever repeated itself (vol. 26, 146).

By claiming that Pushkin expressed the national spirit of the Russian people through his cosmopolitanism, Dostoevskii cements a tradition that originated with Gogol's assertions about the universal character of Pushkin's genius. Treading in Dostoevskii's footsteps, the Soviet critic I. S. Braginskii attempts to describe the specificity of the West-East synthesis in Pushkin's poetry. Braginskii characterizes the oriental influences in Pushkin's post-1823 works by pointing to a qualitative difference between eighteenth-century oriental stylizations, where "the East served as a mere decoration," and Pushkin's ability to synthesize of western and eastern elements in his poetry.

Contrary to these assertions about the ingenious character of Pushkin's Orientalism, his impersonation of Hafez in "From Hafez" is limited to the poem's surface. In this sense, the impersonation does bear a similarity to the eighteenth-century tradition of oriental imitations. It could be compared, for example, to Jan Potocki's Eastern tales. Potocki's "travel letters," *Voyage en Turquie et en Egypte, fait en l'anne 1784*, contain six oriental tales. They form a compilation of oriental truths signaling an alternative to Europe's false morality.

The oriental form provides a mask for the author, who fills the form with his own meaning. But Pushkin and Potocki have different attitudes towards the Orient. For a writer of his time, Potocki had a sophisticated understanding of the region's cultures. Within the context of his time and his personal interests, Potocki's oriental stylizations substantiate the author's respect for the cultures from which he derives his account. Pushkin, on the other hand, usurps the name of Hafez with the same arrogance that later lead him to dismiss Persian poetry as "childish and ugly." Even though "From Hafez" operates as a very skillful imitation, Pushkin's oriental stylization does indeed amount to nothing more than a masquerade.

Braginskii compares the West-East synthesis of Pushkin's later poetry to the achievement of Goethe's *West-Oestlicher Divan*. There is, however, a discernible disparity between Pushkin's attitude towards Hafez's text in "From Hafez" and Goethe's attitude towards the Persian original. Goethe, whose *Divan* overflows with admiration for Hafez, best describes his relationship to the Persian poet in these lines from a poem titled "Nachbildung" (Imitation):

> In deiner Reimart hoff ich mich zu finden,
> Das Wiederholen soll mir auch gefallen,
> Erst werd ich Sinn, sodann auch Worte finden;
> Zum zweiten Mal soll mir kein Klang erschallen,
> Er muesste denn besondern Sinn begruenden,
> Wie dus vermagst, Beguenstiger vor allen! . . .

> In your own mode of rhyme my feet I'll find,
> The repetitions pleasure shall incite:
> At first the sense and then the words I'll find,
> No sound a second time will I indict
> Unless thereby the meaning is refined
> As you, with peerless gifts, have shown aright! (35)

Medieval Persian literature recognized intertextuality as one of the principles underlying literary activity. Oriental poets used to incorporate other poets' texts into their own as a way of giving new poetic expression to the same thought.[7] Goethe's reference to this practice in the quoted passage from the *Divan* illustrates how the German poet bridges the gap between western and eastern cultural traditions by putting himself in the line of Hafez's imitators. The deeply felt similarity of ideas and images between Goethe and Hafez comes from the former's appreciation of the meaning that he discovers—through the mediation of a translation—in the Persian poet's work.

When the two great nineteenth-century Slavic poets first ventured into the field of literary Orientalism—Mickiewicz in "Crimean Sonnets" and Pushkin in his eastern narrative poems—they found their feet in the rhyme of Byron. They engaged in a practice much like the Middle Eastern *tadmin* (poetic dialogue), even though the voice their poetry echoed belonged to a Westerner. In contrast, "From Hafez" does not have an audible voice of a poetic predecessor. Pushkin's Persian imitation contains no trace of Hafez the man and the poet. Pushkin's reference to the Persian poet in the Caucasian cycle does not have the character of a poetic "pereklichka" (exchange). Pushkin obviously had some knowledge of the Persian poet, but he uses it to conceal his own message under the cloak of the stylized text. Since "Delibash" has already communicated the same message, Pushkin's ghazal amounts to nothing more than a literary game. In contrast to Potocki's imitations, "From Hafez" is free of any civic concerns. Upon closer scrutiny, therefore, Pushkin's dialogue with the culture of the Orient appears to consist of no more than a passerby's detached remarks. He assumes the guise of a Westerner who never doubts his superiority vis-à-vis the Orientals and their cultural heritage. Showing no regard for the cultural substance that originally filled this form, the Russian poet arrogantly empties the meaning out of the oriental form. N. B. Potokskii writes in his account of the Arzrum expedition that "Pushkin was one of the first to put on a Cherkess dress, he armed himself with a saber, a dagger, a pistol; imitating him, many peaceful people were buying Caucasian attire and armor from the Cossacks" (Veresaev 9). In "From Hafez," Pushkin similarly puts on the coat of Hafez's poetic form. The oriental stylization functions as a mere decoration.

Dressed in a Cherkess outfit, Pushkin still belongs unequivocally to the Russian military forces dispatched to the Turkish border to fight for Russia's imperialism. That being said, his literary imperialism poses a more complex phenomenon. The story Pushkin tells in "From Hafez" does not promote imperial conquest. Although Pushkin's annexation of the literary Orient in this poem may be described as imperialist in nature, his Caucasian poetry features a conspicuous refusal to sing the praises of Russian troops.

Pushkin's refusal to endorse Russian expansionism on the occasion of the 1829 war with Turkey becomes even more apparent in light of his later, wholehearted poetic defense of Russian imperialism. Just two years after his return from Arzrum, Pushkin penned two poems that invert the anti-militarist message of "Delibash" and "From Hafez." Along with a poem by Zhukovskii, a slim, September 1831 volume titled *On the Taking of Warsaw* contained Pushkin's "The Borodino Anniversary" ("Borodinskaia godovshchina") and "To the Slanderers of Russia" ("Kleviatnikam Rossii"). This publication celebrates the Russian victory over the Polish national uprising that broke out in November 1830. In "To the Slanderers of Russia," Pushkin polemicizes with the Polish rebellion's Western European supporters. In a statement worthy of a right-wing conservative, Pushkin lets it be known that Poland, because it is a Slavic country, belongs to the domain of Russia's internal affairs. "The Borodino Anniversary" sounds the same tones. It presents the Poles' fight for national independence as an act of anti-Russian aggression. By transforming conquest into an act of self-defense, Pushkin resorts to the same strategy that the lesser poet Andrei Murav'ev uses in his "Tavrida." Pushkin takes the presumed Western European aggression to task with a vengeance:

> Ступайте ж к нам: Вас Русь зовет!
> Но знайте, прошеные гости!
> Уж Польша вас не поведет:
> Через ее шагнете кости! (13.1, 273-74)

> Why don't you attack us: Russia challenges you!
> But you should know, invited guests!
> Poland will not lead you any more:
> You will have to step over her dead body!

In a reversal of his position at the time of the Caucasian military campaign, the Russian bard now stands ready to defend tsarist Russia in its one-sided confrontation with the Poles. More important, he identifies himself with the military effort and sings the glory of the victorious Russian army. Not a trace remains of the confusion from "Delibash" about who is fighting whom. There is a clear division between a "my" (we Russians), "vy" (Western Europe), and "oni" (the Poles). Pushkin willingly participates in all the actions of the "my" directed against the threatening "oni." In contrast to "Delibash," "The Borodino Anniversary" features verbs that are in the first-person plural.

The poet's skepticism towards the Caucasian campaign parallels his dubious attitude towards General Paskevich, the commander-in-chief of Russian forces in the southeastern theater of war. Tynianov first observed that irony tints Pushkin's portrayal of General Paskevich in "Journey to Arzrum." (201-3). At the beginning of the account, Pushkin's describes his visit to Ermolov, Paskevich's predecessor and bitter critic. This description and the poet's references to the general in the text of "Journey" deliver unambiguous evidence of Pushkin's own antipathy towards Paskevich. However, when Pushkin looks at Paskevich through the prism of the 1830 events in Poland, he sees him in an entirely different light.

Pushkin wrote "The Borodino Anniversary" upon learning that General Paskevich's troops had taken rebellious Warsaw in August 1831. Apart from overtly positive references to Russia's military might, the poem contains words of praise for the commander of the Russian forces. Pushkin musters great patriotic fervor when welcoming the general's military victory over Warsaw; Paskevich enjoys the designation "powerful avenger of malicious calumnies." Pushkin backtracks even further by now giving Paskevich credit for his victories in the South. He refers to him as "the one who had tamed the hills of Tauris" and "to whom Erevan had paid hommage." Finally, the Warsaw-Borodino comparison finds a parallel in the comparison of Paskevich to Kutuzov, the legendary Russian general who defeated Napoleon.

The two ostensibly antimilitarist poems, "Delibash" and "From Hafez," preceded the publication of "The Borodino Anniversary" and "To the Slanderers of Russia," whereas the latter two preceded "Journey to Arzrum." The two accounts of the Arzrum expedition, one poetic and the other written in prose, bracket the glorification of Paskevich in "The Borodino Anniversary." This framework makes the statements contained in both sets of poems appear somewhat tentative.

Ewa Thompson identifies an "inferiority complex" as an element that contributed to the fierceness of Pushkin's attack on Poland (76). Harsha Ram, who, in contrast to Thompson, downplays the poems' biting chauvinism, sees them as signaling "a new kind of politics," one based on the assumption of "a profound cultural fissure between Russia and western Europe" (214). Although the latter explanation does have merit, the common vice of political opportunism may have additionally fueled Pushkin's imperialist zeal. The circumstances of Pushkin's life in 1831 differed significantly from those of 1829. Soon after he returned from the Caucasus, the poet began to feel restless again. In a letter to Benkendorf, dated January 7, 1830, Pushkin once more pleads for permission to travel abroad:

> Until I am not yet married, and have not begun my government service, I would like to undertake a journey to France, or to Italy. In case I could not receive permission to do so, I would like to request a permission to visit China with a mission that is preparing to travel there.[8]

Like before, the authorities denied Pushkin permission to travel. Shortly thereafter, Russia's prodigal son married. At the time he penned the two Polish poems, Pushkin lived with his bride in Tsarskoe Selo, close to the court, where Zhukovskii was employed as a tutor. Pushkin may have conceived the tribute to Russia's military power as a gesture born from the need to improve his relations with the tsar and Russia's military-political establishment (Tretiak 237). Whatever the motivation, Pushkin did not change his 1831 opinion of Paskevich radically enough to make beautifying editorial corrections to the text of his travel account published in *Sovremennik* in 1835. This intriguing ironic twist raises several questions that point to new ways of interpreting both sets of texts.

First of all, how sincerely did Pushkin support the Russian military intervention in Poland? His poetic reaction to the collapse of the Polish national uprising has been interpreted as a genuine expression of his anti-Polish feelings. Wacław Lednicki writes that

> Pushkin was an enemy, a ruthless enemy, but also a methodical, conscious enemy . . . . Pushkin was a poet of all Russia, a sincere and conscious bard of its power; an apologist of its imperial might. (56)

Certain textual clues speak in favor of Lednicki's interpretation: Pushkin's poetry identified Poland as Russia's long-time adversary as early as 1824. In an unpublished fragment, "To Count Olizar" ("Grafu Olizaru"), the poet emphasizes that an adversarial relationship has divided the two Slavic nations for centuries. Indeed, the words describing Poles in "The Borodino Anniversary" and "To the Slanderers of Russia" echo what Pushkin stated earlier when addressing Olizar. In 1831, he merely expressed the Russo-Polish antipathy in much stronger terms.

And yet the sudden transformation of Pushkin's position vis-à-vis current developments impedes a finalizing judgment of his political sympathies. In an unpublished fragment of the introduction to "Journey to Arzrum," Pushkin complains about the criticism that he faced upon his return from Arzrum: "I was given a serious scolding in a political newspaper because, after my return, I published a poem which did not deal with the taking of Arzrum" (8. 1, 741). The poet's reaction to the criticism coming from the likes of Fadei Bulgarin may have taken the form of an odic praise of the might of Russian arms. In the two Polish poems, Pushkin demonstrates his ability to assume the role of a court poet, should he so choose. But he also leaves open the possibility that, with the turning of the page, General Paskevich, the national hero, will change into a figure of a lesser stature.

Serious corrections are needed to Tynianov's reading of Pushkin's Arzrum prose and poetry as a political statement expressing the poet's antimilitarist sympathies. Sandwiched in between the publication of the two parts of the Arzrum text, the odic praise lavished on Paskevich for the taking of Warsaw dilutes Pushkin's supposed oppositionist sentiments. If read not as an "ironic protest against war" (Tynianov 196), but rather as superficially apolitical, the Arzrum texts do not document the poet's engagement as a champion of the peaceful coexistence of nations. Instead, they record his condescending imperial view of the Caucasus. Why spill blood, Pushkin seems to be asking, over a culturally backward and therefore nonthreatening area that could be easily colonized with the samovar?

Monika Greenleaf suggests that the inconsistencies in Pushkin's politics formed a part of his strategy as a poet. She argues that

> what Pushkin learned from Byron . . . was the possibility of juxtaposing in a single work utterly different, simultaneous points of view on the same matter. The jumps from style to style marked the movements of a mercurial subjectivity. (Greenleaf 45)

Greenleaf quotes the example of "The Prisoner of the Caucasus," where a sympathetic attitude towards the plight of the mountaineers in the narrative poem's prologue stands in stark contrast to the poem's epilogue. Greenleaf continues that

> this was no longer "normative" or even "aesthetic" irony, but irony that brought together utterly different discursive perspectives within the same ostensible narrative framework and did not even begin to articulate a decision. (45)

Although textual as well as chronological boundaries separate the Arzrum texts and Pushkin's Polish poems, the works present the reader with a situation analogous to the pattern suggested by Greenleaf. Pushkin subverts attempts to pinpoint his texts' definite message. While in the Caucasus, against the background of the East, Pushkin defines himself as an inhabitant of European Russia, and he willingly adopts the trappings of Western European Orientalism. In confrontation with the West, his position assumes the distinctive characteristics of antiwestern Russianness. These two discursive perspectives create a sum that is the space of modern Russian culture, which Pushkin embodied perfectly.

The Return

Ivanov Razumnik, one of the main ideologues of the Scythian movement that emerged in Russia at the beginning of the twentieth century, praised Pushkin's "To the Slanderers of Russia" and "The Borodino Anniversary" for their depth of historic introspection (26). Modern Scythianism presented a conception of Russian historical identity grounded in the duality of the Russian people's national character, defined as half-European and half-Asian. Scythianism affirmed the Asian element within Russian civilization. Razumnik identified Scythian themes in Pushkin's two anti-Polish poems. These poems define Russia's position vis-à-vis Western Europe in negative terms. In contrast to them, the Caucasian cycle's last poem, "The Don," opens up the possibility of a positive definition of Russia's peripheral inbetweenness.

Дон

Блеща средь полей широких,
Вон он льется! . . . Здравствуй, Дон!
От сынов твоих далеких
Я привез тебе поклон.

Как прославленного брата,
Реки знают тихий Дон;
От Аракса и Евфрата
Я привез тебе поклон.

Отдохнув от злой погони,
Чуя родину свою.
Пьют уже донские кони
Арпачайскую струю.

Приготов же, Дон заветный,
Для наездников лихих
Сок кипучий, искрометный
Виноградников твоих.

Glistening among wide fields,
There it flows! ... Greetings to you, Don!
From your distant sons
I am bringing you regards.

As a celebrated brother,
Rivers know the quiet Don;
From Araxes and Euphrates
I am bringing you regards.

Having rested from a strenuous chase,
Sensing that their homeland is near,
The Don horses are drinking
From the Arpachai stream.

Please prepare for us, cherished Don,
For the spirited riders
the bubbling, sparkling juice
of your vineyards.

In the first line of "The Don," the river glows in the sun among the flat fields, an image that contrasts starkly with the mountainous scenery that Pushkin leaves behind. His subject's reaction to the sight of the Don is reminiscent of the sighting of land after a long sea voyage. Like a sailor who has been waiting for the first glimpse of dry land, Pushkin's traveler exclaims, "There it flows! . . . Greetings to you, Don!" (Von on l'etsia! . . . Zdravstvui, Don). In addition to welcoming the sight of the river, the traveler salutes the Don on behalf of its sons who are still far away—the Don Cossacks fighting in the war against Turkey—and on behalf of the two rivers of the South, the

Araks and the Euphrates. This greeting indicates the direction in which the traveler proceeds: he is returning home from his sojourn in the South, going from Asia back to Europe. Pushkin significantly does not describe a return to a European metropolis, but to the wide, open spaces of the Don delta.

Each of the three rivers mentioned in the first two stanzas of Pushkin's poem represents a cultural space that has grown up around it over centuries. The Araks and the Euphrates, two major rivers of the South, stand for the traditions of the ancient Orient. The Araks, which rises in Turkish Armenia, was known in ancient times as Araxes. The river's valley has been mentioned as the possible location of the Garden of Eden. The Araks forms the center of an area that also incorporates Mount Ararat, where Noah's ark came to rest and where he was supposed to have planted the first vineyard. The Euphrates rises in the mountains north of Erzerum and flows across the mountains of Turkey into Syria. It belongs to the category of rivers known as the great ancient "givers of life" (Rand McNally 54, 64). The greeting conferred on the Don acknowledges the course of Pushkin's journey and asserts the Russian river's position within the poem's hierarchy of rivers.

The Don originates in the heart of Russia. It flows southward into the Azov Sea. On the south side of the Don delta stands the ancient fortress town of Azov, founded in the sixth century B. C. as a Greek colony, which adopted as its name the Greek version of the river's name, Tanais. Tanais came under the Genoese, and it was eventually taken by the Turks. It was not until 1696 that the Don delta came under Russian domination with Peter the Great's capture of the town.

Jan Potocki, whose Caucasian travelogue Pushkin cites in the text of "Journey to Arzrum," mentions the Don in his account:

> I continued along the banks of the river Don, although without ever seeing the bed of this king of all the rivers of Scythia, of this Tanais, as famous in the works of the Greek poets, as in the works of their historians, and which I crossed repeatedly following Herodotus, Strabo, and Ptolemy. (17)

Potocki sees the river Don through the texts of the ancient Greeks. Pushkin refers to the Don as the renowned brother of other rivers. The Russian word *proslavlennyi* corresponds to the French "fameux (dans les poetes grecs)" of Potocki's description; the fame stretches back to the times of the ancient Greek accounts recalled by the Polish traveler. Potocki's Scythia refers to the land of the Scythians (Greek: *Skythai*; Russian: *Skify*), ancient tribes that were pushed out of Asia and that inhabited the steppes north of the Black Sea. Pushkin adopts this ancient genealogy for the Don.

The Don forms a boundary of familiar territory; it provides a passage to "our" side of the cultural divide. At the same time, stepping into the wide expanses of the Don steppe, Pushkin expands Russia's cultural space to the prehistorical period. Through the mediation of the Greeks, he incorporates the heritage of the ancient Scythians into Russian semiosphere.

The Don creates the outer boundary of a territory that is *cultured, ours, safe*. The poem that forms the finale of Pushkin's cycle marks the poet's departure from what could have become a rediscovered Garden of Eden. Yet the journey possesses the trappings of a longed-for-return. Pushkin leaves the Caucasus feeling that *their* space, the space beyond the Don, is hostile and dangerous: when he looks back, he sees only a "malicious chase."[9] The conclusion of Pushkin's journey contrasts with the resolution of Mickiewicz's oriental voyage. Mickiewicz celebrates Crimea, and his last sonnet offers the reader a Crimean panorama. The final poem of Pushkin's 1829 Caucasian cycle celebrates his return home. The river takes the traveler not away from, but back to an earthly paradise, a safe haven from an evil pursuit. The culminating point in Pushkin's journey lies in the experience of a homecoming, of a prodigal son's return intimated in the cycle's last poem.

Given the pilgrimage writing's re-emergence around the time of the Caucasian poems' publication, how does Pushkin's journey relate to the pilgrimage pattern of travel? Russian medieval pilgrimage accounts omitted descriptions of the pilgrim's return journey, similarly to western and Greek accounts. For example, the twelfth-century account of Abbot Daniil's pilgrimage to the Holy Land, which became a prototype of Russian pilgrimage writing, contains inventories of holy places visited along the way to Jerusalem. It culminates with a description of the celebrations of Easter Sunday and ends with a list of names of Russian dignitaries for whom the Abbot prayed at the Holy Sepulcher. Daniil conformed to a convention that originated from the perception that the journey's climax occurred with the arrival and the religious celebration that coincided with an Easter entry into Jerusalem. The pilgrim was a witness to Christ's crucifixion and resurrection. This experience created a basis for his

Figure 9a: An illustration from Jan Potocki's *Voyage dans les Steps d'Astrakhan et du Caucase.* (Paris, 1829). Potocki's book was among the sources cited by Pushkin in his "Journey to Arzrum." Between pages 126-27.

Figure 9b: An illustration from Jan Potocki's *Voyage dans les Steps d'Astrakhan et du Caucase.* (Paris, 1829). Between pages 154-55.

own spiritual renewal that should not be overshadowed by a description of the journey back home.

The journey of Mickiewicz's "Crimean Sonnets" may not consciously imitate the pilgrimage pattern, but it nonetheless conforms to it. The Traveler/Pilgrim arrives in Crimea, and, through the meditation of the mystery behind natural phenomena, he arrives at a new understanding of the self. This moment represents not only the high, but also the final point of the journey's description. In contrast to Daniil and Mickiewicz, Pushkin starts his journey in the Caucasian cycle from what conventionally would have been the point of arrival. The passage described is the poet's journey back home, and the awaited moment of arrival is not associated with a far-away destination. The medieval pattern of pilgrimage writing became diluted in the centuries after Daniil. It certainly was not part of the norm in nineteenth-century accounts—neither Murav'ev nor Norov conform to it. Nonetheless, Pushkin's noticeable reversal of the paradigm is quite intriguing. But even though Pushkin precludes transcendence from figuring prominently in his itinerary, his journey back home does correspond to the Holy Land pilgrims' affirmation of Russianness. Ultimately, in the Russian Orthodox tradition, the Holy Land pilgrimage is designed to lead the traveler back to the quintessence of his spiritual home, Orthodoxy. But unlike the texts of Murav'ev and Norov and his own anti-Polish verses, Pushkin's Caucasian cycle is relatively free from the undercurrent of crude nationalist/imperialist thinking.

The Russian semiotician Iurii Lotman compares actual cultures to artistic texts constructed on the principle of pendulum-like swings between the "I - s/he" and the "I - I" communicative systems. "But," adds Lotman, "there will be a predominant tendency for the culture to be oriented either towards auto-communication or towards the acquisition of truth from without in the form of messages" (34-35). According to him, with Pushkin, the movement of texts from the West to Russia became less significant. Russia's orientation towards auto-communication increased (150). In the Caucasian lyric cycle, Pushkin clearly delineates the border between the East, Russia, and the West. Eastern cultural influences in the cycle are insignificant; the area's culture barely touches the surface of some of the poems. More important, even though Pushkin speaks—like Chateaubriand—"eternally of himself," he distances himself from the tropes associated with Western European Orientalism.

Notes

1. Monika Greenleaf points out that Pushkin's voyage in "Journey to Arzrum" fails to produce an outcome comparable to that of the "rite of passage" (139, 154).

2. The order of the poems listed in the 1957 edition of Pushkin's works agrees with the order indicated by Izmailov. However, the list does not include "Olegov schit." This omission further confirms the doubts expressed here about this poem's place in the 1829 cycle.

3. Verified biographical information about Hafez is scarce. One author writes that "to say that Hafez was born in Shiraz around the year 1320 A.D., practiced as a professional poet with some connections with several successive rulers' courts there, had an intimate knowledge of the Koran and past Persian literature, composed some five hundred ghazals and a handful of poems in other verse forms, was famous in his own lifetime, and died in A.D. 1389 or 1390, practically exhausts the indisputable facts of the poet's life" (Hillmann 3).

4. V. Eberman writes: "In the course of the entire nineteenth century, along with translations made directly from Eastern languages, Arabic and Persian, pioneered by A. Boldyrev, a student of Silvestre de Sacy, later professor of Oriental languages at the Moscow university [1811-1837, I.K.], and the editor of the first Arab and Persian anthologies in Russia, many translations were made from Western languages" (Eberman 111). However, apart from Boldyrev and Senkovskii in St. Petersburg, Russian Orientalists did not show much interest in tackling literary translations from the original languages of the East.

5. A Persian poet may introduce a wide array of themes into a single ghazal, such as "admonitions and counsels, condemnations of religious hypocrisy and externalism ... warnings against worldly fortunes, glory and power, the beauty of life, the mystery of existence, the ever waiting hands of fate, the vicissitudes of our brief tenure," etc. (Nakosteen, "Introduction," xxx).

6. Hillmann reviews the "long-standing indictment" of the ghazal's alleged lack of unity (8-9).

7. In his introduction to the volume of Hafez' poetry, Annaniasz Zajączkowski notes that an analysis of the ghazals of Hafez reveals the presence of many echoes, allusions, and "borrowings" from several prominent poets. Zajączkowski points out that the notion of plagiarism did not really exist in the East (37-38).

8. Quoted by N. L. Stepanov (377).

9. I derive the notion of a culture's boundary, and related terminology from Iu. M. Lotman's essay "The Semiosphere."

CONCLUSION

Far more than they fight, cultures coexist and inter-
act fruitfully with each other. It is to this idea of
humanistic culture as coexistence and sharing that
these pages are meant to contribute, and whether
they succeed or not, I at least have the satisfaction of
having tried.

E. Said, *Humanism and Democratic Criticism*

The concept of Orientalism that Edward Said articulated in 1978,
twenty-six years before this passage appeared in print, continues to
retain some appeal, especially given the current geo-political situation. But Said's innovative position also spawned a problematic legacy. Orientalism exposes a system of denigration that endowed one
group with agency and discursive control over another group. In
doing so Said's theoretical construct replicates the same mechanisms
of devisiveness that it brandmarks. It falls to the academic to inves-
tigate the past and comment on the present in a way that draws a
line between the discourses of power and the various modalities of
powerlessness. This analytical practice has grown to rely on an
increasingly reified and exclusionary critical idiom.

Only with the publication of *Humanism and Democratic
Criticism* did Said fully acknowledge the importance of a critical
humanistic interpretive practice that refrains from jumping right
into "general . . . statements about vast structures of power or . . .
vaguely therapeutic structures of salutary redemption" (61). In
Humanism and Democratic Criticism, Said concedes that "the risks
of specialized jargons for the humanities, inside and outside the university, are obvious: they simply substitute one prepackaged idiom
for another" (72). He proposes to counteract this growing tendency
by returning to the philological interpretation of texts based on close

textual analysis. The "process of reading and philological reception," he states unambiguously, "is the irreducible core . . . ."; and

> reception is based on ijtihad ["personal commitment and extraordinary effort" (68)], close reading, hermeneutic induction, and it entails troping the general language further in one's own critical language with a full recognition that the work of art in question remains at a necessary final remove, unreconciled and in the state of integral wholeness that one has tried to comprehend or to impose. (71)

Such close textual interpretation forms the basis for a critical practice that is a "technique of trouble," namely humanism (77). With "enlightenment and emancipation" as the ultimate goals, Said urges the humanist to

> accept responsibility for maintaining rather than resolving the tension between the aesthetic and the national, using the former to challenge, re-examine and resist the latter in those slow but rational modes of reception and understanding which is the humanist's way. (78)

Said uses *Humanism and Democratic Criticism* to prescribe crystal-clear guidelines that this author finds gratifying. They correspond very closely to the analytical method developed and used here. This study integrates a philological attentiveness to language with the type of humanism that does not impose essentializing patterns upon the phenomena described. Rather—like the humanism rediscovered by Said—it embraces an opening towards the world in its diversity. Through the adoption of a critical and questioning attitude, it holds forth the possibility of a positive engagement both with the texts analyzed and with the surrounding reality. Although this monograph does accept the orientalist-postcolonial continuum's basic framework, it also elucidates the need to revise one of Saidian Orientalism's fundamental assumptions: that behind all nineteenth-century European travel to the Orient there lurked a Eurocentric desire to expropriate the Other and thereby deploy travel literature as just another weapon of cultural hegemony.

Most of the Polish and Russian writers whose texts figure in this study did, to be sure, assert their Europeanness, usually in a self-conscious manner stemming from their own marginalization within Europe. However, they used this strategy for a variety of purposes.

For Anatoly Demidoff, it served as a vehicle to legitimize conquest. This Russian aristocrat produced a French-language account of his 1837 Crimean journey that presents Russian dominance as beneficial to the regions incorporated into the empire. Demidoff applauds the fact that "the youngest and least-known part of Russia" finally stands open for exploration and exploitation. "Who can say how many ages," he asks rhetorically,

> saw invasion, ravage, and destruction succeed each other on these immense plains up till the day the great empress Catherine . . . proudly pushed the confines of the empire up to the shores of the Black Sea, which was now surprised to bathe a land peaceful and Christian! The genius that seized these regions for their own good bequeathed her plans to her glorious successors. (ii)

None other than Tsar Nicholas I encouraged Demidoff's expedition. In his travel account, Demidoff praises the notoriously oppressive autocrat for granting "wise protection to all without the distinction of race or religion" (iv). Demidoff doubtlessly intended his French-language description's pragmatic approach to prove to the world that Russia, just like any other western power, was spreading the light of civilization by expanding her imperial rule. Writing in the 1830's, Demidoff employed a strategy that evinces a striking similarity to present-day Russian politicans' assertions that they, too, are fighting terrorism by carrying out a ruthless pacification policy in Chechnya.

To reiterate, however: such discursive tendencies did not preclude a wide variety of individual approaches taken by Russians and by Poles as they traveled to the territories of the East. As Tsvetan Todorov wisely points out, membership in a group does not predetermine one's attitude towards others. "The "flaws of individuals," concludes Todorov,

> like those of societies, are just as intrinsic as their greatest merits. It is thus up to each individual to try to make the best prevail over the worst . . . . Wisdom is neither hereditary nor contagious: one attains it more or less but always and only alone, not by virtue of one's membership in a group or a state. The best regime in the world is never anything but the least bad, and even if it's the one under which we live, everything still remains to be done. Learning to live with others is part of this wisdom. (399)

The sentiment expressed by the great Russian poet Aleksandr Griboedov in a letter he wrote from Crimea contrasts with the crude imperialist dogmatism espoused by Andrei Murav'ev or Anatoly Demidoff. "On this burnt-out spot," Griboedov observes,

> the gothic likes of the Genoans once ruled. They were replaced by the herdsmen customs of the Mongols, with an admixture of Turkish grandeur. We succeeded them, the universal followers, and along with us the spirit of destruction. Not one building has been spared, there is not one part of the old town that has not been pillaged and dug up. What's to be said? We are ourselves showing to the future nations that will succeed us, when the Russian race disappears, how they should deal with the remains of our existence." (180)

In the quoted passage Griboedov translates the physical distance that separates him from Russia proper into a critical distance towards Russian imperial expansion. This ideological position brings him certainly closer to the Pole Mickiewicz than to his fellow Russian Murav'ev, who was also touring Crimea at the same time in search of poetic inspiration.

For Poles, voluntary journeying eastward often represented the exact opposite of the involuntary *voyage orientale*, that is, exile to Siberia at the hands of the tsarist police state. The latter embodied complete bondage, while the former offered the opportunity to assume and articulate the position of a subject. But the examples scrutinized in this study make it clear that Poles' individual oriental journeys were multifarious in nature. In contradistinction to the broad perception of a unified Polish national literature, Polish literature of travel to the Orient reveals strong centripetal tendencies at work within this culture. While Adam Mickiewicz, a political exile, portrayed eastern travel as a fully liberational experience, Juliusz Słowacki, traveling as a free man, could not shrug off the specter of bondage.

Even though he was steeped in the cultural heritage of the West, Mickiewicz was capable of engaging the cultural traditions of the East in a non-imperialist, dialogical way. His own grounding in the traditions of Enlightenment humanism and his upbringing in an area of great cultural diversity helped him make this connection. The sonnet, a literary form born from the dialogue between the East and the West, provided him with the perfect means to this end. His

Sonnets stand out as an enduring example of a great work of art that boasts a perfect harmony of form and content. Most important, *The Sonnets* still provide a model of how not to give in to despair, and of how to find a positive way of relating to a changing world by entering into a dialogue with that which is perceived as other. "Modern thought and literature begin with the invention of the sonnet" Paul Oppenheimer asserts (3). Mickiewicz's *Sonnets* encapsulate much of what still today deserves to be salvaged from the modernist project.

WORKS CITED

Anikita, Hieromonach (Shikhmatov, Sergei Aleksandrovich). *Puteshestvie ieromon-akha Anikity po Sviatym mestam Vostoka v 1834–1836 godakh.* Saint Petersburg, 1891.

Annenkov, P.A. *Materialy dlia biografii A. S. Pushkina.* Moscow: Sovremennik, 1984.

Baratynskii, Evgenii. "Tavrida A. Murav'eva." *Moskovskii telegraf* 13 (1827). 325–31.

Batten, Charles L. *Pleasurable Instructions: Form and Convention in Eighteenth-Century Travel Literature.* Berkeley: U of California P, 1978.

Beauvois, Daniel. "Jean Potocki's *Voyages*: From Mythic Orient to Conquered Orient." In *Henaurme siecle: A Miscellany of Essays on Nineteenth-Century French Literature,* edited by Will L. McLendon. Heidelberg: C. Winter, 1984. 13–27.

Becker, Seymour. "Russia Between East and West: the Intelligentsia, Russian National Identity and the Asian Borderlands." *Central Asian Survey,* vol. 10, no. 4 (1991). 47–64.

Benda, Lucjan. "Pierwiastki arabskie w twórczości Adama Mickiewicza." In *Adam Mickiewicz.* London: Polskie Towarzystwo Naukowe, 1955. 269–80.

Bhabha, Homi K. *The Location of Culture.* London: Routledge, 1994.

Bielawski, Józef. *Klasyczna literatura arabska.* Warsaw: Dialog, 1995.

Billip, Witold. *Mickiewicz w oczach współczesnych: Dzieje recepcji na ziemiach polskich w latach 1818–1830: Antologia.* Breslau: Ossolineum, 1962.

Bloom, Harold. "Freud and the Sublime: A Catastrophe Theory of Creativity." *Contemporary Critical Theory,* edited by Dan Latimer. San Diego: Harcourt, Brace, Jovanovich, 1989.

Boehmer, Elleke. *Colonial and Postcolonial Literature.* Oxford: Oxford UP, 1995.

Borowski, Leon. *Uwagi nad poezją i wymową i inne pisma krytycznoliterackie.* Edited by Stanisław Buska-Wroński. Warsaw: Państwowy Instytut Wydawniczy, 1972.

Bowman, Glenn. "Christian Ideology and the Image of the Holy Land: the Place of Jerusalem Pilgrimage in the Various Christianities." In *Contesting the Sacred: The Anthropology of Christian Pilgrimage,* edited by John Eade and Michael J. Sallnow. London and New York: Routledge, 1991. 98–121.

Boy-Żeleński, Tadeusz. *O Mickiewiczu.* Cracow: Czytelnik, 1949.

Braginskii, I. S. "Zametki o zapado-vostochnym sinteze v lirike Pushkina." *Narody Azii i Afriki* 4(1965): 117–26.

Brückner, Aleksander. *Jana hr. Potockiego prace i zasługi naukowe.* Warsaw: Nakład Gebethnera i Wolfa, 1911.

Burke, Edmund. *A Philosophical Enquiry into the Origin of Our Ideas of the Sublime and the Beautiful.* London: Routledge and K. Paul, 1958.

Burkot, Stanisław. *Polskie podróżopisarstwo romantyczne.* Warsaw: Państwowe Wydawnictwo Naukowe, 1988.

Bystroń, Jan. *Polacy w Ziemi Świętej, Syrji i Egipcie 1147–1914*. Cracow: Orbis, 1930.

Carr, Annemarie Weyl. "Icons and the Object of Pilgrimage in Middle Byzantine Constantinople." *Dumbarton Oaks Papers*, 56 (2002). 75–92.

Chateaubriand, François René. *Beauties of Christianity*. Translated by Frederic Shoberl. Philadelphia: M. Carey, 1815.

———. *Travels in Greece, Palestine, Egypt and Barbary During the Years 1806 and 1807*. Vol. 1, Translated by Frederic Shoberl. London: H. Colburn, 1812.

Chodźko, Aleksander. *Poezje*. St. Petersburg: Nakładem autora, drukiem Karola Kraya, 1829.

———. *Le Drogman Turc Donnant les Mots et les phrases les plus necessaires pour la conversation: Vade mecum indispensable a l'armee D'orient*. Par A.Ch. Paris: Benjamin Duprat, 1854.

———. *Specimens of the Popular Poetry of Persia, as Found in the Adventures and Improvisations of Kurroglou, the Bandit-Minstrel of Northern Persia*. Orally collected and translated, with philological and historical notes by Aleksander Chodźko, Esq. London: Printed for the Oriental Translation Fund of Great Britain and Ireland, 1842.

Chojecki, Edmund. *Wspomnienia z podróży po Krymie*. Warsaw, 1845.

Chrisman, Laura and Patrick Williams. "Colonial Discourse and Postcolonial Theory: An Introduction." In *Colonial Discourse and Post-Colonial Theory. A Reader*, edited by Laura Chrisman and Patric Williams. New York: Columbia UP, 1994. 1–20.

Chwalba, Andrzej. "Historię trzeba pisać od nowa." *Tygodnik Powszechny*, no. 34, August 24, 2003: 4.

Clark, Katerina and Michael Holquist, *Mikhail Bakhtin*. Cambridge, MA: Harvard UP 1984.

Danilewicz, Maria, ed. *Listy Adama Mickiewicza do Antoniego Edwarda Odyńca i innych adresatów*. Warsaw: Arkady, 1989.

Demidoff, Anatole de. *Voyage dans la Russie meridionale et la Crimée par la Hongrie, la Valachie et la Moldavie exécuté en 1837*. Paris, 1840.

Dernałowicz, Maria. *Juliusz Słowacki*. Warsaw: Interpress, 1985.

———. "Wstęp." *Kronika rodzinna*, by Władysław Wężyk. Warsaw: Państwowy Instytut Wydawniczy, 1987. 5–30.

Dixon, Megan. "How the Poet Sympathizes with Exotic Lands in Adam Mickiewicz's *Crimean Sonnets* and the *Digression* from Forefathers' Eve, Part III." *Slavic and East European Journal*, vol. 45, no.4 (2001): 679–694.

Dostoevskii, F. M. *Polnoe sobranie sochinenii*. Leningrad: Izdate'lstvo Nauka, 1990.

Drohojowski, Józef. *Pielgrzymka do Ziemi Świętej, Egiptu, niektórych wschodnich i południowych krajów. Odbyta w roku 1788, 89, 90, 91*. Cracow, 1812.

Druzhnikov, Iuri. *Prisoner of Russia: Alexander Pushkin and the Political Uses of Nationalism*. Translated by Thomas Moore and Ilya Druzhnikov. New Brunswick: Transaction Publishers, 1999.

Eberman, V. "Araby i Persy v russkoi literature." *Vostok* 3 (1923): 108–25.

Fieguth, Rolf. "O jedności kompozycyjnej sonetów odeskich i krymskich." In *Adam Mickiewicz i kultura światowa*, edited by Stanisław Makowski. Warsaw: Wydawnictwo Uniwersytetu Warszawskiego, 1999. 91–100.

Florensky, Pavel. *Iconostasis*. Translated by Donald Sheehan and Olga Andrejev. Crestwood, NY: St. Vladimir's Seminary Press, 1996.

Fonkich, Boris L. "Russia and the Christian East From the Sixteenth to the First Quarter of the Eighteenth Century." In *Modern Greek Studies Yearbook*, edited by Theofanis G. Stavrou. Vol. 7 (1991): 439–61.

Freud, Sigmund. "Mourning and Melancholia." In *A General Selection from the Works of Sigmund Freud*, edited by John Rickman. New York: Liverwight Publishing Corp., 1957. 124–40.

Gasparov, M. L. *Ocherk istorii ruskogo stikha: Metrika, ritmika, rifma, strofika*. Moscow: Nauka, 1984.

Gibb, H. A. R. *Arabic Literature: An Introduction*. London: Oxford UP, 1926.

Goethe, Johann Wolfgang von. *West-Oestlicher Divan (West-Eastern Divan)*. Translated by J. Whaley. London: Wolff, 1974.

Gomolicki, Leon. *Dziennik pobytu Adama Mickiewicza w Rosji, 1824–1829*. Warsaw: Książka i Wiedza, 1949.

Greenleaf, Monika. *Pushkin and Romantic Fashioning. Fragment, Elegy, Orient, Irony*. Stanford: Stanford UP, 1994.

Griboedov, A. S. *Polnoie sobranie sochinenii*. Edited by N. K. Piksanova. St. Petersburg: Akademia Nauk, 1917.

Grintser, P. A., ed. *Vostochnye motivy: Stikhotvorenia i poemy*. Moscow: Izdatel'stvo Nauka, 1985.

Hammer-Purgstall, Josef von. *Literaturgeschichte der Araber*. Vol. 1. Vienna: Kaiserl. königl. Hof- u. Staatsdruckerei, 1850.

Herder, Johann Gottfried. *Outlines of a Philosophy of the History of Man (1784)*. Translated by T. Churchill. New York: Bergman Publishers, 1966.

Hillmann, Michael C. *Unity in the Ghazals of Hafez*. Minneapolis: Bibliotheca Islamica, 1976.

Hokanson, Katya. "Literary Imperialism, *Narodnost'* and Pushkin's Invention of the Caucasus." *The Russian Review* 53 (July 1994): 336–52.

Hołowiński, Ignacy. *Pielgrzymka do Ziemi Świętej*. Vilnius, 1842.

Hony, H.C. *A Turkish-English Dictionary*. Oxford: Clarendon Press, 1957.

Ivanov, Razumnik. *Ispytanie v groze i bure. Aleksandr Blok: Skify. Dvienadtsat* Berlin: Skify, 1920.

Ivinskii, D. P. *Kniaz' P. A. Viazemskii i A. S. Pushkin*. Moscow: Filologia, 1994.

Izmailov, N.V. "Liricheskie tsikly v poezii Pushkina kontsa 20–30 godov." *Ocherki tvorchestva Pushkina*. Leningrad: Izdatel'stvo Nauka. Leningradskoe Otdelenie, 1975. 213–270.

Janion, Maria. *Życie pośmiertne Konrada Wallenroda*. Warsaw: Państwowy Instytut Wydawniczy, 1990.

Kalinowska, Izabela. "The Dialogue Between East and West in the *Crimean Sonnets*." *The Polish Review*, vol. 42, no. 4 (1998): 429–36.

———. "The Sonnet, the Sequence, the Quasida: East-West Dialogue in Adam Mickiewicz's *Sonnets*." *Slavic and East European Journal*, vol. 45, no.4 (2001): 641–659.

Kamionka-Straszakowa, Janina. *Zabłąkany wędrowiec: Z dziejów romantycznej topiki*. Wrocław: Ossolineum, 1992.

Khohklova, N. A. *Andrei Nikolaevich Murav'ev—literator*. Saint Petersburg: Rossiiskaia Akademia Nauk, 2001.

Kleiner, Julusz. *Mickiewicz*. Lublin: Tow. Naukowe KUL, 1948.

Koropeckyj, Roman. "Orientalism in Adam Mickiewicz's *Crimean Sonnets*." *Slavic and East European Journal*, vol. 45, no. 4 (2001): 660–79.

Krachkovskii, I. *Ocherki po istorii russkoi arabistyki*. Moscow: Akademia nauk SSSR, 1950.

Królikiewicz, Grażyna. "Symboliczność i elegijność w lirice Słowackiego." In *Juliusz Słowacki—poeta europejski*, edited by Maria Cieślak-Korytowska, Włodzimierz Szturc, and Agnieszka Ziołowicz. Cracow: Universitas, 2000. 72–87.

Kubacki, Wacław. *Z Mickiewiczem na Krymie*. Warsaw: Państwowy Instytut Wydawniczy, 1977.

Kukulski, Leszek, ed. "Wstęp." In *Podróże*, by Jan Potocki. Warsaw: Czytelnik, 1959. 5–17.

———, ed. "Wstęp." In *Podróże po starożytnym Świecie*, by Władysław Wężyk. Warsaw: Czytelnik, 1957. 5–40.

———. "Posłowie." In *Podróże po starożytnym Świecie*, by Władysław Wężyk. Warsaw: Czytelnik, 1957. 243–54.

Kużma, Erazm. *Mit Orientu i kultury Zachodu w literaturze XIX i XX wieku*. Szczecin: Wydawnictwa Naukowe Wyższej Szkoły Pedagogicznej, 1980.

Landa, S. S. "'Sonety' Adama Mitskevicha." In *Adam Mitskevich: Sonety*. Leningrad: Nauka, 1976. 225–300.

Layton, Susan. *Russian Literature and Empire: Conquest of the Caucasus from Pushkin to Tolstoy*. Cambridge: Cambridge UP, 1994.

Lednicki, Wacław. *Aleksander Puszkin: Studja*. Cracow: Nakładem Krakowskiej Spółki Wydawniczej, 1926.

Lewak, Adam. "Czajkowski, Michał (Sadyk Pasza)." Polski slownik biograficzny. Cracow: Polska Akademia Umiejętności, 1938. IV: 155–59.Lotman, Iu. M. "O semiosfere." In *Trudy po znakovym sistemam*. XVII. Tartu, 1984. 5–23.

Łużny, Ryszard. "Księcia Piotra Wiaziemskiego romans z Polską i z rewolucją." *Z notatników i listów księcia Piotra Wiaziemskiego*. Edited by Ryszard Łużny. Cracow: Wydawnictwo Literackie, 1985. 5–17.

Majeska, George P. *Rusian Travelers to Constantinople in the Fourteenth and Fifteenth Centuries*. Washington: Dumbarton Oaks Research Library and Collection, 1984.

Mickiewicz, Adam. *Dzieła wszystkie*. Warsaw: Nakładem Skarbu Rzeczpospolitej Polski, 1936.

———. *Dzieła: Wydanie narodowe*. Cracow: Czytelnik, 1955.

———. *Dzieła: Wydanie rocznicowe*. Warsaw: Czytelnik, 2000.

———. *Sonety Adama Mickiewicza*. Czesław Zgorzelski, ed. Wrocław: Ossolineum, 1976.

Mickiewicz, Władysław. *Żywot Adama Mickiewicza*. Poznań: Polskie Towarzystwo Przyjaciół Nauk, 1929.

Mucha, Bogusław. *Adam Mickiewicz czasów emigracji i Rosjanie*. Łódź: Wydawnictwo Uniwersytetu Łódzkiego, 1997.

Murav'ev, Andrei Nikolaevich. *Puteshestvie ko sviatym mestam v 1830 godu*. Saint Petersburg, 1832.

———. *Tavrida*. Moscow, 1827.

———. "Znakomstvo s russkimi poetami." Vol. 2, *A. S. Pushkin v vospominaniiakh sovremennikov*, edited by V. E. Vatsuro. Moscow: Khudozhestvennaia Literatura, 1985. 44–45.

Nadezhdin, N. I. Review of *Puteshestvie k sviatym mestam v 1830 godu*. *Teleskop*, 11:18 (1832). 245–54.

Nakosteen, Mehdi. "The Structure, Contents and Origin of the Ghazal (Sonnet)." *The Ghazalinnat of Haafez of Shiraz*. Boulder, CO: Este Es Press, 1973.

New Catholic Encyclopedia. San Francisco: Mc Graw-Hill, 1967.

Norov, Avraam Sergeevich. *Puteshestvie po Sviatoi Zemle v 1835 godu*. Saint Petersburg: 1838.

Ogrodziński, Władysław. "Ignacy Pietraszewski (1796–1869): Życie i dzieło." In *Ignacy Pietraszewski: Uroki Orientu*. Olsztyn: Wydawnictwo Pojezierze, 1989. V–XXXV.

Oppenheimer, Paul. "The Origin of the Sonnet." *Comparative Literature*, vol. 34, no. 4 (Fall 1982): 289–304.

———. *The Birth of the Modern Mind: Self, Consciousness, and the Invention of the Sonnet*. Oxford: Oxford UP, 1989.

Ouspensky, Leonid and Vladimir Lossky. *The Meaning of Icons*. Translated by G. E. H. Palmer and E. Kadloubovsky. Crestwood, New York: St. Vladimir's Seminary Press, 1989.

Pietraszewski, Ignacy. *Uroki Orientu: Wspomnienia z wojaży (1832–1840, 1860–1862)*, edited by Zygmunt Abrahamowicz. Olsztyn: Wydawnictwo Pojezierze, 1989.

Piwińska, Marta. "Człowiek i bohater." In *Problemy polskiego romantyzmu*, vol. 2, edited by Maria Żmigrodzka. Wrocław: Ossolineum, 1974. 47–100.

Poklewska, Krystyna. "Romantyczny podróżnik, czyli rzeczywistość w poezję przemieniona. O wierszu 'Na szczycie piramid.'" In *Juliusz Słowacki—poeta europejski*, edited by Maria Cieślak-Korytowska, Włodzimierz Szturc, and Agnieszka Ziołowicz. Cracow: Universitas, 2000. 128–38.

Polevoi, Nikolai. Review of *Puteshestvie ko sviatym mestam, v 1830 godu*. *Moskovskii telegraf* no 9 (May, 1832), 525–41, continued in no. 13 (June 1832), 217–33.

Ponomarev, S. I. "Ierusalim i Palestina v russkoi literature, nauke, zhivopisi i perevodakh (Materialy dlia bibliografii)," *Sbornik Otdeleniia Russkago Iazyka i Slovesnosti Imperatorskoi Akademii Nauk* 17 (1877): 1–127

Potocki, Jean. *Voyage dans les steps d'Astrakhan et du Caucase*. Paris, 1829.

———. *Voyages en Turquie et en Égypte, en Hollande, au Maroc*. Paris: Fayard, 1980.

Pratt, Mary Louise. *Imperial Eyes. Travel Writing and Transculturation*. Routledge: London and New York, 1992.

Przybylski, Ryszard. *Podróż Juliusza Słowackiego na Wschód*. Cracow: Wydawnictwo Literackie, 1982.

Pushkin, Aleksandr. *A Journey to Arzrum*. Translated by Birgitta Ingemanson. Ann Arbor: Ardis, 1974.

———. *Polnoe sobranie sochinenii v desiati tomakh*. Moscow: Izdatel'stvo Akademii Nauk, 1958.

Radziwiłł, Mikołaj Krzysztof. *Podróż do Ziemi Świętej, Syrii i Egiptu*, 1582–1584. Edited by Leszek Kukulski. Warsaw: Państwowy Instytut Wydawniczy, 1962.

Ram, Harsha. *The Imperial Sublime. A Russian Poetics of Empire*. Madison: University of Wisconsin Press, 2003.

———. *Prisoners of the Caucasus: Literary Myths and Media Representations of the Chechen Conflict*. Berkeley: Berkeley Program in Soviet and Post-Soviet Studies, 1999.

Rand McNally Encyclopedia of World Rivers. Chicago: Rand McNally, 1980.

Reychman, Jan. *Podróżnicy polscy na Bliskim Wschodzie w XIX w.* Warsaw: Wydawnictwo Wiedza Powszechna, 1972.

———. "Zainteresowania orientalistyczne w środowisku Mickiewiczowskim w Wilnie i Petersburgu." In *Szkice z dziejów polskiej orientalistyki*, edited by Stefan Strelcyn, 69–93. Warsaw: Państwowe Wydawnictwo Naukowe, 1957.

———. "Podróż Słowackiego na Wschód na tle orientalizmu romantycznego." Warsaw, 1959. Unpublished manuscript.

Rymkiewicz, Jarosław Marek, Dorota Siwicka, Alina Witkowska, and Marta Zielińska. *Mickiewicz: Encyklopedia*. Warsaw: Horyzont, 2001.

Sahas, Daniel J. *Icon and Logos: Sources in Eighth-Century Iconoclasm*. Toronto: U of Toronto P, 1986.

Said, Edward. *Orientalism*. New York: Random House, 1978.

———. *Culture and Imperialism*. New York; Knopf, 1993.

———. *Humanism and Democratic Criticism*. New York: Columbia UP, 2004.

Savel'ev, P. "Vostochnye literatury i russkie orientalisty." *Russkii vestnik* 2/1 (1856):115–124; 2/2(1856): 270–278; 3/1 (1856): 28–38.

Sawrymowicz, Eugeniusz. *Kalendarz życia i twórczości Juliusza Słowackiego*. Wrocław: Ossolineum, 1960.

Schimmel, Anemarie. "The Genius of Shiraz: Saadi and Hafez." *Persian Literature: Columbia Lectures on Iranian Studies*, edited by Ehsan Yarshater, no. 3. New York: The Persian Heritage Foundation, 1988.

Schlegel, A. W. "Vorlesung über das Sonnett." In *Geschichte des Sonnetts in der deutschen Dichtung*, by H. Welti. Leipzig: 1884. 241–50.

Segel, H. B. "Mickiewicz and the Arabic *Qasidah* in Poland." In *American Contributions to the Fifth International Congress of Slavists*. The Hague: Mouton, 1963. 279–300.

Senkovskii, Osip. *Sochinenia*. Saint Petersburg, 1859.

Shepherd, Naomi. *The Zealous Intruders: The Western Rediscovery of Palestine*. London: Collins, 1987.

Silverman, Kaja. *The Subject of Semiotics*. New York: Oxford UP, 1983.

Ślisz, Andrzej. *Henryk Rzewuski: Życie i poglądy*. Warsaw: Krajowa Agencja Wydawnicza, 1986.

Sloane, David A. *Aleksandr Blok and the Dynamics of the Lyric Cycle*. Columbus, OH: Ohio UP, 1988.

Słowacki, Juliusz. *Dzieła*. Wrocław: Ossolineum, 1952.

———. *Dzieła wybrane*. Wrocław: Zakład Narodowy im. Ossolińskich, 1983.

Spiller, Michael. *The Development of the Sonnet: An Introduction*. London:

Routledge, 1992.

———. *The Sonnet Sequence: A Study of Its Strategies.* London: Twayne Publishers, 1997.

Stam, Robert. *Reflexivity in Film and Literature: From Don Quixote to Jean-Luc Godard.* New York: Columbia UP, 1992.

Stankiewicz, Edward. "Sound and Sight in the *Sonety Krymskie* of Adam Mickiewicz." In *For Wiktor Weintraub: Essays in Polish Literature, Language and History: Presented on the Occasion of His 65th Birthday,* edited by Viktor Erlich. The Hague: Mouton, 1975. 496–98.

Stavrou, Theofanis and Peter R. Weisensel. *Russian Travelers to the Christian East from the Twelfth to the Twentieth Century.* Columbus, OH: Slavica, 1985.

Stepanov, N. L. *Lirika Pushkina.* Moscow: Sovetskii pisatel, 1959.

Sterne, Laurence. *A Sentimental Journey Through France and Italy by Mr. Yorick.* Berkeley: U of California P, 1967.

Sumption, Jonathan. *Pilgrimage:. An Image of Medieval Religion.* Totowa, NJ: Rowman and Littlefield, 1975.

Swidziński, Jerzy. "'Sonety Krymskie,' czyli sposób artystycznego łudzenia despoty.'" In *Spotkania literackie: Z dziejów powiązań polsko-rosyjskich w dobie romantyzmu i neoromantyzmu,* edited by Bohdan Galster and Janina Kamionkowa. Wrocław: Ossolineum, 1973.

Abdulla El Tayib. "Pre-Islamic Poetry," In *Arabic Literature to the End of the Umayyad Period.* edited by A. F. L. Beeston, T. M. Johnstone, R. B. Serjeant, and G. R. Smith, 22–111. Cambridge: Cambridge UP, 1983.

Tertz, Abram (Andrei Sinyavsky). *Strolls with Pushkin.* Translated by Catharine Nepomnyashchy and Slava Yastremski. New Haven and London: Yale UP, 1993.

Thompson, Ewa M. *Imperial Knowledge. Russian Literature and Colonialism.* Westport, CT: Greenwood Press, 2000.

Todorov, Tzvetan. *Bakhtin and the Dialogical Principle.* Translated by Wlad Godzich. Minneapolis: U of Minnesota P, 1984.

———. *The Conquest of America: The Question of the Other.* Translated by Richard Howard. New York: Harper Perennial, 1992.

———. *On Human Diversity. Nationalism, Racism, and Exoticism in French Thought.* Translated by Catherine Porter. Cambridge, MA: Harvard UP, 1993.

Tretiak, Józef. *Mickiewicz i Puszkin.* Warsaw: Nakładem księgarni E. Wende i Sp., 1906.

Uziębło, Gerard. "Kilka słów o orientaliźmie Adama Mickiewicza." *Ateneum* (Warsaw), vol. IV (1889), 132–43.

Vatsuro, V. E. "Epigramma Pushkina na A. N. Murav'eva." In *Pushkin: Issledovaniia i materialy: 13. Sbornik nauchnykh trudov.* Leningrad: Nauka, 1989. 222–41.

Veresaev, V. *Pushkin v zhizni.* Moscow: Sov. Pisatel', 1926.

Viazemskii, Petr Andreevich. *Fon-Vizin.* Saint Petersburg, 1848.

———. "Pamiati Avraama Sergeevicha Norova." *Russkii Arkhiv* 1869 (7). 068–074.

———. *Polnoe sobranie sochinenii.* Saint Peterburg 1878.

————. *Puteshestvie na Vostok, 1849–1850.* Saint Peterburg 1883.

Walicki, Andrzej. *Philosophy and Romantic Nationalism: The Case of Poland.* Oxford: Oxford UP, 1984.

————. *Poland Between East and West: The Controversies over Self-Definition and Modernization in Partitioned Poland.* Cambridge, MA: Harvard UP, 1994.

Watt, W. Montgomery. *The Influence of Islam on Medieval Europe.* Edinburgh: Edinburgh UP, 1972.

Weisensel, Peter R. "Russian Self-Identification and Travelers' Descriptions of the Ottoman Empire in the First Half of the Nineteenth Century." *Central Asian Survey* 10/4 (1991): 65–85.

Weiskel, Thomas. *The Romantic Sublime: Studies in the Structure and Psychology of Transcendence.* Baltimore: The Johns Hopkins UP, 1976.

Wężyk, Władysław. *Podróże po starożytnym świecie. Część pierwsza.* Warsaw, 1842.

————. *Podróże po starożytnym świecie.* Edited by Leszek Kukulski. Warsaw: Czytelnik, 1957.

White, Hayden. "The Noble Savage Theme as a Fetish." In *Tropics of Discourse: Essays in Cultural Criticism.* Baltimore: Johns Hopkins UP, 1978. 183–96.

Wilkins, Ernest. "The Invention of the Sonnet." *Modern Philology,* 13 (1915), 463–95.

Wilkinson, John, ed. *Jerusalem Pilgrimage 1099–1185.* London: Hakluyt Society, 1988.

Williams, Patrick and Laura Chrisman, eds. *Colonial Discourse and Post-Colonial Theory: A Reader.* New York: Columbia UP, 1994.

Wolff, Lary. *Inventing Eastern Europe. The Map of Civilization on the Mind of the Enlightenment.* Stanford: Stanford UP, 1994.

Wysłouch, Seweryna. "O malarskości *Sonetów krymskich.*" In *Księga Mickiewiczowska,* edited by Z. Trojanowiczowa and Z. Przychodniak. Poznań: Wydawnictwo Naukowe UAM, 1998. 35–51.

Wytrzens, Guenther. *Pjotr Andreevic Vjazemskij: Studie zur russischen Literatur- und Kulturgeschichte des neunzehnten Jahrhunderts.* Vienna: Verlag Notring, 1961

Zajączkowski, Annaniasz. *Gazele wybrane Hafiza.* Warsaw: Państwowe Wydawnictwo Naukowe, 1957.

————. *Orient jako źródło inspiracji w literaturze romantycznej doby mickiewiczowskiej.* Warsaw: Państwowy Instytut Wydawniczy, 1955.

Zawadzka, Danuta. "O 'Sonetach krymskich' Adama Mickiewicza." *Mickiewicz. W 190-lecie urodzin. Materiały z sesji naukowej: Białystok, 2–4 grudnia 1988.* Białystok: Dział Wydawnictw Filii UW w Białymstoku, 1993. 119–29.

Zgorzelski, Czesław. *O lirykach Mickiewicza i Słowackiego: Eseje i studia.* Lublin: Towarzystwo Naukowe KUL, 1961.

INDEX